UNDERCOVER

A TRUE STORY

JOE CARTER
UNDERCOVER

CENTURY

1 3 5 7 9 10 8 6 4 2

Century
20 Vauxhall Bridge Road
London SW1V 2SA

Century is part of the Penguin Random House group of companies
whose addresses can be found at global.penguinrandomhouse.com

First published by Century in 2016

www.penguin.co.uk

A CIP catalogue record for this book is available from the British Library.

ISBN 9781780895024

Typeset in India by Thomson Digital Pvt Ltd, Noida, Delhi
Printed and bound in Great Britain by Clays Ltd, St Ives plc

Penguin Random House is committed to a sustainable
future for our business, our readers and our planet. This book
is made from Forest Stewardship Council® certified paper.

MIX
Paper from
responsible sources
FSC
www.fsc.org   FSC® C018179

Dedication

To the most caring, loving and brilliant mum. Thank you for single-handedly raising the most beautiful and talented children. They make me proud every day and I love them so very much. I am sorry that I let you all down.

Acknowledgements

Thank you to:

Stephen Ainscough for starting me on the journey.

To Paul, Claire, Tom and Mary and the gang at Newman Street.

Sharmaine Lovegrove for connecting me to the right people and enthusing soooo much about my writing.

And a huge thank you to Ajda Vucicevic at Random House for your constant support, guidance and reassurance.

And of course to Boo.

Foreword

I recall like it was yesterday – the first words that Joseph Dominick Pistone delivered to the hushed auditorium at the FBI Academy in Quantico. I was sat in the stalls exchanging niceties with the men either side of me, part of a select class of undercover officers. I felt honoured and privileged to have been invited on their esteemed undercover course and, as we awaited the talk, a general sense of excitement settled over us. The most famous undercover officer in the world – the first person to infiltrate the Mafia in New York – was about to deliver a lecture.

Donnie Brasco, as was his alias, had been part of one of the most complex and intricate operations of his generation. It had lasted six years and had almost cost him everything.

The entire audience was in awe of the man and his remark-able achievements as a UC. He had the class in the palm of his hand, without uttering a single word.

When he finally spoke, his words were slow and considered: 'Anyone in this room who is becoming an undercover officer to get away from their boss, or is running away from a nagging wife or screaming kids . . . Anyone who is here to hide from any problems they have in their own lives . . . Then I tell you one thing – you are in the wrong place, you are on the wrong course, and there is the door.' He paused whilst people took in the gravity of his words.

The words he spoke, I have come to realise, were true; they were spoken from the heart. He knew all this because he had been there. And before too long, I would learn – the hard way – just how true they were.

Prologue

It was thirty years, three months and eight days since I had stood with over 200 new recruits, been sworn in to serve my queen and country, and promised to protect the people of London.

I was now sat in a comfy chair at the Hilton hotel surrounded by business men and women conducting meetings and interviews, sipping green teas and cappuccinos, with their Apple MacBooks laid out on the tables in front of them. None of them knew who I was, or why I was there, clutching a crisp white envelope that contained my warrant card.

I was going to hand it in and walk away from a job that I had devoted the best part of my life to. I had never imagined that it would end in this way, with such despair, such unhappiness, and with so much anger and heartache.

There was only one reason I was there: my ex-detective inspector, the only person that I still trusted, had asked to meet me on 21 December. He knew that this was my last day – this was to be the end of my thirty-year police career. I had spent the past twenty years working undercover; I had received over thirty-five Chief Constable's and Judge's Commendations for bravery and dedication to my work. I was overwhelmed by sadness and a sense of futility. I thought of trust and support and camaraderie, all the things that I could no longer look to my colleagues for.

It had been a week since I had been told by a twenty-something-year-old kid from HR that I wasn't entitled to an exit interview with the chief constable as I didn't fit the criteria. I looked at him, dressed in his Hollister jumper, Primark skinny jeans and cheap shoes. I thought to myself that he had no idea who I was or what I had done. I wanted to sit him, his supervisor and the other 'luvvies' from HR down, and tell them my story. Explain to them what I had done in my service, the people I had hurt, the number of times I'd risked my life to put baddies behind bars. That I thrived on danger – the more dangerous the situation or nastier the person, the more I would want to do the job. I wanted to tell them my story.

I looked him up and down, took a deep breath and said, 'Do you know what? You're right, I'm sure the Chief has much better things to do.'

In any other walk of life or career, I was certain that I would have been sat down and somebody would have picked my brains, unloaded all the contacts I had accrued over two decades. They would have listened, and documented the knowledge and experience I had of sensitive operations and undercover techniques. Made notes of the tactics I had used that had been successful, and those I implemented that had failed. My head was full of twenty years of detailed information that I had collected working undercover throughout the world. But not a single person spoke to me: no exit interview, no debrief from the unit head, no one from my department even said goodbye.

Of course, I was sure they were all glad to see the back of me. Although we'd had a huge amount of success in the undercover unit, and had never before put so many top-echelon criminals 'away' for serious offences, I knew that certain senior officers wanted me off the premises. I brought success, but at a risk to them and their spotless CVs. They were always concerned when I was deployed; they worried about the job going wrong, the money getting stolen, or bad press about the tactics used. I never felt they had any genuine concern for my safety or me. Their number one priority was their own reputation. With me out of the way, that meant that there was one less thing that could prevent their path to promotion.

I knew that I wouldn't get any big send-off, that there would be no collection amongst my peers to buy me a retirement present. I'd witnessed colleagues in the past, who had done little to nothing in a thirty-year career, receiving Mont Blanc pens or nasty cut-glass decanters. There wouldn't even be a card for me, adorned with handwritten comments from people I barely knew and certainly didn't care for. No drunken slaps on the back or speeches from insignificant and boring senior officers chronicling my career over thirty years that they had no personal knowledge of. But most of all, there was one thing that really got to me, the thing that hurt the most and would stay with me forever. There was not one single person to say: 'Joe, thank you.' I realise, now, that's all I wanted: someone – anyone – just to say something, to give me a little sign that what I had done mattered. That I hadn't wasted my life.

I had sacrificed a marriage and hurt so many people on the way. I wanted to be told it wasn't all for nothing. I just wanted someone to say thank you.

One

It was 1984, and the early months at Chiswick Police Station were not filling me with joy. I seemed to go from day to day, shift to shift, without feeling I had any direction to my life. Shifts became all too familiar. We would all parade into the briefing room before a shift. We would be asked to produce our appointments. We would all then hold out our wooden, leather-strapped truncheon, our silver whistle on a chain and our up-to-date, ruled-off pocketbook. At this stage, the sergeant would read us our postings and what time our 'refs' (refreshment meal breaks) would be taken.

I would invariably be posted to the furthest beat from the station. I would walk there aimlessly, not really knowing what I should actually be doing to fill my eight hours, and then wander the streets in a daydream for most of the shift. I was only ever awoken from this when the radio would shout my number to take a call. This used to startle me, and almost amounted to an inconvenience. I was aware that all the decent calls – the meaty ones, the ones with any action – were always taken by the cars. The walkers were left with rubbish. The old lady who wanted to report her cat missing. The family who were being kept up all night by their neighbours blasting Bob Marley until the wee small hours.

When I walked into these houses, flats or bedsits, I knew everyone was thinking that they had sent the work experience boy to deal with their problem. I was nineteen, I had only been in the police for three months, and it was clear to see that I was in the wrong job. I was always polite; I had been brought up to treat people with respect. I had no prejudices and believed in the moral values of right and wrong. I always managed to deal with each situation professionally. I would normally get a cup of tea and slice of homemade Victoria sponge from the dear old ladies. They were grateful for a natter and I always left with 'such a lovely young man' ringing in my ears.

My police career was going nowhere. I was coming up for my three-month probation report. I thought I'd had a right score, as the station's football manager was my reporting sergeant. That meant he was responsible for signing off my probation reports. Without being big-headed, I was a half-decent footballer. I was fit and played to an alright standard.

Undercover

The rivalry and competition between police stations in the 1980s and 90s was huge. On a Thursday at any of the police sports clubs in London, the pitches would be full of rival teams, playing competitive football and taking it very seriously. The bar afterwards was a place for banter, and rubbing the noses of a rival nick in the sand if they had been on the receiving end of a Chiswick and Brentford defeat.

This is where my naivety showed. I knew my three-monthly report was imminent, and the skipper had said we would have a chat. I just didn't expect it after five pints of light and bitter in the bar.

My sergeant was a smart-looking man. He was about thirty-eight years old, with a short mop of jet-black hair and a matching, thin moustache. He was slim and wore police-issue spectacles, which he let fall to the end of his nose. He loved a drink and was a sucker for Fuller's ESB. It was our local brewery in Chiswick, and as he used to say, 'It would be rude not to.' He put his arm around me, like an uncle would at Christmas after one too many glasses of port. He said, 'I've checked your work return for the last three months and noticed that you've only reported six people for traffic offences. Why is that?'

Quick as a flash I countered him: 'Traffic really isn't my thing and I like to use my discretion. I tend to give verbal warnings to those that have committed minor infringements.' There was a verbal-warning book held in the police station that catalogued the names and details of the offences for which members of the public had received a warning. My skipper patted me on the back and said, 'You were our best player today, son. Well done. We'll go through your report tomorrow.' I thought no more of it, finished my pint and revelled in the celebrations of another victory for the nick.

When I think back, playing for the nick was the only part of the job I actually enjoyed. I lived for Thursdays – we were allowed off early ahead of time to play, and came into late shift after the match had finished, and if lucky we were let home early from night duty to sleep.

The next shift at the nick I was called into the sergeant's office. He told me to sit down and was not his normal self. He passed my three-monthly probation report across the table. He told me to read it. I opened it and read what he had typed. It was not pleasant reading. He said that I was not progressing as he had expected. He said if I continued the way I was going he would not recommend that I got through my probation. My arrest figures were poor and my traffic offences were disgraceful. Even worse, he commented that I had told him that I preferred to issue verbal warnings rather than report people for traffic violations. However, having checked the verbal-warning register, he saw that I had not made a single entry. The last line of the report read: *I recommend this officer is placed on monthly reports and is spoken to by the chief superintendent.*

He looked at me and said, 'Is there anything in there that isn't true?' I paused and stuttered before I feebly said, 'But I thought you were my mate?' It sounded pathetic and naive and childish. He said that the Chief would be seeing me tomorrow, and to make sure I had some reasons for my poor performance so far. I learnt a big lesson that day, a lesson that would stand me in good stead throughout my thirty-year police career: *Never, ever trust any of your colleagues*.

I wasn't sure what I should do next. Maybe call it a day; I wasn't enjoying being a policeman and I had never wanted to be one in the first place. This was down to my mother. I could kill her . . . why had she insisted that I filled in the forms to join the Met? I can hear her even now, saying: 'If you don't, I can only see you being locked up by them.'

I needed to think over my options, and there was only an hour left of my shift. As I contemplated going back out to walk down those last sixty minutes, I bumped into Eammon, who had just come in from the back yard. Eammon was a lovely, gentle man; he was softly spoken, and everything he did was done in a calm way. He was the first Eammon I had ever met – not a common name, but one you associate with a librarian or maybe a farmer. However, Eammon was a detective and an experienced one, though I only knew this because he played for the football team. I had not had any professional dealings with him. In fact, I had never set foot inside the Criminal Investigation Department (CID) office. I knew it was at the end of the corridor on the first floor. The door was always closed, and the detectives that worked there were not the approachable type.

Eammon asked what was up. I explained that Skip had put me on monthly reports and it was very unlikely that I would pass my probation. And to top that, the chief superintendent wanted to see me.

Eammon looked at me and said, 'Don't worry about that. Meet me in The Barley Mow at two thirty and I'll help you out.' Then he skipped up the stairs and disappeared out of sight.

I was a bit taken aback by Eammon. I didn't really know him; we had exchanged a few pleasantries whilst getting changed for football, but no more than that. But I knew I fancied a pint, and I was intrigued to find out what Eammon might say.

When the shift finished, as ever the entire relief went for a drink in the pub next door. I made my excuses, turned left out of the nick and walked along the alleyway behind the High Road towards the quaint Barley Mow pub. I had only been in there once before, and as I walked in this time I saw Tommy Cooper – a tower of a man – having a drink with his wife. He looked at me, and he had a twinkle in his eye. He was holding court, and on any other day I would've loved to listen to his tales.

I walked past him and his entourage and saw Eammon nursing a pint, sat on his own at a table. I asked him what he wanted, but he said he was fine and that the rest of the CID office would be joining him in a while.

I ordered my pint and sat down. He looked at me and said, 'You don't want to be a policeman, do you? You're thinking of throwing the towel in.'

I stared at him as I took the first gulp of my lager top. It felt like I was talking to an older stepbrother. 'That's exactly right, Eammon. I don't think this is the job for me.'

'You don't have to walk the streets and be told when to eat and when you can use the Gents. There is another job in the police – the brains behind everything that happens.'

'What job is that, Eammon?' I asked. 'And what makes you think I can do it?'

He told me the CID were a family, and they stuck together. They solved all the crimes and put right the 'fuck-ups' that the 'helmets' made. 'We think differently, we act differently and we speak to people differently. It's not an "us and them" mentality with the public. We need them on our side if we're going to get results. I know it sounds like I'm slagging uniform off, but what I'm trying to say to you is the CID is a totally different job. If you want I'll help you as much as I can to join us. What do you think?'

I said to him: 'Anything is better than what I'm doing now – anything.'

He asked what shift I was on tomorrow and I told him I was early again. 'Perfect,' he said. 'That gives you at least three hours before the Chief will call you in. Tomorrow morning stand on Chiswick Common Road, and at about seven thirty a blue Maestro will drive towards the High Road. You stop that car and check the driver's documents. You'll find he's disqualified from driving and has a fake licence. Trust me, and when the Chief calls you up, you'll either be in the charge room or interviewing the prisoner with me.' Eammon wrote down the car number and a name on a Fuller's beer mat that he'd ripped open. He shook my hand and said, 'Don't let me down now. See you in the charge room in the morning, and not a word to anyone.' Then he patted me on the back and walked round to the other bar, and left me with my thoughts.

For some strange reason, the chat with Eammon had really given me a lift. But how did he know such precise detail and why was he helping me? For now, all I knew was that to keep the Chief off my back, nothing was better than a crime arrest apparently off my own initiative. If he didn't find out, then I certainly wasn't going to tell him.

I decided against joining the rest of the relief and instead went back to the section house, which was supposed to be my home.

Two

I was tossing and turning all night in fear that I would sleep through my alarm. My state-of-the-art, digital-radio alarm clock, fitted with a large snooze button, was perched on the wooden-topped stall that stood next to my bed. The alarm was a recent addition to the few personal objects I had in my room in the section house.

I had the full-length poster of Fiona Butler approaching the tennis net, with her racket in her right hand. She was lifting her skirt with her left hand to reveal she wasn't wearing any knickers under her white tennis attire. This poster filled the entire length of my bedroom door.

I had a single bed, and had removed the police-issue orange-and-purple blanket and replaced it with a Paddington Bear

9

duvet cover and pillowcase. Quite sad really, for a Metropolitan Police officer approaching his twentieth birthday. I had a black-and-white picture of my mum and dad, looking like film stars in the early 1960s, and some birthday cards from my younger brothers and sisters. It wasn't cosy and it felt nothing like home.

This was my sad room on the fifth floor of the Brentford section house. This was the hall of residence occupied by young male and female police officers, or occasionally older residents who had found themselves in marital difficulties and for whom this was their only solution.

There was a sink in each room which was metal and had corrosion around the taps and smelt of urine. The fact of the matter was, most people used their sink as a lavatory as they couldn't be bothered to walk the length of the corridor in the middle of the night to empty their bladder. It was far more convenient to take the two steps from one's bed, step on your tiptoes and use the sink for a wee whilst running the cold water tap. Far from hygienic, but very practical and rewarding.

The toilets consisted of two urinals that stunk to high heaven and two individual toilet cubicles, which were permanently soiled and not conducive to having a relaxing ten-minute, peaceful sit-down. The toilet paper was tracing paper and was lethal, so it was essential that you had your own roll of Andrex in your room. There was also a single bath, which had the enamel wearing off around the plug area and was never washed by the previous bath-goer. There were three individual showers, which were adequate; the shower curtains smelt rancid and I would only ever shower wearing flip-flops, but they were powerful and hot.

Undercover

My alarm was set for 5.05 a.m., but I had glanced at it regularly since 4.10. I was sure that I was going to over-sleep and miss the opportunity of making my first arrest on the back of Eammon's tip-off. I couldn't face another turn in the bed and jumped out at 4.45, grabbed my towel and ran to the shower. This was the first time since I had finished at Hendon Police Training College that I was excited about going to work. I had a super-quick shower and got dressed in my uniform in no time. I normally left it until the last moment to leave my room, but I was starting up my car at 5.10.

It was only a ten-minute drive from the section house past Kew Bridge and over Chiswick roundabout to the nick. I decided I'd make a short detour and check whether the motor that Eammon had described to me was parked on or around Chiswick Common Road. I'm glad I did, as the excitement it gave me when I spotted it was ridiculous. I was onto some-thing; I had a cause, a reason to be. I was gonna nick some-one. I would have to caution them, put the handcuffs on them. The control room would hear my voice, asking for the van to come and collect a prisoner. Yes, today was the day.

I got to the parade room early – well early. I had already booked out a radio, one that I knew worked, not one of the dodgy old ones that I would purposely book out sometimes to avoid hearing the control room dispatching work.

The inspector allocated beats, and although Chiswick Common Road wasn't on the beat I'd been allocated I had to walk that way to get to mine, which as usual was at the edge of our territory. I walked out of the station with a bounce in my step.

I had fifteen minutes to be in position. I didn't want to be late; I couldn't contemplate missing him. I was going to nab this fella and make it the first of many, many arrests for me.

Like clockwork, the Maestro chugged along the road. The driver couldn't have seen me stood behind one of the large horse chestnut trees that lined the pavement. In September conkers would fall in abundance from the branches; today, they provided the perfect screen for me to step out from. The look on his face resembled what I imagined would be the look of a train driver when someone stepped out in front of his or her train. There was instant shock and he brought the car to a stop.

I went through all the pleasantries with the driver. I noticed how nervous he was, fumbling in his wallet for his driver's licence. He handed me a very new, pristine paper licence. It had the correct colours and font, but the paper did not feel right. I looked at him as I rolled the paper between my thumb and forefinger. I said, 'You going to tell me where you got this from, Mr Smith?'

'I needed a licence 'cos I lost mine for three years for drink driving. I won't fuck you about.'

I told him I was arresting him for producing a fake driving licence and for disqualified driving.

Before I cautioned him, I asked him if there was anything else he wanted to tell me. He pointed to the boot and said there was some 'tom' in there. I didn't have a clue what he meant, but I opened the boot to find a yellow cotton moneybag containing all sorts of jewellery: necklaces, rings, bracelets and two big chunky watches. I could've shouted out loud – here was a bag of stolen jewellery. I later found out, without declaring I hadn't got a clue, that 'tom' was short for 'tomfoolery', which meant jewellery.

I nicked him for handling stolen goods and then called up the station asking for a van to convey a prisoner and myself to the nick. The control room immediately asked if I was with anyone else. I said I was alone. I had the prisoner handcuffed, a bag of tom and a forged driving licence, all before 7.45. I was so chuffed; it felt really good.

The van driver pulled up, took one look at Mr Smith and said, 'Harry, what have you been nicked for this time – I thought you were going straight?!'

Three

Chiswick Police Station was a lump of a building that sat on the corner of tree-lined Linden Gardens and the bustle of Chiswick High Road. It was a typical 1970s structure that added no class to the High Road, and no awards would have been collected by the architect. It served its purpose: it was full of uniform officers and detectives responsible for policing the streets and solving the crimes that were committed locally.

This was my place of work, the first police station that I'd been posted to since I passed out from Hendon Police Training School. I should've been excited; I should've been the keenest officer ever to enter that station. Eager to walk the streets, greet people, help them. Eager to arrest as many people as I could, and make the streets of Chiswick a safer place. But that wasn't me. I didn't want to be there. And I don't mean Chiswick – I just didn't see myself as a police officer. I had never planned to be one, yet there I was, not even reached twenty years old, with a huge responsibility on my shoulders.

There was a four-team system that operated to cover the twenty-four-hour period. The teams were called reliefs, and I was allocated to 'C' relief. There was a uniform inspector in charge of each relief and four sergeants. The remainder of the relief was made up of PCs, of whom there were about ten. The shifts were: earlies (6 a.m. until 2 p.m.), lates (2 p.m. until 10 p.m.) and night duty (10 p.m. until 6 a.m.).

The relief pecking order was an established and engrained culture, and you had to understand and acknowledge your position in it. The lowest of the low were the probbies, the new probationary PCs who had been allocated to each relief. Then there were the walkers, those PCs who had yet to be given a driving course – who therefore, by default, spent eight hours a day walking their assigned beat. If they were lucky, during the last few hours of a night shift they might get picked up by one of the cars.

The next in line was the van driver – he was the 'elder' of the relief who was often the person with the longest service. The van driver, as well as attending emergency calls, had the responsibility of collecting and transporting all the prisoners from wherever they were arrested to the police station. Our van driver always wore his police flat cap tilted to the back of his head. He kept the keys for the precious van on the aerial of his police radio, which was clipped onto the breast of his police tunic. He often smoked roll-up cigarettes, and bragged that he could roll one while taking a call at break-neck speed.

The kings of the relief were the area car drivers. They were the PCs who had passed the advanced driving course, and who on each shift were allocated an operator to answer all calls over the radio and keep a detailed log of the calls the car had dealt with. These men loved nothing more than to drive at ridiculous speeds, to get to every call dispatched from Scotland Yard as fast as they could. The ones that were really up themselves would wear standard black driving gloves, which, when not on their delicate hands, would be hanging out of their tunic breast pocket.

I had no aspirations to be any of these people, and some of them I felt sorry for. I appreciated their individual skills – after all, it's not easy to steer a police car safely through the streets of London at ninety miles per hour. But to me they were caricatures, desperate to be known as the best. If truth be told, they would often get themselves to the call in lightning-quick time, but the driver was far from the best at dealing with the incident and often wouldn't get his hands dirty. He would stay in the car and let his operator deal with whatever the incident was.

The person who really made the relief tick was the leader, the man at the helm – the inspector on the team, or the guvnor, as he was referred to. In the short time I spent in uniform, it was always a male guvnor. My inspector was a man's man, with hands like shovels and a big heart. And he had a story to tell. He had fought career criminals toe to toe in the 1970s and 80s, and was now in the twilight of his career. He had been 'busted' back to uniform after a colourful and traumatic career as a detective on the Flying Squad, amongst other postings. He had a misdemeanour whilst a detective inspector and his punishment was losing his position as a detective and reverting to being a 'helmet'. Punishment enough for a career detective. But I must say, it never dampened his appetite for work or his desire to put the baddies away, and his enthusiasm was infectious.

I grew fond of him, and he taught me a thing or two about the way to get a job done. He taught me the Ways and Means Act, which was not an Act of Parliament but rather the unofficial rules we adhered to so that a situation was dealt with, a person arrested or a crime solved. It was not always textbook, but it always got a result.

I remember one September morning, it was about eleven o'clock and I was on my way into the front office of the police station. I'd been walking for the past four hours in the depths of Strand-on-the-Green, taking in the autumn air and the silence of the river. A call sounded over the radio about an armed robbery at the NatWest bank, where two suspects had made off wearing blue overalls. The guvnor ran to the tall grey gun cabinet that stood in the front office. He had the key on the duty inspector's key ring. I saw him open the cabinet and grab two small revolvers and a fistful of bullets.

He shouted for me to jump into his Austin Allegro. No sooner had I sat in the passenger seat than he threw me both guns, and put his huge fist over my lap and dropped the bullets. I looked at him in amazement and said, 'What am I supposed to do with them?'

He looked at me and laughed. 'Load the fucking things, otherwise they won't go bang.' He leant over and released the barrel that held the bullets. I could see that there were chambers for five bullets. I was shaking as I placed them into the first revolver.

I went to load the second one, and it dawned on me that there was only the two of us in the car and I was now loading a second gun. 'Who is this one for, guvnor?' He took a brief sideways look at me and said, 'Just load it.' As I loaded the second revolver, a voice crackled over the radio saying that the two men had last been seen going into the underpass of the A4 at Sutton Court Road. We were within fifteen seconds of there. He shouted at me to tell control we were taking the exit of the subway riverside. The Allegro flew across the A4 and screeched to a halt on the upslope of the subway.

I was a nineteen-year-old boy, who had never before in his life handled a gun, and I was now sat with two I had loaded in my lap, listening to the female radio operator saying at least one of the male robbers was in possession of a sawn-off shotgun. Was I really in this situation? Should I actually get out of the car?

The guvnor grabbed one of the revolvers and leapt out of the car, screaming at me to join him. I put the gun in my waistband and jumped out. He shouted at me to get the other gun. I showed him my waistband and he shouted that it wasn't much good in there. We were now stood shoulder to shoulder on the upslope of the subway, both holding police-issue revolvers. I could hear the guvnor breathing heavily. I looked at him and said, 'What do I do if they come up the slope, guvnor?'

'Shoot them, and shout as loud as you can "Stop! Police!"'

I took a deep gulp and prayed that I wouldn't see two men dressed in blue overalls coming out of the safety of the under-pass carrying a sawn-off shotgun. I prayed that I wouldn't have to shoot someone, prayed that if I did that I would miss them but they wouldn't shoot me. It's amazing how many thoughts can rush through your head in seconds.

I looked at the two-handed grip the guvnor had on his gun and tried to replicate it. As the seconds ticked by, the guvnor starting to creep down the slope and told me to follow him. We'd got to the right turn to the underpass when two teenage boys in smart school blazers came out. Both of them were visibly shaken and put their hands up in the air. The guvnor growled at them to lie down and asked if anyone else was in the underpass. Both boys said no but were apologising pro-fusely. The guvnor then turned the corner to view the subway, and all that was there was a ray of sunshine illuminating the far end of an empty, robber-free subway. I could've shouted out loud I was so happy.

The guvnor came over to me, put his arm around me and walked me up the slope back to the car. He took the gun from my hand and could see I was shaking. 'I think you deserve a drink for that,' he said. 'Now get back in the car and let's try and find these robbers.' Thankfully, we never did find them.

Four

I realised that if I put the effort into my police work then I would reap the benefits. I now had a bounce in my step; my sole focus was to nick as many people as I could for decent criminal offences. I had a target – I now knew I wanted to be a detective. I didn't want to wear the uniform, or 'fancy dress' as some of the older detectives used to call it. I wanted to don a suit, work on the first floor of the nick, and rub shoulders with all the other detectives in the pub at lunchtime. I had Eammon's words echoing in my ears: 'If you talk to people nicely, you'll be surprised what they'll tell you.'

I wasted no time in my quest, and it took me only three months and many, many arrests to get out of uniform and start my CID apprenticeship. There was an easy route to take, but that involved joining the Masons, and as a good Catholic boy with a lack of interest in boys' clubs I declined that route. Instead, I stuck to hard work and nicking lots of villains. I worked with many seasoned detectives; I picked up good techniques from some and discarded many from others. It was on-the-job learning, and there was nobody in that police station that was working harder than me.

My efforts were rewarded with an early posting to the crime squad. I was now able to wear my own clothes, and I started growing my hair long and trying to do everything to not stand out as a police officer. I started meeting contacts and sources in pubs, and listened to them tell me what was going on amongst villains in the area. We had a very simple technique, and it would be as effective now. We would do at least one search warrant a day, based on intelligence. We would crash through an unsuspecting villain's door early in the morning, seize whatever we were there to find. Nick them, interview them, and convince them that it was in their best interests to help us out. Inevitably this would lead us to the information for the search warrant for the following morning. It was not rocket science, but it worked.

I was beginning to make a name for myself, and had gained a good reputation as a thief-taker. I progressed to the district crime squad, where I was in competition with other prospective detectives: it was awash with testosterone. I kept my head down and was lucky enough to have some decent informants, but I was at a disadvantage because I had declined the offer to 'join the square'. At that time, the CID was controlled by the Masons, and I'd chosen not to join. However, I was very fortunate that, against all odds, my hard work was rewarded and I passed an interview at the age of twenty-one to become a detective.

It is fair to say that being a detective in the 1980s was full of fun and excitement. There were real characters in the police in those days. There was a sense that you could rely on each other, that your team or partner had your back. So very different from the experiences I encountered in the last decade of my police service, when at every opportunity your colleagues would do whatever they could to catch you out and drop you in the 'proverbial'. No one had your back; in fact, you most definitely had to watch it.

I was given a really decent posting, a proper posting – I was going to Harrow Road Police Station in West London. This was an imposing red brick building that sat on the Harrow Road, surrounded by black railings. Ten stone steps led up from the pavement to the huge black front doors. The building was set on five floors, including the basement, and it had history; you could sense the stories that the walls of the rooms held.

The Harrow Road station had quite a reputation in the 1980s, and the uniform officers took no shit. They ran the streets and ensured that the locals knew that. They didn't suffer fools gladly and there was – very much – an 'us and them' mentality. It appeared to be the uniform versus the world. The problem was, they struggled to see the difference between the hugely lawful and supportive community, and the bad guys. It is fair to say that some of the challenges that faced the police were huge.

Undercover

I was one of eight new DCs at Harrow Road, and it was an exciting opportunity to make a name for ourselves and the department. There were four teams in the CID office, with a detective sergeant in charge. The night shift was always frantic and incredibly busy. It was the responsibility of the night duty detective to prepare the night duty occurrence book – or the OB, as it was known. This was a typed report that was left in a ring binder in the office to notify the day shift detectives what had occurred overnight, who had been arrested and dealt with, and most importantly what prisoners were sat in the cells awaiting interview and investigation. You could tell the lazy detectives from the industrious ones by the number of prisoners that were handed over in the morning. If you had an old-school detective who saw night duty as a way to have a late drink away from his wife and catch up on a few hours' sleep in the DI's office, then there would be maybe eight to ten prisoners in the cells. All the detective needed to write was: *Placed in cell to sleep.* The industrious ones, however, would do all they could to leave the minimum amount to interview.

Every single day, six out of the eight new detectives – who were spread evenly across the four teams – would rush into work. Most of us lived in the suburbs, and my drive took between one and a half and two hours, each way. I always left home before six and drove as fast as I could to get in first, so that I could sign for the interesting prisoners from the OB. This meant two things to me: a guarantee of overtime and an opportunity to 'roll over' a suspect (get them to admit offences, and also have the potential of an informant). I had learnt in my very early days that if you talked to people the right way, they would respond. I also knew that the most successful police work was based on the best intelligence.

CID was based on the first floor. Before you entered the main office, you had a small interview room on your right and a small galley kitchen, where cups of tea and coffee were made. This area should have been condemned as a health hazard. It was not a tidy office in any shape or form. Every detective had their own desk, with a three-tier set of locked wooden drawers that slotted underneath and a three-tier set of plastic in-trays that sat on the desktop.

On my team, I had a dynamic new DS who was a ringer for the TV presenter Richard Keys. He was a good man, and a good supervisor and detective. He allocated the work evenly and always pitched in to help. I worked alongside another two new DCs. One we all referred to as the Commander, as even back then we knew he was destined for high places and better things. He was educated – well, certainly more than I was – and had an air of rank about him. He was a very good detective and a talented chief. Then there was a really tenacious local fella from an Irish background. He was a quick thinker and steady as the day is long – he was like a bloodhound, and never gave up on a case. You certainly wouldn't want him on your trail if you were a criminal. We all worked really well as a team, and spent long, long hours together at work.

Our supervisor, Jack, was a great character; he was a Celt, and coming to the end of a long and distinguished career.

He had served on the Flying Squad and was a true leader – he had the respect of the office without really having to do too much. Their office was called the Pips Club, as a uniform inspector had two silver 'pips' on his or her epaulette to show their rank.

Every day, there were two tasks that the detectives on duty had to complete. Firstly, once the supervisor had completed his meetings and attended to all necessary matters for that day – a detective would be allocated to take the boss to the pub, or a number of pubs. Jack was very slight of build and wasn't a great lover of solids, but he would easily drink eight to ten pints of bitter each lunchtime. Some people enjoyed the chaperone task, but others dreaded it, because if he didn't like you or thought you weren't good at your job, he would tell you.

Then, at 5 p.m., all detectives on duty would down their tools on hearing the words 'The Pips Club is now open.' There was a huge double cabinet full of booze in his office; we would all have a drink and talk to each other, taking the piss and showing the camaraderie you have in a close-knit team, like detectives did in those days. It made for great team spirit and bonding, and it would always be a thing of amusement to see what state Jack was in – or more importantly his chaperone – would come back in. Work would always get finished, the prisoners in the cells would be dealt with, and those that wanted to continue drinking would take the short trip across the road to the Elephant pub. It was the task of the night duty CID to ensure he and his car got safely home so that he could drive in the following morning. For us, the pattern was the same every day.

We played hard, but we also worked very hard. Drinking was a huge part of the detective culture and if you got the balance right between work and drink that was the recipe for success. We got through a tremendous amount of work in those days, and I used my time wisely to recruit a number of good informants.

Five

Harrow Road was a vibrant and extremely busy place to work, and competition was fierce to be the best detective. I was learning so much, and I was enjoying my time at the station. Time flew past, and securing a place on the crime squad had given me a well-earned break from the daily toil of interviewing the prisoners left in the cells every morning. It also got me away from the daily allocation of crimes to investigate that had occurred overnight in the area. I was now free to run whatever operations I wanted. This was the type of work I thrived on.

In that part of West London at the time, it was crucial to have the ability to blend in with the community, otherwise you stood out a mile. By now I had hair down my back and sported a ponytail. I always had a penchant for decent clothes, and dressed different to my colleagues. I had my own approach to police work, and I was an individual and a leader rather than a follower. I got the job done – it wasn't always textbook, but it was successful. I was a true believer in talking to the baddies, getting down on their level and trying to learn what it was like to be a villain. I found that they warmed to me, and I had a great talent for getting them to talk to me. I probably saw a lot of me in them; if I hadn't taken a different path, I may have been in the same position as them.

One day, out of the blue, I received a phone call from Mary, asking me for a favour. I had known her many years – she was a great detective and she would often disappear for days, apparently working for the Yard, but no one would ever ask any questions about the specifics of what she was doing. She told me she wanted me to meet someone at a local pub and fill him in about a particular housing estate on my patch. She said it would be worth my while.

The man in the pub was about thirty-five years old. He had long straggly hair, and a very rugged face with a scar the length of his forehead; he had numerous tattoos and wore a battered brown leather jacket and black half-fingered gloves. There was a Jack Russell on his lap, as Mary had said there would be. He shook my hand and, without asking me what I wanted, bought us both a large Lamb's Navy Rum. He was very polite, and quizzed me about the set-up on the estate and the individual bad guys controlling it. I was acquainted with all the players and rattled off everything I knew. Our meeting ended with him telling me that if I saw him around to ignore him, but that he had no doubt, from what Mary had said, we would meet again in the future. I watched him walk out the door, and forty-five minutes after meeting him, I was none the wiser about who he was or what he was doing. What I did know was that I liked him.

Six

It was déjà vu as I stepped off the District and Circle line at St James's Park and looked out for the sign to 'The Park and Broadway'. I thought I looked class as I shuffled my way up the stairs, pulled my warrant card out of my trench coat pocket and briefly flashed it at the rather rotund black lady, who gave me a beautiful smile as she allowed me through the barrier.

I had made this exact journey three months previously, although it hadn't ended the way I had envisaged. I'd got the phone call from my Irish friend Mary, saying that SO10 wanted me. On that day at the Yard, it had ended in embarrassment. I'd licked my wounds, however, and was now returning to be interviewed again to become a Level 1 undercover officer.

I went through security, which isn't what it is today, and took the Victoria Block lift to the fifth floor. The fifth floor at the Yard was known as the 'corridor of power' – there was plush carpet leading to double wooden doors, and portraits of previous commissioners adorned the walls. I felt out of place, uncomfortable – perhaps even nervous. Not of the forthcoming interview, but at the thought of bumping into a very senior officer, who might question what a pony-tailed no-one like me was doing on this illustrious corridor.

I pushed through the double doors and quietly made my way to the last but one office on the left-hand side. I knocked and heard a voice tell me to come in. There were three men sat in the room. In the middle was a very smart-looking man in his early forties, sporting jet-black, well-coiffured hair and a perfect black moustache. He was slim and wore his suit well, and he oozed confidence and charisma.

Next to him was a large white man who had mauled me three months previously – he was about sixteen stone, had a mop of brown hair, and wore clothes like your dad would. He didn't like me, that was clear, and I wasn't convinced by his cockney accent. I knew that this man had a fantastic reputation, but I felt that he didn't want me on his team. The third man had a smiley, lived-in face. I could see he'd done more than a few rounds in the boxing ring, and he had the hands to match.

The DCI, who I will call the Mexican because he reminded me of a baddie from one of the old westerns my dad would watch, started proceedings. He said, 'I know you made an appearance a few months ago, but we're going to pretend that didn't happen. You're in role now, react to what you see and hear.' He then pointed to the TV sat on the drinks cabinet beside me. 'I'm a paedophile and I'm watching two eight-year-old girls in their knickers on video, and I've got copies of this video for sale, if I'm happy with you.' He then undid his flies. 'I'm gonna have a wank. Are you, or what?!'

I didn't even pause for breath. I took one look at the television and another at the Mexican unzipping his flies and said, pointing at the TV, 'That is nice, very nice, but a fifty-year-old geezer playing with a shrivelled-up cock does nothing for me. I'll buy the video, but please, put your cock away.'

He smiled and said, 'That'll do for me, Joe. You're in. Alan here will take you down to the main office and explain what happens next.'

I stood up and was joined by the man with the huge hands. He shook my hand with a vice-like grip and said, 'I'm Alan. You done good there, son.'

This was the start of my journey as an undercover officer.

Seven

I was now a Level 1 undercover officer. I was a national resource, but at that time in the 1990s no one worked full-time in the role, apart from the handful of staff who ran the SO10 office. When specific operations were initiated, you would receive a phone call from the 10 office and tentative enquiries would be made to ascertain if you could get released from your day job. At the time, the majority of UCs worked on specialist squads or in busy CID offices, and undercover work was an extracurricular activity. You had to seek the support and release of your day job boss to allow you to go off and work undercover.

Undercover work was exciting: it came with definite risks, huge challenges and even greater rewards. We all craved to do this work full-time; it was like a dream job, and I'm sure that most people would thrive on the adrenalin that comes with these deployments. But the fact was, at this time, it was more like a hobby. You had to complete the eight to ten hours on your day job before you deployed into the seedy undercover world. It was an unspoken area of policing – no one asked you where you were going that evening or indeed, when you returned, where you had been. When we were together as a group of UCs, we looked like a motley crew, and you certainly wouldn't have thought we were in mainstream policing. The truth was, it was the most exciting challenge that policing held at the time.

I had recently been promoted to detective sergeant and had been posted to a very busy South London station. I was now both a supervisor and a UC, and I knew which one of the two roles excited me more. Whenever I received a call from the 10 office, I was invariably able to deploy, and so I started my apprenticeship as a new undercover officer. I went out and performed supporting roles and made cameo appearances, doing whatever I was asked to do. I was used on many operations, and the main problem I found at the beginning was convincing myself that the baddies had no idea I was a policeman pretending to be a villain. Once you overcome this, the skill is being yourself and staying calm. I loved this type of work and saw every different operation as a challenge.

There were now strict rules being placed on the police for stopping and searching people, and prisoners could only be kept in custody for set periods of time. There were specific requirements placed on interviewing suspects, including the fact that they had to be offered a solicitor. There was no doubt the pendulum had swung in favour of the villains rather than the police. There was no longer fear or trepidation about being arrested. Undercover work was one of the only ways to beat the bad guys at their own game. It was dangerous, but the rewards were fantastic. I also knew that I was good at it and wanted to do more and more deployments.

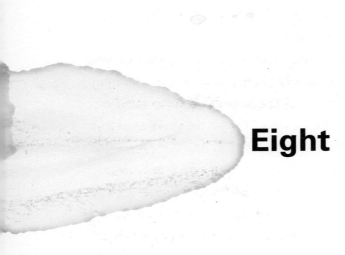

Eight

It was the mid-1990s and I was desperately trying to juggle my role as a supervisor on one of London's busiest squads, my undercover career, and life as father of a young family.

I hadn't been married very long, and Sarah and I had a new child and had recently moved into a new house in an unfamiliar area. My wife knew no one, and both sets of our parents were hundreds of miles away, so there was no support network for her to rely on. In truth, she knew very little about my work and even less about the fact that I was working undercover. We were close and talked a lot – that's if I wasn't at work – but those conversations never actually involved my job. In theory, Sarah and I should have sat down and discussed the pros and cons of me pursuing a role as a UC. In reality, all I had said when posed the question about family, was: 'My wife fully supports me becoming a UC.' That was far from the truth, but I knew that the lack of her support or knowledge of the role was not going to stop me.

I'm sure these pressures are exactly the same as all of you reading this book have previously or are currently experiencing. We all deal with pressures in different ways. It's the decisions that we make that shape our lives and those of the ones we love the most. I'm not sure I always made the right decisions.

The Flying Squad was one of the elite branches of Scotland Yard, and it was split into four offices covering geographical areas of London. The squad was set up in October 1919, and over the years had gained a reputation for courage and determination in tackling the most violent of London's armed robbers. The office I worked at was on a leafy suburban street in London, surrounded by properties worth millions of pounds. It was a picturesque setting and the perfect base to conduct investigations from. The Flying Squad was often the pinnacle of a detective's career, and many returned after taking promotion.

I had joined just as the Squad took responsibility for investigating the epidemic of 'steaming' offences, where large groups of males were entering banks and building societies to intimidate and terrorise staff, before leaving with as much cash as it was physically possible to steal. It wasn't really the type of offence that I had envisaged I would be investigating.

The London office was headed by a team of senior officers. On the first day I arrived, I was called by one of them into his office. He asked me to close the door and told me that now I was on the Flying Squad I was on the most elite squad in the country. He said my days of swanning around as an under-cover officer – with my long hair, in my flash cars – were over. He wanted all my attention focused on leading a successful team. I didn't like this man; I didn't like the way he dressed, the fact his suit jacket was too big for his slopey shoulders. I didn't like the fact his teeth were too big for his mouth, and I didn't like the way he was talking to me. Even his name – Justin – wound me up. But there was no way I was going to let him see my dislike. I assured him that he'd get 100 per cent from me, and that I was excited about my time on the squad.

The formalities were completed by him telling me that he was sending me on a firearms course, followed by a tactical advisers' course, so that I could supervise armed operations. The man made my skin crawl, and I couldn't find a single thing that I liked about him. He held his hand out and I looked at it, paused slightly before shaking it, and left his office. I rubbed the sweat from his palm off on my trousers as I walked down the corridor. I knew that I needed to stay one step ahead of this man, but I didn't think that would be too difficult.

I have to say that shooting was not my forte, and the thought of carrying a gun didn't excite me in any shape or form. It was a necessity on the Flying Squad, but some of the guys absolutely loved carrying one. To me it was a pain; the weight of the gun in its holster would damage any good-quality belt, and if you wore it in a shoulder holster it would crease the shape of your jacket. My gun was always in my car, in the pocket behind the driver's seat, where I sat, and I hoped that it would stay there throughout any operation. The fact of the matter was, I was a very poor shot. I don't think I could've hit a barn door, let alone one of South East London's top robbers as he was fleeing from a van or a bank he'd just robbed.

One of the funniest moments on the Squad, and what made me realise that the office wasn't equipped to deal with steamers, took place in the Home Counties. It was a Monday morning in the pedestrian-controlled area of a delightful garden city. The team was sitting in wait for a group of criminals that we'd had intelligence on for some time. We were holed up in offices opposite and adjacent to a well-known high street building society. Minutes after opening, between eight and ten fit black men in their early twenties ran into the building society. Within seconds they were over the counter one by one, pushing staff onto the floor and grabbing money.

Like coiled springs, we exited the comfort of our hideout to confront these robbers, all of whom were unarmed. The ensuing mayhem was like a darts team chasing a group of young sprinters. It's fair to say that most of our team were overweight; they loved a pint every night and chasing young robbers wasn't on their wish list. A few of the guys ran maybe fifty yards before throwing their metal asps in the direction of the fleeing criminals in desperation. We did manage to arrest one or two of the robbers, as some of us could run, and luckily none of the building society staff was injured.

It was just another typical day on the Flying Squad when I received a phone call from Don, my best pal who worked as a sergeant in the SO10 undercover office. He told me that a request had come in from overseas for assistance with an operation. It would require maybe a week in Europe every two months assisting one of their UCs.

It was a long-term, deep infiltration into a gang of serious criminals and businessmen in Holland and Belgium who were responsible for the production and supply of a large percentage of the Ecstasy tablets that had flooded the European cities. These men were a close-knit group, some of whom funded their criminal friends to run the illicit labs where the high-grade pills were made. They had proved almost impossible to investigate by conventional policing methods. The only way to find out exactly how these people conducted their business was to get amongst them. To become part of their network; to befriend them and encourage them to believe that we could enhance their criminal activity. It was a very important international operation – a fantastic new challenge.

He said he and the boss thought that it was perfect for me, and that he'd look after me on the job. Don was one of the handful of people that I trusted. We worked well together, and seemed to know what each other was thinking or what the other would do before he did it.

Don was a meticulous man, and his life was a complete contrast to mine. He was a year older than me, but he wasn't married and didn't have kids. He lived in a pristine show home in South London and he suffered severely from OCD. His house was immaculate, and you would never believe that anyone actually lived there, let alone him and his girlfriend. There was literally no sign of life in his house, and until I met his girlfriend – now his wife – I didn't believe she existed. Don was good Old Bill, and had trodden a very similar path to me in proving himself as a detective in London. It was a dog-eat-dog world and he was street savvy like myself. He had put a lot of villains behind bars the hard way.

He knew the issues that I had with my supervisor on the Flying Squad, but the timing couldn't have been better as my boss was off for at least four weeks following a minor operation. Both Don and I knew the detective inspector who was in temporary charge whilst he was away, and we got on well with him. Don also said that he would 'mark the card' of the Flying Squad superintendent (who just happened to be an ex-UC) so a request would be made for me. All in all, the job had my name written on it. In the 1990s the only time a UC was directly supervised was when they travelled overseas for an operation, otherwise your 'handler' was on the other end of a phone.

I wasn't really enjoying my time on the Flying Squad and it's fair to say that it hadn't lived up to its reputation. There were some very good, keen detectives on the Squad, but they were outbalanced by a number of people who had returned for a second posting but were still stuck in the ways of the 1980s. I found it frustrating, and I was obstructed in a number of operations that I wanted to conduct.

The DI agreed to release me, and he said that he had received a call from the superintendent at the Yard, who was aware of the operation and supported my release. I knew I was now bombproof, and had 'top cover' for the inevitable aggravation that I would get when the boss returned.

The following week, Don and I met with the two handlers who had flown over from Holland to talk to my boss about the operation. The undercover officer was not allowed into Scotland Yard, and he and I would meet once the formalities of this meeting was over. The two handlers were gentlemen and they both had the same name, but one was 6'4" tall and the other 5'6" small, so they were known as Big Luuk and Small Luuk. I liked them from the moment I met them. They were warm and friendly, laid-back and constantly smiling. They had been in their jobs a number of years and it showed. It was like having your two favourite uncles around who you hadn't seen for years.

Don and I and the two Luuks went and met the UC in a bar not a million miles from the Yard. He was a big guy; he made Big Luuk look not so big. He wore leather trousers that didn't leave a lot to the imagination, and he had a head like a pit bull. He and I got on from the moment he squeezed my hand and introduced himself as Hans. We spent until the early hours talking, drinking and joking, and also coming up with a plan for the operation. By the end of the night, it felt like we were the best of friends. Don spent most of his time talking to the Luuks, and they agreed when we would travel over on the first deployment.

It was far too late for me to get home, and there was no way I could drive, so they paid for a hotel room for me for the night. I said my goodbyes, as I had to be up and away early the next morning to return to the reality of my day job on the Flying Squad. We agreed that we would see each other again in two weeks' time in Holland. The next fortnight seemed to take an age to pass.

Nine

I woke up ten minutes before my alarm was due to go off at 5 a.m., doing my best not to wake up my wife as she slept next to me. I jumped in the shower, brushed my teeth and then went into the utility room to put on the clothes I had laid out the evening before. I crept out of the house and was sat in the car as the alarm on my phone went off indicating it was now five. My packed case had sat in the boot since nine o'clock the previous night. I liked the smell of the leather in the Mercedes that I'd been given to use on this trip. This car had proved lucky for me in the past, and I hoped it would continue.

I drove the forty-five minutes to Don's house without encountering any traffic. He was looking out the front window of his Brookside Close–style house as I pulled up. He went straight to the boot, and when he then opened the passenger door we realised that we both had the identical red Ralph Lauren jacket on. 'We must co-ordinate our wardrobes before the next trip,' I said, laughing at him. Before I could drive off, he had to go through his OCD routine of checking for his passport, three denominations of money, and the reference number for the tunnel. Just as I was about to drive off, he leapt out of the car and quickly tried the door of the highly polished car that sat on his drive, to confirm it was indeed locked.

The Channel Tunnel had only opened a couple of years earlier, in May 1994, and I had never had the occasion to use it. I wasn't quite sure what to expect. We were in plenty of time when we pulled off the M20 at junction 11a and handed our passports to the lady in the cubicle. She handed me a letter to place on the interior mirror of the car I was driving, and we were told our train was in fifty minutes and it would be announced in the service area. We grabbed a coffee and agreed that it was far too early to eat.

Don had got us each a thousand pounds' worth of French francs, Belgian francs and Dutch guilders for the trip. Like a dad handing his son weekly pocket money, he gave me an envelope of crisp notes in the three separate currencies. The remainder of the time was taken up with him arguing with me about the fact that I had not purchased the kit that was required by French law to apply to the headlights of the car, or the spare bulbs and emergency triangle. I was not in the slightest bit concerned by this, but for Don it was another thing he was stressed about.

Undercover

Our number was called and I followed a line of traffic onto a train platform and into the shuttle. I was told to park, apply my handbrake and keep the windows open. It was a strange experience sat on a train inside one's own car. In thirty-five minutes the shuttle quietly arrived in Calais, and the doors opened and all the cars made their way tentatively off the train.

Don and I had agreed that we would stop at Cité Europe and fill up the car with booze, as we both knew that we would not be in the mood on the return journey. We looked like a couple of luvvies from the King's Road; neither of us wanted to push the trolley. We argued amongst ourselves as to whether Tesco was cheaper than Carrefour. We opted for Carrefour and stocked up on Cellier des Dauphins and J. P. Chenet, along with a number of cases of Export 33. I also grabbed a Reblochon cheese, but I knew I'd have to wrap it over and over again and hide it from Don, as it would truly stink the car out.

We filled the vast boot with our booze, and as expected Don stacked them in a neat and organised manner. He wanted to ensure the boxes were positioned so that in six days' time, on our return, he could take his from the right and mine would sit on the left. But I knew that as soon as we started driving, his excellent organisational skills would be made irrelevant, as the cases would move around, and it would be a free-for-all on Sunday.

It's hard to believe now that for a journey to Holland, three different currencies were required. We made sure that we stopped in Belgium for breakfast so we could spend their francs. The breakfast consisted of lovely hunks of bread, a pot of butter, some Gouda cheese and two bowls of jam. We both fancied sausage, egg and bubble, but as a substitute this was very tasty. We washed it down with fresh coffee and cigarette smoke. Neither Don nor I smoked but it appeared that everyone else in France and Belgium did, wherever they were.

We continued our journey to the south of Holland, and carefully made our way to the address of the house where Don was going to stay with our handlers. In preparation, Don had purchased a detailed map of the area the week before, from the National Map Centre on Caxton Street, opposite the Yard. Don was probably – no, definitely – the most organised and professional person I knew; everything he did was meticulously thought through. In fact, he and I were complete opposites, except that he had similar sartorial style to me.

We were greeted like long-lost relatives, and the smell of fresh coffee filled the kitchen/dining room. Hans and both Luuks were there, and we discussed the plan for the next six days. The rules when working overseas are that if it is an operation on behalf of that country, you abide by their laws and their protocols. The briefing was very laid-back; Hans wanted to get my face known in the area and there were many bars that he wanted to visit. I must admit it didn't sound too stressful. The conversation between Don and the two handlers involved which restaurants the three of them would eat at over the next few days. Tall Luuk said, 'Remember, Don, if you don't eat or drink you die. This is very important.'

I grabbed my case from the boot of my car and put it into Hans's vehicle. We drove the half an hour or so to his apartment. It was a large, loft-style, open-plan affair with exposed brickwork; apparently it had formerly been a bakery, and there was a stream running down the side that used to turn the large wheel for grinding the flour. The main thing was there were two bedrooms, both with en-suite, so our modesty would remain intact.

Hans and I spoke as if we had known each other for years, but it was incredible that not once did we speak about our own families. This ensured that we didn't blur the lines. All Hans knew was who I was as an undercover officer, and nothing about the real me.

We went out that evening much later than we would have in London. It appeared that most local people would eat a meal with their family or friends at home, before heading out to enjoy many drinks later on. The Dutch people put us to shame: they were polite, educated, and knew how to get the work–life balance right. Everyone spoke English – most of them very well. They also knew how to have a good time and could drink. Unbeknown to me, it was the lead-up to Carnaval in this part of the Netherlands. This tradition was associated with the Catholic faith and took place over three days prior to Ash Wednesday. In modern-day Holland, the carnival has continued without any association with religion, and is a time for people to enjoy themselves. Roads close, businesses shut, and many people take a week's holiday to celebrate in the bars and restaurants. There is a certain style of music that is played in the bars, and lots of dancing. The Dutch don't need a reason to party, but for the next few days they had the perfect excuse.

I was introduced to many people whose names I would never remember, but they were all so friendly it seemed the perfect place to work. We partied into the night, and their appetite and endurance were far greater than mine. I told Hans I was spent and needed to sleep – after all, it was 3 a.m. He agreed, and we both hit our beds feeling a little worse for wear.

Amazingly, I managed to sleep until 9 a.m., which was surely a record for me. Hans was still asleep, and I made an abortive attempt at filling the coffee percolator, then instead settled for a glug of orange juice to wash down two paracetamol. I rang Don, but he didn't pick up. I was later to find out that he and the Luuks hadn't gone to bed until 4.30 a.m. The fridge looked a tad devoid of food, so I slipped on a pair of joggers and took a stroll into the town, which was only five minutes away. It certainly cleared my head, and I bought some fresh bread, butter and a selection of cut meats and cheese, along with some fresh milk.

By the time I got back, Hans was up and the strong smell of coffee filled the apartment. He was in his training gear and he looked huge; he wouldn't have been amiss on Muscle Beach in LA. He invited me to come to the gym, and against my better judgement I accepted. It is no exaggeration to say he ruined me in the gym; he made me lift weights and do repetitions that I'd never done before. I was fit – football fit – and I wasn't carrying any weight, but I couldn't and didn't lift weights. There were women in the gym with bigger muscles than I could dream of having. He certainly was a strong boy, and I was glad I had him in my gang.

We spent the remainder of my stay visiting as many places as we could. We drank a lot, ate plenty and met many, many people, but slept very little. We worked well as a team and the handlers were very grateful for the hours that we put in.

The journey home seemed a lot longer than the way there. We were both weary, and Don said the two Luuks could party for weeks and his body could not cope with another six days like that. He said that he'd insisted that they went and saw their families, just so that he could stay out of the pub.

I wore my sunglasses all the way back, not because it was a sunny March morning, but because my eyes were so tired and sore. We were both glad when we arrived at Calais. Although we were early, we were sure that if it wasn't busy we would be allowed on an earlier train. We showed our passports and were directed into a small garage area that was controlled by British customs officers. All Don would say is: 'I fucking knew it – it's because you've got those glasses on.' We were subjected to a full and thorough turnout. They had everything out of the boot; they opened the cases of beer and put the car up on the ramp. It was as if they genuinely expected to find something.

Don was being pleasant and answering all their questions, but I had taken a different approach, and apart from showing them my passport didn't give them the time of day. It was a good forty-five minutes that they kept us in the garage, and they ran sniffer dogs over all our luggage and purchases. I'm surprised the dogs could smell anything, as the Reblochon cheese truly stunk after six days in the boot. The whole garage smelt of it. They told us that they were finished with us and the car, but no one apologised for delaying us. I could see that one of their Geltex high-visibility jackets was hanging over a chair near the boot of our car. I saw the look on Don's face as he knew exactly what I was going to do.

I unwrapped a few of the plastic bags and removed the circular cheese, then dropped it into the right jacket pocket and quickly secured the Velcro fastener. We drove out of the garage and were waved through the secondary checkpoint and onto the shuttle. Don did not say a single word until the train started moving towards England. He looked at me and shook his head: 'I cannot believe you did that. You are such a cunt.' We burst out laughing, and the laughter continued for most of the journey. We both knew this had been our first visit of many to Holland, and we were more than pleased with the way the operation had started.

Ten

On returning from a spell away you are filled with guilt. Guilt that you have put your family, and everything that was planned for the past six days at home, in second place. Guilt that you abandoned your office, colleagues and investigations, and have had no contact with your team for that time. All these things prey on your mind.

You know that you are part of an international investigation targeting a team of criminals responsible for the production and distribution of the bulk of Ecstasy tablets in Europe. It's an operation that poses significant danger and challenges. But you know that no one will care about that, and you won't be able to discuss the case or fight your corner when you're told that you're not pulling your weight or that you've let the team down.

I knew that I would be returning regularly to Holland, and I realised that my position in my day job would become more difficult. I also understood that I had the small issue of my supervisor to deal with on his return to work.

I arrived home and all was fine; my wife didn't have time to worry about me – her life was chaotic and much busier than mine. She had a home to keep, the kids to deal with, and all the clubs and teams and football matches to ensure they got to. Her job was far more difficult than mine, and she did it very well. No matter how busy she was, she always read to the kids at bedtime, a talent that she had mastered to perfection. If in exceptional circumstances I was around to read at bedtime, I would always be told, 'You don't do the voices like Mum does.' I know she enjoyed reading to them as much as they loved the way she told each story. I was very lucky to have such a good wife; she was a lovely person, and an even better mum. I have always thought how lucky the kids were to have her.

I arrived back in the Flying Squad office on the Monday morning. I had dumped my washing at home and had an evening with the kids, and I was on the road at 7 a.m. I wanted to make sure that I was on top of everything before the bosses landed at nine. I kept my head down over the next three weeks, and worked longer hours and harder than anyone else in the office. I wasn't going to give them a single reason to criticise me. The only thing that suffered was my family and the amount of time I spent with them. I would literally go home, climb into bed when everyone was asleep, and then get up the following morning and leave before anyone was awake.

One particular evening, I was in the office alone at about 8.30 when I heard the combination door to the office open. It was Justin and the main Flying Squad driver returning from a late meeting at the Yard. The driver, Steve, was a lovely man and a very talented driver; he popped into the office and we chatted for ten minutes. He invited me down the pub for a few pints, but I told him that I had work to finish. He pointed down the corridor to Justin's office and whispered that he'd been sat outside a pub in Victoria waiting for him to finish a few pints following his meeting. He said that on the way back he'd had a moan-up about me, amongst others, and had described me as a prima donna. Steve laughed, but told me to watch my back and disappeared to enjoy a few pints.

About fifteen minutes later, I heard a door close and footsteps down the corridor. Justin came into the office, stood behind me and held on to the back of my chair. I could smell alcohol on his breath and cigarette smoke on his cheap raincoat. He leant forwards and spoke quietly but through gritted teeth: 'You think you're a clever fucker, getting that job through while I was away. Well, your days are numbered and I'm on your case. You better watch your back. I don't know who you think you are, but you're a nobody in this office.'

I was so angry, and I wanted to grab his scrawny face with my hand and smash it into the wall, but there was no way I would give him the pleasure. In any case, I knew the office was covered by cameras. So I didn't say a single word, I just turned around and stared deep into his eyes. He found the silence awkward and muttered under his breath – 'fucking prima donna' – as he left the office for the night.

I shook my head in disbelief. This was the hypocritical man who had had two undercover officers working for him for three months, helping him infiltrate a team of robbers. The man was an idiot, and I knew I couldn't work for him for much longer. I had always been taught that revenge is a dish best served cold, and these were the thoughts that I held in my head for my journey home late that night.

I made half a dozen more trips to Holland in the company of Don, and on both occasions we were subjected to an extensive and prolonged turnout on our return journey. It appeared that the customs officers were having the last laugh over the Reblochon incident and not us. It added an extra hour and a half to our estimated journey time, and Don would say, 'Who's the funny one now, you div?' I knew he was right, but it still made me chuckle, sitting in that garage in Calais.

The operation was progressing very well and we had been invited by the targets to go to Spain on a trip to celebrate the sale of a number of restaurants by one of the individuals. The trip had been approved, and of course Don was coming along to ensure that I didn't get into any trouble. We flew to Barcelona, and Don met up with the two handlers while Hans and I hired a car and drove an hour up the coast to meet the seven targets. These guys were all – bar one – older than us, and they ran successful businesses as well as their criminal enterprises. The majority of their daily life was made up of drinking and womanising.

Undercover

We booked into our hotel, which was chic and classy. It didn't feel like a holiday hotel – more of a boutique place. The high season had come to a close, and the normal hustle and bustle of a Spanish seaside town had disappeared weeks before. The temperature was warm without being sunbathing weather, but you could still feel the lovely, therapeutic heat on your skin. It was a welcome change.

Hans made contact with the guys and told me that we were meeting at 8 p.m. for a celebration dinner at the only fish restaurant that was still open. We spent the next few hours wandering around the cobbled streets of this once-busy fishing port. I admired the wooden window shutters and the pastel colours of the painted terraced houses that overlooked the narrow streets. I found myself staring at the elderly ladies who sat on wooden stools outside their houses making detailed and intricate linen handkerchiefs and napkins with their weathered hands. I loved the gold hoops that hung from their ears, and the shimmer of gold that adorned their teeth when they smiled at me. I knew that these women were the backbone of the families that lived inside these beautiful houses.

We had a really pleasant afternoon, and then we had an hour or so to get ready before we wandered down to the fish restaurant. The evening was really warm – in fact, it felt like the temperature had gone up. The seven of them were sat outside underneath an awning, at a large table overlooking the harbour. The white linen tablecloths were covered in bottles of wine and ashtrays, but no food had been eaten yet. There was no doubt that these men had started the celebration early. We were greeted with cheers and shouts of 'God Save the

Queen.' They were in high spirits, and enjoying the Spanish wine and beer.

The table was like a scene from the film *Goodfellas*. Sat at the head of the table was Arthur – it was his celebration, and he was the reason that we had all travelled to this beautiful spot in Spain. He was a hard man, a man that had clearly fought many physical battles in his time, and his face bore the evidence of that. He was now a successful businessman, and he owned a number of restaurants and a bar. He was the number two in the organisation, and the main financial backer. The number one target hadn't been able to travel to Spain, as a rival drug distributor had recently shot him in an attempt on his life.

The most difficult member of the group to judge was Ludo. He rarely said a word and I always felt uncomfortable in his company. I avoided him as much as I possibly could. He watched everyone and listened far more than he ever talked. Arthur's best friend, Pieter, was an over-tanned skinny man in his mid fifties, who wore open-necked shirts and Italian hand-stitched loafers without any socks. He had a huge horizontal scar that ran down his chest and was always on view behind the huge, gold letter 'P' that hung from a ridiculously heavy belcher chain. This man was the mouthpiece of the group, and he came from a large Gypsy family. He was volatile and uncouth and racist. I really didn't like him.

We spent the night drinking plenty and picking at *gambas*, paella, stuffed peppers, cheese *croquetas* and calamari. For these men the food was a side dish to the main course, which was the alcohol. The evening got louder and the wine flowed freely. The meal finished when three cars pulled up on the harbourside. We were all given a balloon of Lepanto Gran Reserva, which I was assured was a top Spanish brandy. We didn't sit and gently sip and appreciate such a wonderfully delicate and expensive drink, but knocked it back in two glugs.

The bill was paid in cash by Arthur, from a vast amount of money he kept in the black leather manbag that he had on the table in front of him. We drove in convoy out of the town and into the Spanish night, disappearing into the countryside. There were three of us in each executive taxi. After about thirty minutes, we turned off the road onto a long, windy dirt track that dropped down into a valley. We drove through a large set of gates to an illuminated ranch-style building. I could see a very slim South American–looking male stood outside, as if he was awaiting our arrival. He was dressed in a tight-fitting black suit, and he had a mop of black hair that was combed back; it glistened under the lights.

I wound down the windows to hear the chorus of crickets making quite a noise under the pitch black of the sky, which was illuminated by the thousands of stars that were clearly on display. Arthur was in the lead car, and he got out and engaged in a heated discussion with the South American for a few moments. He then removed a wad of money from the leather bag, and handed it to the slick-looking male before shaking his hand. He gestured for us all to get out of the cars and join him. We stood on the wooden veranda and Arthur explained that everything was paid for, that we had the place to ourselves and to have fun. I was listening to him as I saw the brake lights of the three cars disappear into the darkness.

I was near the back of the nine of us as we wandered into the building. It was wooden from top to bottom, but there was a Hawaiian theme to the bar area. The room opened up to reveal about twelve girls dressed only in their bikinis – some wearing high heels and a few barefooted. They were sat on a long, high-backed pine bench, and all of them were smiling. I was stuck in that moment as I surveyed the different nation-alities, hair colours and shapes of the ladies. I found myself focusing on a red fluffy bow that a tall blonde girl had on the front of her stiletto-heeled shoes.

Arthur put his arm around me and said, 'Have as many as you want – it's my gift to you.' I leant on the bar as I tried to work out the enormity of my problem. I was stuck in the middle of nowhere in a brothel surrounded by beautiful pros-titutes and seven criminals, with the go-ahead to do whatever I wanted with whomever I chose, and it was all paid for. As I was going through my thought process, I ordered a San Miguel and watched Arthur grab the two youngest girls by the hand. They climbed up a short flight of stairs and disap-peared behind a heavy velvet curtain.

A very petite oriental girl came and stood next to me, and asked me to come and sit down with her. She was tiny, and had flawless skin and silky black hair that went down to the middle of her back. She grabbed my hand and made to lead me away. I handed her my glass of beer and told her to take it and I would join her after I'd used the bathroom. I watched her walk slowly and seductively over to a booth, and she blew me a kiss as I stood watching her. I walked towards the entrance and saw an illuminated top hat, which I presumed indicated the Gents.

Undercover

As I walked in, Ludo was in there looking at himself in the mirror. He was sweating profusely and was wiping the condensation off his silver-rimmed round spectacles. He put his glasses on the ceramic sink and splashed cold water on his face. He was about fifty-eight years old and had a hair-style like a monk, with nothing on top but short cropped at the sides. He had a very large, solid, protruding tummy that had been earned over many years in bars and restaurants. He wore a short-sleeved, light-blue shirt with a breast pocket that contained his cigarettes. There were sweat marks visible and expanding under his armpits. I looked at him and said, 'Ludo, are you OK?' He dried the water from his face with two or three paper towels, and discarded them in the bin on the floor.

He looked at me in the mirror as he held on to the ceramic sides of the sink, and replied, 'No, I'm not. I don't want to be here. I am on my third marriage to a beautiful thirty-five-year-old girl who I love very much. She will find out about this from one of them. I can't let that happen.'

I looked at him as he straightened his body and let go of the sink. I could see that he meant every word. 'What do you want me to do?'

He turned around to face me, took a step closer and held both my shoulders. 'Please, just get me out of here. I can't stay here.'

I took Ludo outside. I knew there was no phone signal and I couldn't go in and order a cab as the other men would not allow that to happen. We walked the short distance to the boundary of the brothel, where there was a small pergola with a wooden seat, where I presumed the security guard would sit during the summer season. I told Ludo to wait there and I'd be as quick as I could.

I was in the dark apart from a flicker of light that I could see just over the hill of the unmade road. The closer I got to this light, the louder the noise of dogs became. I got to a set of large metal gates, which led up to a huge house that was in darkness, but the flicker of light came from a smaller building slightly to the left. There was an intercom system that obviously controlled the electronic gates. I buzzed it repeatedly but there was no answer, although I heard the sound of a door open and shut and the noise of dogs barking frantically. I then saw the silhouette of a very small man leading two dogs down the long driveway.

'*Ayudame, por favor*,' I said to the man, who was barely managing to hold the dogs with his right hand as he shone the torchlight into my face. He didn't say a word to me, but turned on his heels and headed back up the hill with the dogs as I repeated myself: '*Por favor.*' I heard the door open again, and then a few minutes later it shut and the tiny silhouette reappeared down the driveway. The man opened the gates with a key fob when he was about twenty-five feet away. In a German accent he said, 'You want some help, my English friend?'

I explained the predicament I was in and asked him if I could use his phone to call a cab. He said that he could do with a break from the house and agreed to drive me back.

I'd been gone about fifteen minutes by the time I climbed into a large red Mercedes that looked like it was very seldom driven. The man knew the short drive to 'the house of the ladies', as he described it. We pulled up alongside Ludo, who was exactly where I'd left him. A huge smile erupted across his sad face and he climbed into the back of the car. He was patting me on the shoulder over and over and thanking me. I told him that it was Dieter he needed to thank and not me. We drove back into Blanes and we both invited Dieter into a tiny tapas bar for a few drinks.

The bar was full of local people, and surprisingly busy for the early hours of the morning. There were two huge hams on stands on the counter, and the air was full of thick cigar smoke. Ludo bought the largest Cohiba cigar for himself and handed another to our new friend Dieter, who rolled it in his hands and then held it to his nose and savoured the smell. We drank beer and brandy, and after about an hour Dieter said he must get back to the 'big house'. Ludo gave him a handful of pesetas and placed another Cohiba in his pocket. We both thanked him for his help. He left the bar with half the lit cigar hanging out of the side of his mouth.

Ludo was so genuinely grateful for me getting him away from the brothel. He told me that I had saved his marriage. We drank and enjoyed each other's company, and he told me many stories and opened up to me about his wasted days spent in a Belgian prison. We were definitely getting close and a trust was forming, a bond that I hadn't previously had with him. Ludo was the quietest of the seven, and I was always worried about the quiet ones, as they listened far more than they spoke.

I had got up to order us two more brandies when the door crashed open, and the bar fell silent for a moment as Hans filled up the doorway. I walked towards him, realising that I had completely forgotten about him. It hadn't even entered my head that I had left my colleague, my teammate, my partner behind. He grabbed me around the throat with his right hand and pushed me against the wall. He was a strong man, much stronger than I was or ever would be. He said through gritted teeth, 'Don't you ever do that again. I would not have left you there.' He released his grip and lowered me slightly so my feet were now in full contact with the floor of the bar.

I knew he was absolutely right. I had made a selfish decision earlier that night. Not only had I done Ludo a massive favour, but I'd also got myself out of a very difficult situation. I hadn't given any thought to anyone but myself. Ludo had been my ticket to get us both out of the brothel. In fact, it should have been the three of us driving away together in Dieter's car. I apologised to Hans, and like a true professional he assessed the atmosphere of the bar. He could see Ludo sat in the corner and knew that I must have done it for a reason. He went and sat with Ludo, and shouted over to me to order a large brandy.

I wanted to give the two of them enough time to talk to one another before I returned with the drinks. By the time I sat back down, Hans had accepted a Cohiba and was chatting freely with Ludo. The three of us talked and talked for the next two hours, and there was no doubt we had made huge inroads into Ludo and he had opened up to the two of us. I asked the bar owner to order a taxi for Ludo, as his hotel was a little further away than ours and he was not in a fit state to walk. He insisted on paying the bar bill, and hugged me as I put him in the back of the car.

Undercover

We watched the taxi disappear up the hill, and then Hans and I started walking back towards our hotel. It had been a very long night, but I felt particularly sober and focused. I apologised to Hans, and promised him that I would never let him down again. He was very understanding and realised that out of his difficult evening there was a positive outcome. He said Ludo was a great ally for us to have and he now trusted us, and that wouldn't have happened if I'd stayed there.

I looked at him and smiled and said, 'Anyway, Hans, tell me what happened to you when I left you?' He smiled back at me and said, 'I used all the skills I have learnt to deal with the situation professionally.' I nodded in admiration as I said, 'Very good answer, Hans.'

We said goodnight and climbed the stairs to our first-floor rooms. I looked at my watch as I took it off and placed it on the bedside table. It was four in the morning and I could hear the sound of the birds beginning to wake up outside. Moments later, I was fast asleep in the luxurious, white Egyptian-cotton sheets of the huge king-size bed.

Eleven

I felt more and more unhappy on the Flying Squad, and the supervisor of the unit had made it clear that he wasn't going to make my stay there a comfortable one. I needed to have an escape plan. The work wasn't what I expected it to be and I really wasn't enjoying my time there.

Don phoned me up out of the blue and said that the head of the undercover unit wanted to see me. As normal when a boss wants to see you, I racked my brains for what I'd done wrong. I quizzed Don about the reason for the meeting, but he told me not to worry and to be in his office at four o'clock. I knew the DCI of the undercover unit reasonably well; he was a proper detective and had excelled in his time on the Flying Squad in South London. He was a man's man and someone that I felt you could trust as a boss. He wasn't flying through the promotion ranks and using the undercover unit as a paragraph on his CV; he believed in the unit and was a very safe and capable pair of hands to deal with the complexities of some of the operations.

I got to the Yard with five minutes to spare and abandoned my car in the chaos of the basement car park. I went straight up to the fifth floor, walked past the main office and down to the end of the corridor and the door marked *Detective Chief Inspector SO10*. The door was open and the boss was busily working at his desk. The office was set up considerably different from my last meeting in this office, when his predecessor had interviewed me to become an undercover officer. I knocked tentatively and he told me to come in and shut the door. He had a pot of coffee on a percolator and he poured us both a cup. We talked about football, as he was an avid Wimbledon fan and knew that I loved the game.

After the pleasantries had finished, he asked me if I knew why he'd summoned me to come up to the Yard to see him. I told him that I hadn't got a clue, which was the truth. He explained that funding had been put aside to set up an infiltration unit as part of SO10. It would employ full-time UCs to deploy on long-term infiltrations. He said that Don was in the process of setting up the unit, but that he wanted two supervisors to run it. He described it as the 'crown jewels' of the department, and that it had to be run by experienced UCs and tactically astute detectives. He said that he wanted me to be the second supervisor in the unit. Don and I would report directly to him, and the work would involve national and international operations.

I was flattered, to say the least, by the offer. SO10 was internationally recognised as the centre of excellence for undercover operations. The supervisors that worked in the SO10 office were at the top of their game and were held in high regard. The DCI told me that there were two vacancies coming up in the new year due to retirements, and that initially I would work in the main office at the Yard but after a maximum of three months I'd be on the infiltration unit. I was not to say a word to a soul, and even when I started at the 10 office I was to keep his plan to myself. He told me that Don knew everything, so the secret was between the three of us. I was completely shell-shocked; I had just been offered the best job in the Metropolitan Police, a job that many people would have given their right hand for. I was a very lucky man.

Before I left his office, the boss told me that I could relax a bit now about that idiot who was causing me all the aggravation on the Flying Squad. He told me that he had always thought he was a wanker. I shook his hand, and he said I needed to keep my head down as the transfer would be agreed by the bosses and I need do nothing further.

I skipped down the corridor like a schoolboy and poked my head into the main SO10 office to see if Don was about. He came to the reception counter and I asked him if he had a minute for me. He grabbed his coat, and we left the Yard and went to our favourite cafe by St James's Park tube station. The coffee in this place was the best, as all the staff were proper Italians, but I really didn't like the tall thin glass cups. I sat next to Don and gave him his glass; he looked over at me and said, 'I understand congratulations are in order.' We then spent the next fifteen minutes talking about how my name had been suggested for the job. He said that Michael, the DCI, had insisted that he needed the two most capable staff in charge of the new unit and that he wanted continuity for the future. Don said that the boss had asked him if he would be happy to work with me if he could get me released from the Flying Squad. Michael knew that Don and I were close, and that we worked well as a team. Don told him that I would have been his first choice and that he couldn't have asked for a better partner. Don said that in a five-minute conversation the deal was done. Michael had phoned the head of the Flying Squad, an old friend of his, who agreed to let me go. There was never a shortage of detectives who wanted to join the Flying Squad, so it was easy to agree.

I thanked Don for all his support and told him how excited I was about the prospect of running the unit with him. I felt proud, grateful and humble. I knew that I wouldn't tell a soul – just in case, for some reason, the transfer fell through – but I had everything crossed that it would go through smoothly. I now didn't care about the aggravation I was getting on the Flying Squad. He was irrelevant to me, inconsequential, and I would do my best to keep out of his way. I would be professional, and keep my head down and my nose clean until the transfer was complete. My escape plan had been prepared for me and I was looking forward to completing it.

Everything seemed to be going fine; I was ticking the days off and getting the job done. Christmas was upon us, and I had received a phone call from Michael to say that I'd be starting at SO10 in January but that no one was going to be told until a few days before Christmas.

We were fast approaching the Squad's Christmas lunch. These lunches were traditionally very boozy affairs; they were often a time when pent-up frustrations aired themselves following too much red wine and lager. This particular lunch was in a rather lovely part of London. As usual, it had been an early start and the inter-team rivalry within the office was apparent. There were heated discussions over which team had the most 'pavement' jobs off, which team hadn't had any, and which team had put which gang of robbers away for the longest stretch in prison, and so on. It was all a very macho rivalry.

I had learnt over the years never to drink wine at these functions. I always stuck to beer and was acutely aware of the detectives who would quaff red wine like it was water. It was always them that seemed to collapse onto their meal or be involved in any incidents that occurred. At this particular lunch I noticed that Justin was in the red-wine gang; the conversations from the three or four of them were getting louder. It was his role during the dessert course to stand up and say a few words. It wasn't a difficult task to rally the troops and thank them for all their hard work. Well, it is very difficult when you have drunk far too much red wine. He stood up to deliver his speech and he looked dreadful. He wasn't a well-dressed man at the best of times; the suits he wore just hung off his slopey shoulders and looked cheap and creased. The best item of clothing he possessed was the silk Flying Squad tie that hung halfway down his shirt. He began to speak, but the words wouldn't come out in any semblance of order. He was getting barracked, and the harder he tried to regain control, the more raucous everyone got. I just sat there quietly thinking to myself what a complete knob the man was. He was publicly humiliating himself. One of his mates stood up and rescued him by delivering a well-timed anecdote.

The meal was descending into carnage as port and brandy bottles were placed on the table. I decided that I had seen and heard enough for one day. I told the six members of my team that I was going to the Gents and I'd see them in the wine bar two doors down where I'd buy them all a drink. I went down the steps into the basement, where the fully refurbished and plush toilets were. I went to one of the urinals and rested my forehead on the antique white tiles whilst I emptied my bladder. There was a loud crash and Justin half fell through the door, helped by one of the other, more sensible, officers from the office. He saw me straight away and made his way over to the urinal. He was slurring his speech: 'Here he is, the so-called best undercover officer in London . . . fucking prima donna is what you are, a fucking prima donna.'

I ignored him, and turned and walked to the sink area to wash my hands. He followed me and made a grab for my arm, but missed. I washed my hands whilst he shouted at me, telling me my days were numbered and that I wasn't fit to be on the Flying Squad. He detested the fact that I hadn't worn a Flying Squad tie to the meal and said I had let the Squad down. I dried my hands on two or three paper towels and carefully placed them in the Brabantia silver-and-black bin.

I stopped in the middle of the toilets for a moment, and all the pain and unhappiness this man had caused me over the last eighteen months overwhelmed me. He was a nasty man;

he had done all he could to ensure I knew I wasn't welcome. No one would have criticised me for doing what I was about to do. I didn't want any witnesses; I'd just ask the others to step outside whilst the 'boss' and I had a chat. Fuck it – what had I got to lose? In fact, a lot of people would thank me, would even shake my hand. He made another lunge for me as I stood there. Now was the time. I had thought about this moment in my head; I was going to smash him straight between the eyes. I could feel the pain as my knuckles crashed into the bridge of his nose. I could hear the sound of his nose breaking and see the inevitable blood that would splatter over his cheap and tatty shirt. He deserved everything that he was going to get.

He stumbled, and as I looked at his dishevelled and pathetic state, I knew what I was going to do. I'd show him who was the better man. I looked at him and winked. I patted him on the shoulder and said 'Look after yourself. Make sure you get home safely.' I put £20 in his pocket and asked him get a cab before he got himself into trouble or hurt.

I walked out of the pub and joined my team in the wine bar. These were hard-working detectives who were good at their jobs. They had covered my back whilst I was away working undercover, and I insisted that I get the bill in the wine bar as a way of thanking them. I didn't utter a word about the antics in the toilet, and to this day only three people know what happened in there.

I was happy to make it through Christmas and glad to see the back of that year. The new year brought a new job and a new challenge, and it heralded a new era in my career. I was excited for the future.

Undercover

I did have one ongoing undercover job that I wanted to finish before I started on the infiltration unit. An operation that would see me cross the water to Belfast, to finalise buying up to five kilos of heroin. It was a job that filled me with worry, a job that couldn't be taken lightly. There was a huge amount of planning and logistics that went into an operation of this nature. There were huge dangers, and lots of pressure on me to ensure that it was successful, as money and time had been invested to get the investigation to its current stage. Deploying in Belfast was a new challenge that took things to another level of danger and high risk. I always liked to be put under pressure to test my skills to the limit, to see if I had the bottle. This was going to test me to the core. This was a big operation, and I knew that I had to finish it.

Twelve

It was just before I started at the infiltration unit, whilst still at the Yard, that I was sent to Belfast. We landed at the city airport carrying only hand luggage. I was travelling with Don, my cover officer and best friend. As usual, he was anal about certain things. He kept telling me to take my sunglasses off, as he feared that they would trigger a stop by Special Branch. It was one of his pet hates, me wearing sunglasses indoors. As usual, and much to his annoyance, I ignored him.

I gripped my leather holdall tightly as we exited airside into the arrivals lounge. If I am to be truthful, I was a little bit apprehensive about this trip. Belfast was an unknown place to me. All I knew of it were the daily news bulletins and the scenes of carnage that accompanied them. It had been suggested by the Royal Ulster Constabulary that we stay at the Europa Hotel in the city centre, but Don said staying at Europe's most bombed hotel wasn't in his plans. He had booked us into the Culloden hotel in Holywood.

We had an important job to do. It had been some time since a UC had been deployed in Belfast, and there was a particular risk when it came to buying five kilos of heroin. A large amount of drugs in any situation, but especially so in this close-knit community where crime and drugs were controlled by those with guns and paramilitary power.

It was only a month since the much publicised and contested Good Friday peace agreement, and the political and religious tension could be cut with a knife. I was aware of the Troubles, the bombings, the murders and the Catholic–Protestant divide. But nothing could prepare me for the reality of the situation. The huge wall along Cupar Way that divided the Loyalists of the Shankill Road, their Union Jack flags flying, from the people of the Falls Road with their tricolour flags everywhere. The hand-painted murals of the UVF, the IRA and the UFF proudly adorned the walls of the different areas.

It was a new world to me. I felt safe across the water dealing with all sorts of nasty people – career criminals, drug dealers, murderers, conmen, rapists, and men who would think nothing of stabbing or glassing you in the face. But to me this place was different; it was the unknown, and it smelt of violence. I was apprehensive but I didn't want to show it.

We were met at the airport by a big man with big hands and a huge smile. Mick was the detective sergeant from the UC office and he immediately apologised for the absence of his DI, who was known to both Don and me. He was an infamous character, a hard-drinking, hard-working detective who had worked undercover in his own maverick style – a style that we had both been critical of in the past. However, now I had witnessed Belfast for what it was, I understood a little bit more why he had decided to go it alone and do it his own way.

Mick drove us through the city, pointing out various places where colleagues, friends and even family members had suffered or died as a result of the bombings and killings by Republican terrorists. It was incredible to listen to the matter-of-fact way such atrocities were being spoken about. It was as if this was a normal occurrence, a geographical hazard, a way of life. I kept thinking about it, as I sat in the back of the Ford Mondeo: why the city was divided, why it was a problem that was ingrained in the make-up of families. I stared out of the window in silence.

Mick explained to us that this deployment was being taken extremely seriously, that there was to be a full briefing later that evening and any meetings by me would be covered by an armed surveillance team. The team wanted to see me so that there could be no mistaking me for any of the targets. Don looked at me to acknowledge I was happy with this before he nodded his agreement to Mick.

Mick then said that we would meet the team shortly, as we were going for a liquid lunch. He said we could relax; a friend of theirs ran the pub and it would be full of 'our people'. We'd be meeting the team that was supporting my deployment, the people that would have my back should things go wrong. He said they'd worked together for years and were good men. It was a comforting feeling to know that we were all in this together, that we had a common purpose. It put me at ease.

We were introduced to a very attractive DCI, who was overseeing the operation, and she said she'd heard a lot about the two of us and was looking forward to running the job. She said that we'd talk about the specifics later, in her office.

The pub had a buzz about it and was full of big men drinking pints of Guinness and lager, all of whom were involved in one way or another in my deployment in their city. As I understood it, I would be at the centre of this team. They had never met me before, but they would be ensuring my safety at every turn. Standing there in the warmth of that Belfast pub, I felt like they would be there for me and for the success of the job.

It would be fair to say that after about five pints I was a tad windy about how long this liquid lunch might last, and Don was of the same opinion. Mick told us not to worry and to have another pint. In fact, before we could agree, he thrust another pint of Harp into our hands.

I pushed my way through the throng of drinking and talking men to the Gents, to relieve myself. To my right, standing at the other urinal, was a man who I had not seen or spoken to. Without introduction, he turned to me so that our eyes met, then in a soft Belfast accent he said, 'Just so yous know, you'll be on your own out there.' He turned back towards the wall, shrugging his shoulders as he refastened his belt. 'We know you're a Fenian. Nothing personal.'

He turned away from the urinal, washed and dried his hands, and left the toilets without another word. I stood there, numb, resting my head against the wall and trying to digest what had just been said to me. In his calm, non-threatening voice, this stranger had let me know in no uncertain way that he knew I was a Catholic, and if anything should go wrong I was on my own. Turning away from the wall, I laughed aloud in disbelief as I realised the magnitude of the situation I had put myself in. I left the toilets and returned to the bar. I ran my eyes around the room to see if I could spot the man amongst the faces, but he was nowhere.

Don handed me my pint. I took a big gulp and looked at him and said, 'I've got a feeling this job's going to fall out of bed.' I knew then that I wasn't going to tell him what had been said until we were both safely on the plane back to Gatwick.

I'd play this one out in my own way. I would ensure that the only people I would be talking to following the scheduled briefing would be Don and the taxi driver who took us from our hotel back to the airport. I would explain that the targets had got cold feet about meeting me. It would only be two people that knew the truth about why we never completed the trade for the heroin.

Once I'd made my mind up that Don and I were flying back to the relative safety of London, I allowed myself to relax and forget what had just happened. I had made the decision that I didn't want to deploy in Belfast. It was me and me alone that was calling the shots. I liked working on my own – I thrived on it – and felt confident in my own ability. That wasn't an issue. But Belfast was different; it was on another level. Being on my own here, with the possibility that I would have no backup, was a risk I wasn't willing to take. Belfast had made me feel isolated and out of control, even though it was only a short distance across the water. I was out of my comfort zone, surrounded by people I didn't know and had never had to rely on to get me out of a sticky situation.

The failure of this operation would be placed squarely on my shoulders, but that would be something I would have to deal with. I knew that not all jobs would end this way and I had other jobs to be getting on with. I couldn't dwell; Belfast was now a thing of the past, and it was history. I needed to concentrate on my next job.

Thirteen

I tucked my car away just off Church Hill Lane in Woodford Green, knowing I was early. I sat in my car and sipped the strong takeaway latte that I had insisted the Cypriot café owner put two extra shots into. It tasted bitter, but gave me the boost that I craved following the tedious journey that morning. In ten minutes, I was due to be picked up and transported to Snaresbrook Crown Court to give evidence. As I waited, I closed my eyes and allowed myself to remember the reason I was sat where I was . . .

I was in my car outside a café just off Green Lanes, waiting to meet two Albanians. This part of North London was well-trodden territory, controlled by the Turks. Their restaurants, grocers, coffee shops and bakeries formed a large part of the local community. It was known as Little Turkey, and it was amazing how over the years the Turks and the Greek Cypriots had learned to forget their grievances and live as neighbours. Though it is fair to say that most of the Greeks had moved further up the road to Palmers Green, and Green Lanes was now a mix of Turks and Kurds. These communities had their differences and there were constant battles over the heroin business, which was connected to Kurdish separatists in south-eastern Turkey. I had known this place for many years, and it posed a constant challenge for an undercover officer.

To this day, I believe the Turkish gangs are one of the most difficult to penetrate. I had once been told that if a Turk or Russian gangster tells you today is Monday, make sure you check your diary or a calendar. They will look you in the eye and be as convincing as your local priest, but it will, in fact, be Tuesday. I had experienced this in my early days working undercover, mingling in the very cafés and restaurants that surrounded me as I sat there in my car. The area hadn't been a happy hunting ground for me, and I wasn't filled with confidence.

I put this to the back of my mind and ignored the numerous men that came out of the café to take a good look at me, snarling at me as they sucked long and hard on their cigarettes. I could hear their voices saying to themselves: *What is he doing here, on our territory?*

I sent a text message to Endrit, who at the weekend had told me to be at this café. I was five minutes late, but had decided not to sit inside and wait. *I'm here*, is all my message said. I hadn't met Endrit yet, but we had spoken on the phone. His English was good, and he had told me he was from a place called Tropojë in the north of Albania. Whether I believed him was another thing.

You see, I knew from my many visits to Albania that Tropojë was an infamous place – steeped in history, with a reputation for being the wildest place in the country. It was virtually beyond the control of the government, almost a no-go area. It was surely a cunning ploy by Endrit to imply that he was from this area, knowing that no one in their right mind would try and cross him.

I loved Albania; I thought it was a stunningly beautiful country. It was a very proud nation, and had suffered many hardships over the years. The capital, Tirana, was expanding, and the number of cars with British plates that drove on the city's crazy roads was significant.

As I sat there waiting, I found myself thinking about the two people that the Albanian nation had adopted as its own daughter and son. The first was Mother Teresa, and her picture was to be found in the most unexpected places. In the criminal court in Durrës, a painting of her adorned almost the entire wall behind where the public sat. There were souvenirs of her in all the shops. She had been born in Skopje, in what is now Macedonia, and her family moved to Tirana in 1934. She became the country's most famous daughter for all the fantastic charity work she did throughout the world, and she is loved to this day.

A far-stranger adopted child of the country was Norman Wisdom, the famous English comedian. When his popularity waned in the UK, the Albanians continued to love him. It was an affection that had spanned many decades. During the Communist dictatorship, when the public in Albania wasn't allowed to watch many films, Norman Wisdom films were some of the very few allowed to be viewed. He became an outlet for the Albanian people, and a sign of laughter and hope. The country loved the comedian so much that, when he died, the government declared a national day of mourning for him.

I'm not quite sure why my thoughts had turned to these two individuals – possibly because there was such a huge contrast to the character I was about to meet. I knew he would be made of different stuff, and I certainly wasn't expecting any charity or laughter from Endrit in the next few hours.

My phone rang as I locked eyes with the Turkish man who had spent the last five minutes staring at me. It was Endrit's voice, but he was calling from a new number. 'Where are you, Joe?' he said.

'I'm sat in my car outside the café.'

'Good. We will pull up in thirty seconds in a VW Golf. Follow us.' The phone went dead before I could ask a single question. Throughout this short conversation, one of the Turkish men continued staring at me, and as I put my phone onto the passenger seat he knocked on my window. I lowered it as he blurted out, 'Who the fuck are you staring at, mate?'

I continued staring at him as I put the car into drive and said, 'No one.' I pulled away and began to follow the Golf, and I could hear him shouting 'Fuck you' as I closed the window.

As I followed the Golf, I noticed there was a thickset male with close-cropped black hair sitting in the passenger seat – I presumed Endrit was the driver. The passenger had his window slightly open; I could see ash from continuous smoking strewn on the rubber seal where the window joined the door. I followed them further up Green Lanes until we came to a large grocery shop on the corner. I pulled up behind the Golf and parked. Endrit got out, came over to me and opened my door. The other man walked straight into the grocery shop whilst speaking on his phone. Endrit shook my hand and said, 'Joe, it's good to meet you. Sorry about that café.' He pointed at the man on the phone and continued: 'He didn't want to bump into someone who may have been in there.'

As we walked towards the grocery shop, I could smell the gorgeous aroma of freshly baked bread. Endrit said, 'This place does the best coffee and pastries.' I thought he said the word 'pastries' like a true European; I hadn't expected that word to come out of his mouth.

Endrit paused at the entrance and said, 'Joe, one more thing. If Agim asks, I've been out with you before, in Brighton, OK?' I nodded at him and smiled to myself. I now knew that Endrit must be below Agim in the pecking order, and he had obviously exaggerated how long he had known me. This was a really positive step for me, but Endrit was an idiot if he had told Agim that he knew me longer than he actually had, which I was sure he had.

We walked through the shop, under an arch and along a hallway that led to a small square room. There were two old Turkish men sat at a table playing Tawula; they didn't even look up as Endrit and I walked in. In total there were only about ten tables in the room, and Agim was sat at the quietest table in the corner. He was still smoking, although an elderly lady who sat alone at one table shouted at him in Turkish.

He took one more lug on his cigarette, then stubbed it out on the back of an empty packet that I presumed he had just squashed on the table. He spoke in Albanian to Endrit, who then asked me if I wanted Turkish coffee. I told him I'd rather pull my own teeth out, and asked for a latte with an extra shot. Endrit walked the few steps to the counter to order our drinks.

Agim looked at me as he broke off a piece of the packaging from a fresh pack of cigarettes and started flossing between two of his bottom teeth. I looked at them, thinking that a deep polish of his railings really would be money well spent. They were badly stained from years of coffee and nicotine. He continued his flossing as he stared at me, and managed to dislodge what looked to me like a piece of meat. I watched as he inspected it between the thumb and forefinger of his right hand. He seemed pleased with himself. He gave it one more look before he popped the tiny morsel back into his mouth.

All three of us sat at the small round table. There was a small terracotta pot of demerara sugar, and a glass salt cellar with a silver top. It was half full, and I could see pieces of rice nestled amongst the salt. Endrit had brought the coffees over to the table, and he and Agim shared a copper pot containing the unfiltered Turkish coffee. Agim poured the thick coffee into two small cups that sat on battered saucers. It is essential that you let the coffee settle in the bottom of the cup; otherwise you get a mouth full of ground coffee, an experience that had put me off Turkish coffee forever.

Endrit then said, 'Agim wants you to know that his English isn't so good. If there are things he doesn't understand, he will ask me. I have told him how we know each other.'

I nodded but didn't say anything. Agim then spoke broken English in a gruff voice. The first words he uttered were: 'Is Brighton nice, plenty of girls?' I nodded at him, and he laughed aloud and continued: 'I like girls.'

I studied his face. I guessed he was about thirty-five years old; he had crow's feet around his eyes and his hairline was receding. He had a large crescent-shaped scar just underneath his right eye, and I wondered how he'd got it. I lifted my coffee cup and said, '*Gëzuar*.' Both men lifted theirs, laughed and said, '*Gëzuar*. Cheers.'

Agim then looked at me. 'I have two things you might want – the white and I also have the brown, but the brown can cause me problems around here.' I understood exactly what he meant, as for him to be selling heroin at a reasonable level in and around Green Lanes could cause him significant problems with the Turks. I wanted to declare from the start that I was after white.

'I'm after good-quality cocaine. I want it regular and I want it to be a consistent quality. I don't know how much you boys can move?'

Agim told me I didn't need to worry about how much they could move – it would not be a problem. Then he stood up and said, 'Come with me.' He started walking across the small room to a door beside the two old men playing Tawula. I followed him without a care in the world.

This small wooden door led to a hallway. On the left was another door, which he opened. It was a communal toilet, and there was a key on the inside that Agim used to lock the door. He pulled a string cord, which activated the light in the windowless toilet.

Undercover

The two of us were almost toe to toe, and I could see his face in far more detail. His thirty-five years on this earth had probably been tough ones, and they had taken a toll on his features. He took a cigarette from the fresh packet and lit it with a cheap lighter. He looked at me as he took a deep, long suck, held it for too long and then exhaled. I hated cigarette smoke, particularly when it was blown in my face. I said nothing and waited for his next move.

He hesitated momentarily before he said, 'My English may not be so good, but I can tell when a man is scared. You can feel the fear, and I now know you are not. In this world we must be careful. You are a friend of Endrit, so soon we may be friends.' His English was broken, but it was better than he had made out.

He went into the toilet cubicle and began to urinate all over the seat and into the pan. Then he took another drag on his cigarette before flicking it into the toilet. I unlocked the door and shouted back, 'Don't forget to wash your hands!' I knew there would be little chance of this. I would try and remember not to shake his hand when we parted company.

As I walked back to the now-empty table, I knew this had been a test for me. A test to see if I had the bottle, to see if I was scared of these two 'mad Albanian men' from Tropojë or wherever they were from. The fact of the matter was, I didn't care who they were or where they were from. I was going to be better than them. I would try and stay a step ahead, and beat them at their own game. I felt I was going in the right direction.

Agim walked back into the room a few minutes after me, and I could see him wiping his right hand on the right leg of his jeans. He sat down and put three phones on the table. I stopped myself from asking for his number.

I looked across at him and said, 'Agim, I want two to three kilos a week, and I would like to get things going soon. But first, I'd like to get to know you better and take you to a restaurant I like.' I handed him a restaurant's business card. 'Two thirty tomorrow. The food is great. Now if you'll excuse me, I have a long drive back to Brighton, where I should have been an hour ago.'

Endrit had just returned to the room, and I explained I had to go. I stood up and hugged him, purposely holding him longer than felt comfortable, as I knew Agim was watching intently. I patted Agim on the shoulder, thanked him for the coffee and said I looked forward to seeing him tomorrow.

I savoured the wonderful smell of bread baking as I walked through the grocery shop to my car. I knew Endrit would be answering many, many questions from Agim in my absence. I had not planned ahead for that meeting and I'd had no idea how I expected it to go, but I was pleased with how it had turned out. I would be meeting them tomorrow on my territory.

Two months later I was in Finsbury Park, in a restaurant owned by a very good friend of Agim and Endrit. I had become close to the two men since our first meeting, and had purchased reasonable amounts of cocaine from them. Today I was going to purchase two kilos.

We sat at the back of the dark restaurant, with the only sunlight coming from the opened rear door, which Agim used when he went out to smoke one of his constant Marlboro cigarettes or to speak in Albanian on one of his three mobile phones. If things went to plan, it was the last sunlight he would feel on his face for a long time, and this played on my mind.

He came back into the restaurant and sat down. He looked deep into my eyes as he sipped the remnants of his lukewarm espresso and took a last strong pull on the cigarette that he should have finished outside. He exhaled, and I could smell the disgusting combination of years of smoking and coffee on his breath. It made me angry – not the fact that he'd told me the gear wouldn't be here for another half hour, but the fact I could smell, almost taste, his breath.

He shouted to the restaurant owner to lock the front door. He leant forwards from the dirty old sofa we were sat on, and said he had something he wanted to tell me.

I was relaxed, remarkably so. I knew from all the 'trades' I'd previously done that the day when larger amounts of drugs were brought out could be very tense. People got jumpy, nervous and often very aggressive. To me, the fact I was sat alone in a locked restaurant controlled by a man who had previously been described to me as 'the biggest Albanian player in North London' by the young detective sergeant who was running the operation, did not bother me in the slightest.

Agim said in his broken English, 'You know what, Joe? Us Albanians are crazy people. Take me and you. Say last night we go out and have a fight. This morning we drink coffee or *raki*, we shake hands and we are friends again. But there is something wrong in our minds in the way Albanian people are made. Because you know, Joe, if ever you insult my family, the

name of my family, or you double-cross me . . . I will kill you.'
He spat these last four words out, and a splash of his putrid
spittle landed on my right cheek. I wanted to wipe it away but
I wasn't going to move my eyes from his; it was important I
showed no fear, no reaction to this threat. I believed every
word this man had said. I believed he had killed before and
would have no hesitation in killing me, but I wasn't frightened. He continued: 'And, Joe, if I don't kill you then my son
will. And if he doesn't, it is his son who will kill you.'

I let him finish, I held his thoughts in my head longer than I
held his stare. Then I said, 'You know what, Agim. When you
and I sit around a table eating the best fish taken from the sea
in Durrës in your beautiful country, and our families are sat
with us, and we are drinking the success of our long business
together, you will forget about such thoughts.'

The restaurant owner put a jug of *raki* on the table with
three grubby tumblers. I poured three large shots and toasted
to 'our future', and we clinked glasses and Agim repeated
those words.

I knew there would be no future; there would be no family
meals together, no business partnership. It was my job to help
lock this man up, put him behind bars, to prevent him killing
anyone else who might insult his family or double-cross him.
And I certainly wasn't going to allow him to do it to me.

It wasn't long before, following a few frantic phone calls, a
rather sweaty male knocked on the door of the restaurant. He
was only about thirty, and going bald before his time. He had
sweat marks under the arms of the canary yellow, fake Ralph
Lauren polo shirt he wore. He looked frightened as he carried

a Tesco carrier bag limply by his side. He and Agim had a conversation in Albanian. I heard my name being said, and he nervously and somewhat reluctantly shook my hand. Agim wasn't happy, and said that there was a problem. His people in Luton only wanted to release a kilo at a time, just in case anything went wrong.

I took control now. This was my opportunity to dominate these men. I told Agim that wasn't what we had agreed. He had counted my money – the money I had brought because he had told me the previous evening it was definitely on for two kilos. 'And now when I am sat in your restaurant, you talk about double-crossing and things going wrong.'

Agim apologised; he said he had already received a call to say the second kilo would be an hour and half.

It made absolutely no difference to me as an undercover police officer whether he sold me one kilo or two, because he had conspired to sell multiple kilos and his Albanian friend had brought one kilo with him today. However, it was important for me as a 'drug dealer' to show I wasn't happy, to show this couldn't happen again. I grabbed the bag from the man and went to the toilet with it. Agim followed me. In the dirty, small cubicle I put the cracked toilet seat down. I removed the block from the bag and cut through the black masking tape to reveal the white brick inside. I tested the gear, and Agim asked if I was happy. I looked him in the eyes and said, 'What do you think, Agim? I've now got to put myself at risk twice, because this key has to go, then I've got to come back again and do the same.'

Agim replied with the words that confirmed I was in control: 'I'm sorry.'

I left the cubicle with Agim, and sat back down on the sofa to discuss what we were going to do about paying for this first kilo. But before discussions were concluded, there was a huge explosion as the restaurant door was smashed in.

'*Armed police – don't move!*'

I saw many silhouettes bundle in through the sunlight from the back door. Then I was thrown to the ground, a knee in my back as plastic cuffs were squeezed around my wrists so tightly they cut into my skin. My face was squashed onto the dirty carpet. I could see Agim was in a similar position to me, and in between us on the floor was the Tesco bag. Our eyes met, and again I looked deep into his as he spat on the carpet.

The armed officers picked Agim up from the floor and took him out through the back door. As I was left lying there, all I could hear in my head was his voice saying repeatedly: *If ever you insult my family or you double-cross me, I will kill you.*

Fourteen

It was normal practice after finishing an operation to harbour different feelings: thoughts of betrayal, divided loyalties and a sense of sadness. Men such as Endrit and Agim, who minutes before their arrest had seen me as a friend, would instantly hate me, despise me, even want me dead. Sometimes it was good to talk about the way these situations made you feel.

As usual I'd had the obligatory call from Denise, who ran the administration and booking of all psych appointments for the undercover team. She was a bundle of energy and could talk like no one I'd met before. It was a skill to get her off the phone before she had managed to tell you the entire hour-by-hour itinerary of her weekend. But she was a kind lady, and didn't have a bad bone in her body. I'm sure she must have thought I was permanently being followed by the police, as most of my calls would finish abruptly with, 'I've gotta go, Den, the Old Bill are behind me.' This time she had sufficient time to say, 'Don't forget you're with the psycho at one o'clock.' I promised her I'd be there, and teased her that I wouldn't miss it for the world.

It had been a number of years now since it was made a requirement for full-time undercover officers to keep regular appointments with their designated psychologist. If they failed to attend, or the psycho felt they were unfit to deploy, then the operative would be withdrawn from all operations. Some officers found it very therapeutic and rewarding to be able to unburden themselves onto a professional. They made the most of the hour or so they had with the psycho to chat through many personal issues, and following the appointments felt a weight off their shoulders. It's fair to say I wasn't one of the people who embraced the set-up.

I was aware why the system had been imposed. A few years before, a talented and experienced undercover officer had had a breakdown following numerous undercover deployments. He was a man's man, not a shrinking violet, and was probably doing more deployments than anyone else in the country at the time. This was still in the days when operatives didn't work undercover full-time. Most of them tended to have day jobs as detectives working on the busiest specialist squads. They would then be deployed on specific undercover operations as they arose. In the late 1980s, if you were a good operative you could bounce from one undercover operation to the next.

Following a number of incidents, this particular operative ended up being sectioned to a mental institution. It was a harrowing time for him and his family. It was also the catalyst for the Police service to cover their backs and to negate any subsequent claim by an undercover operative having a breakdown as a result of their undercover activities. Therefore, shortly after, the psychologist appointment system was put in place.

I always parked my car away and I liked to walk the last half a mile or so. It cleared my head, not that I had any intention of divulging anything to my psychologist. I had been seeing her for a number of years now and I wondered who got more out of the sessions, her or me. I liked her very much and I have no doubt she was excellent at her job. The fact was I knew far more about her than did she about me.

There was a long path to the Victorian house, which was set back off the road, I admired the beautiful original bay windows where I could see a huge tabby cat sat at the window seat surveying the front garden. I rang the ornate bell and the door was answered by the secretary, who smiled politely, and without uttering a word ushered me into the waiting room. I sat in a high-backed, green-upholstered chair, with lovely padded armrests. I picked up a recent copy of *The Field* magazine from the walnut coffee table and read through 'The Editors' 12 Top Tips for grouse shooting'. I could smell the fresh lilies that were positioned in front of the large mirror above the fire place. This was a tranquil place, a peaceful almost calming room to be in.

I heard the buzzer sound in the secretary's room. I knew from previous visits that the secretary would enter my room shortly. 'If you'd like to go up she is ready for you now.' I returned the magazine to the coffee table and walked up the wide staircase to the second floor. I noticed the green carpet was a tad threadbare in places and wondered why it hadn't been replaced. Margaret, or Maggie as she liked to be called, was waiting at the top of the stairs. 'You always look so brown, where have you been!?' Before a word came out of my mouth and as she shut the heavy door behind me, she told me she was off to Venice at the weekend.

We sat in our usual classic Habitat chairs, it was lovely furniture but it always bugged me because I didn't think it suited this room or indeed the house. I was sat in the bay window which, as usual, was open one notch on the catch. After about ten minutes of discussing the merits of various cities in Italy, she paused and asked, 'Anyway, how are you?' She spoke with a truly soothing Scottish accent; it wasn't harsh, it was soft and gentle. I looked at her and said everything was fine, very busy but I wouldn't have it any other way. She asked me about the relationships I was building with the targets on the operation I was currently deployed on. I explained that one of the targets was confiding in me about the breakdown of his relationship with his father. He clearly trusted me about this as well as the criminality we were doing together.

She asked how this made me feel, the fact he was confiding in me, did I feel uncomfortable about it? I told her it was my job and if he wanted to talk about how he had let his dad down in between him selling me heroin that didn't bother me in the slightest. She paused again and then explained how important maintaining family relations was. She said she was really sad that she and her brother didn't make more effort with each other. She said the longer you allow it to drift apart the harder it feels to mend. She went on to say she felt guilty and that she should've made more effort, and often thought about the times she'd cancelled meeting him for a coffee or supper, saying she was too busy, when really she was just too lazy.

She paused, and I could tell that this situation was clearly bothering her. I stared at her as the tears started to roll down her red cheeks. She didn't speak for what seemed like an age. I wasn't quite sure what to do. I felt uncomfortable; I could see how upset she was, but I did nothing to comfort her. I erred on the side of silence, and sat there and prayed she would stop. She composed herself and pulled a tissue from the sleeve of her cerise cardigan and blew her nose loudly. She shook her head, saying, 'I've promised myself I will make more effort.'

I asked her if there was anything else she wanted to discuss with me. She looked at me with her head tilted slightly to the side. I could see the tracks of the tears on her face. She stared at me with her sharp blue eyes that were red from her crying, but said nothing. She tilted her head slowly from side to side on five occasions, the silence was deafening, and you could hear the tick of the grandfather clock in the entrance hall. I knew if I said nothing in this silence, I would be free to go. As she straightened her head from the fifth tilt she said in her gentle voice, 'No you're fine, I'll see you in three months.'

I got up and went to leave. As I walked past Maggie, she grabbed my right hand with both her hands. She still held the wet tissue, and tucked it back into the sleeve of her cardigan. I could feel the cold of her hands as she held onto me tightly.

'We all have issues, whoever we are. Thank you so much for listening.'

I took a deep breath and said, 'Remember what you said. You're going to make more effort. There's no time like the present – pick up your phone and ring him.'

She looked at me and a smile broke across her face. 'Do you know what – that's exactly what I'm going to do. Thank you, thank you so much.'

As I stepped onto the first step to go downstairs, I heard Maggie pick up the receiver of the phone that sat on her desk. For some strange reason, I felt pleased with myself.

I walked slowly back to my car through the tree-lined avenues, wondering whether I should be more open about what I felt, or what was happening at home or with my family. I stopped in the middle of the pavement and smiled, and said to myself: *Don't be a plum – don't trust anyone.*

It did give me a thought, though, that perhaps it was time I spoke to my son about certain things.

Fifteen

A few days later I was sat in an Indian restaurant sipping an ice-cold Tiger beer, the condensation running down the outside of the thin glass. It tasted so nice, and it was evident from the pleasure on my son's face that he was also savouring the moment. This restaurant had an intimate atmosphere, and the soft furnishings that I sank into held the delicious smells of all the beautiful spices that had been cooked by the Bengali chefs over the years. This was a family-run restaurant, a place in which I'd had many good times.

Charlie was my eldest son – he was sixteen years old, but it seemed like a moment ago that I'd watched him come into this world. I've got to say, the arrival of Charlie was enough to put me off being bedside when any other child entered this world.

We had many scares before he finally landed, many conversations with strange doctors advising me to take my wife out for a hot curry and then go home and make love to her ('That'll help get things going!').

After many false dawns, my wife Sarah went into actual labour, which coincided with the attendance of twelve trainee obstetricians on the ward ('I'm sure Mrs Carter won't mind if we all have a look. Is that OK, Mrs Carter?') Well, my wife didn't know what day of the week it was; to cope with the ever-increasing pain, she'd had more drugs pumped into her than Ozzy Osbourne. Her bed was surrounded by white-gowned, interested obstetricians, all frantically making notes. This was an alien place for me – I hated hospitals at the best of times, and the fear of this birth overwhelmed me.

Without an announcement or explanation, I saw Sarah's legs being put into U-shaped metal holders. The sort you see in a rowing boat to slot the oars into, but these ones sat under her knees. I was then horrified to see a huge set of forceps unwrapped from medical paper. I recall the extreme strength being used on the forceps to pull Charlie out by his head, and then a loud squelching noise as he landed on the delivery table.

I can remember vividly looking at what had come out, thinking, *That's not a baby, it's an alien.* It had a cone-shaped head. I stared at it, but for once I was completely lost for words. I was in shock; it wasn't what I'd expected and I could feel my legs going weak. I had to get out of the delivery room. Without even a thought for poor Sarah, who had just gone through extreme pain, I left and ran to the nearest outside door to gulp in the fresh air. I needed time to comprehend what I had just seen. I was traumatised, I was in shock, I needed to get a grip.

I composed myself and made my way back to the labour room. By now the 'alien' had been checked over and resembled a healthy young boy. He was wrapped up and was given to Sarah to hold.

'Have you thought of a name?' Before the words left the midwife's mouth and before Sarah was aware of the question being posed, I declared, proud as punch: 'Charlie.' My first child was a boy – something I'd always wanted, my eldest being a boy. I was a dad, not to an alien but to beautiful Charlie.

Before I move on to explain why Charlie and I were having a curry together, I want to mention a funny thing Sarah did after the birth. At the end of her bed were her notes, which read: *Delivered, Neville Barnes*. Well, Sarah insisted on sending a thank you card to *Doctor Neville Barnes c/o The Maternity Unit*. She found out when she returned for a check-up that there was no Dr Neville Barnes, but that it was the name they gave to a forceps delivery.

Charlie was a good boy, and a talented one. He was made of different stuff to me and was much more like his mum, which I was pleased with. If I am honest with myself, I was always hard on Charlie; I seemed to find fault with things he did rather than praise all the things he did right. I know that now, but you can't put the clocks back.

I loved Charlie very much and I made sure I told him as often as I could. Charlie was a sensitive kid, and showed his emotions in the way that I never could. It was a strong character trait – a trait that I didn't possess. He had a talent for acting and singing, and he had a way of making words sing when he committed them to paper. A unique talent for writing; a talent that I will never have. He was also an exceptional athlete – he had natural speed and an excellent physique. He was a good footballer, played rugby and could run like the wind; he had the natural ability to excel at most sports, but not the dedication.

Charlie's best friend was an Italian boy named Gino, whose hard-working parents came from Sicily. His mother, a tiny lady, ruled Gino and his younger brother with an iron fist. Gino was a tough kid and another good sportsman, though he wasn't at the top of the leader board academically. He had the reputation of being the 'hardest' boy in school and very streetwise, and him and Charlie were inseparable.

Throughout Charlie's upbringing, he often asked me, 'Exactly what do you do, Dad?' My response had always been: 'I'll tell you when you're older.' Charlie wasn't the type of kid to keep quiet about the fact his dad worked undercover. I didn't want to fill his head with information that could cause him and me problems. What he didn't know couldn't hurt him. He knew I was a detective and worked at Scotland Yard, but beyond that he knew nothing. Now he was sixteen, I thought he was old enough and mature enough to know what I did.

His mum and family were away for a few days, so I'd thought there was no better time than today – over a beer and a quiet curry – to have a grown-up conversation with him. So we were enjoying the taste of popadoms washed down with ice-cold beer when I said to him, 'You know I've always said to you I'd tell you when you're older what I do, son. Well, I think you're old enough and mature enough. This is between you and me, and you shouldn't speak to anyone other than me about it. Do you promise?'

'Course I wouldn't – I promise, Dad.'

'Charlie, I've been working undercover for the last fifteen years.'

He took another sip of his beer and started to laugh – he actually laughed out loud. Then he said, 'Dad, that's so funny.' This wasn't the reply I was expecting. 'Gino said only last night, "You know your dad says he's a detective – well he's not, he's a drug dealer. No one dresses in the clothes he's got or drives the cars he does without being a drug dealer." Dad, that's so cool. Is that why you know *Donnie Brasco* so well?' He sat back, still with a smile on his face, but deep in thought. There was a comfortable silence before he asked, 'Have you ever killed anyone, Dad?'

I stared back at him, and laughed as loudly as he had at me.

Sixteen

What my boy didn't know, and I would never tell him, was the fact that I was running an undercover unit and I had responsibility for a number of dedicated operatives. One of the best on my team was Emma. She had recently embarked on a new operation, and it was part of my job to ensure that she deployed safely and had all the support she needed to fulfil her role.

Emma's new operation was to set up a shop and buy stolen property taken in local burglaries, robberies and thefts. To do this, she needed to blend into the local business community. She had also been tasked to infiltrate a number of drug-supply networks in the area. This was a difficult challenge for anyone, let alone a female on her own.

Undercover

She had chosen a house to live in and had ensured that it looked like a home, not a place occupied by someone who was just passing through. Her days were busy and she had to display all the normalities of a shop owner. She opened the shop every day, and never really knew who would come through the door. For all intents and purposes she was running a normal business – the only difference being that she was buying stolen property. It was arduous work.

Emma had spoken to me at length on the phone, and had asked me to come to a meeting to discuss the operation. She explained that she wanted some ideas on how to expand her current deployment – from buying stolen property to moving into a drugs network. I promised that I would come to the meeting and support her in whatever way I could. Emma was one of a very small number of full-time female undercover officers in the UK. I understood the commitment and devotion entailed in working in a full-time undercover role, and those demands were considerably greater for a wife and mother, which she was.

I had asked Emma if she could bring the meeting a little closer to the M25, as I had to be in Central London that afternoon. She arranged that we meet at the services we usually met at on the M25 with the man in charge of the operation. The two of us arrived half an hour before the scheduled time and discussed where she was at with her deployment, and more importantly what she wanted to achieve. She had been set the task of infiltrating a number of pubs, including a particular bar that was a well-known spot for the organised dealing of cocaine.

She explained that it was uncomfortable for her as a woman to go into the bars on her own – it looked like she was trying to pick-up or was a sad, lonely lady. We discussed many options, and after dismissing a number of suggestions agreed that the best option was for her to have a 'boyfriend' who was an obvious criminal, and who could ease her into any drugs network.

Emma was more than pleased with the plan and she had a big smile on her face when Dave, the man in charge of the operation, appeared. I recognised him immediately but we hadn't seen each other for a number of years. We chatted about how time flies and what the two of us had been up to since we had last met. Dave had been an observer on one of the undercover courses that I had instructed on. He was a nice man and a good detective, although his exposure to undercover work since that course had been minimal. He told me how pleased he was with Emma and the commitment she had given to the job so far. He explained his vision for the operation and the expectations of the bosses. Emma described what she thought was the best way to progress the operation: She wanted to introduce a boyfriend with an overtly criminal profile.

The two of them then discussed various names to fill that role, and the merits and otherwise of these individuals. I excused myself to take a phone call outside while they came to an agreement as to who they wanted. I knew that if Emma was happy, then I would back her choice. The call took longer than I'd expected, and as I sat back down and apologised to them for my absence, I felt both sets of eyes boring into my head. I asked them why they both looked so weird, and had they come up with a suitable person? Dave looked at me and said that, after considering many names, they both wanted the same person. It felt like Dave was fulfilling the role of a judge on *The X Factor*. I said to him, 'Go on, Mr Cowell. Who have you chosen?'

Dave said that both he and Emma wanted me to do the job. I fitted the profile, and they'd only go for someone else if I wasn't interested. I was their first choice, and Dave asked if I'd be up for taking on the role. He knew that I was on a job at the moment, but said that he'd wait to use me if I wanted to do it.

I looked at Emma and asked her if that's what she actually wanted. She said a hundred per cent, if I was able to do it. I could see that they both wanted me, and I told Dave I'd do it as soon as I finished my current job, which had about a month left in it. I informed him that he'd have to phone my boss and officially ask for me. Dave assured me that he'd do that straight away, and that he'd let me know as soon as he had an answer.

I made my excuses as I had another meeting to travel to, but I left both of them with smiles on their faces. Emma said that she had her fingers crossed that I'd be allowed to do the job, and Dave thanked me for coming. I left the service station, unsure as to whether I would be allowed to do the job or not. It was a decision that was out of my hands, and I knew that I'd receive a phone call from my boss once he'd made up his mind. Over the years I'd had hundreds of such requests, but I no longer got too excited. Until I was officially authorised to deploy, such requests were flattering but I had to wait for the official green light.

But Dave must have struck whilst the iron was hot, because as I drove down the A13 through East London my DI rang my mobile. He explained that another request had come in for my services and he wanted me to do this one, as it was alongside Emma. He asked if I fancied doing it, and notified me that it would be a full-time commitment. I said that if he wanted me to do it then I was more than happy to support Emma. He said that he would sort out all the official paperwork and that I should sort out the specifics with Dave. Although I was being cool about the request, I was really happy that I'd been asked for. I knew that I'd throw myself into the new job and make sure that it was a success to the best of my ability.

As ever, I'd agreed to do another operation without a single thought for my family and the responsibilities I had at home. This was not because I didn't care dearly for them – the thought just hadn't entered my head. I should have sat down with my wife and discussed, like an adult and accountable parent, the impact this would have on my family. I guess I was like that, it was very simple, I told them I was becoming an undercover officer and it was never up for discussion. That was that as far as I was concerned. But, as usual, I had accepted in a breath another huge commitment away from the reality of my own world. I really was a very selfish person, and I recognised this but did nothing to change it. Why? Because I could see no further than the challenge of my next operation.

Seventeen

It was a lovely summer's evening, and my skin felt warm and tight from a few hours of sunshine that afternoon. I was looking forward to a couple of glasses of champagne with the lady that I'd shared the last two months with. We had got to know each other well; we talked for hours on end, and were comfortable and very happy in each other's company. It was the first time I'd felt like this for many years. She was a lovely person, she was always relaxed with me, she was herself, she wasn't pretending to be someone or something she wasn't. She was just being Emma, and that's what I liked.

I hadn't been to this wine bar before, but it was 'the place to be' in town. It was always mobbed with a mixture of the affluent, the wannabes, the B-list celebrities, the villains, and the ordinary Joe Public out to show off their tans and enjoy a summer drink or two. There was always a line to get in, and Emma had said that she'd had to spend twenty minutes queuing before. I hated queues, and although it should be an Olympic sport for the British, it was one I'd never participated in.

Emma was getting ready and so I ordered a taxi for 8.30 p.m. I shouted up to her that I was going to get some bits from the shop and I wouldn't be long. But I had no intention of going to the shop. The bar was only a five-minute drive away and I could see that there were already around ten people queuing up. I also saw two large door supervisors dressed all in black, their undersized black shirts rolled up to show their statutory tats and overworked biceps. I pulled up right outside the bar, the roof down on my car, and I beckoned one of the men over.

I didn't move from my seat. 'Listen, fella. I'm up from London and my missus runs a business in town. I'm taking her out for a few bottles of champagne to celebrate me moving up here. I'll be in a taxi. Do me a favour when I pull up – just make her feel special.' I held out my hand to shake his, and squeezed a crisp £50 note into his hand. 'My name's Joe. You'll be seeing a lot more of me.'

He took the bullseye and carefully squeezed it into his tightly fitting black strides. 'Nice to meet you, Joe. I'm Nathan.'

As I drove back to 'our' house, the wind felt nice on my face. I pulled up into the drive; I could smell freshly cut grass, and a waft of barbecued sausages hit me. The house had such a homely feel about it. It was on a quiet street full of normal people – families who I'm sure were proud to live there, on the street where I shared my 'home' with Emma. I sat there for a moment in the car and smiled to myself. Life wasn't so bad. Then I looked up and saw Emma through the bedroom window looking down at me. I was glad she was my missus.

Emma came down the stairs and looked a real picture; she dressed well and looked classy, she didn't try to look younger than she was. She had a penchant for shoes and handbags, and wore them with a touch of style. I told her that she looked lovely and the cab would be arriving in a few minutes. She said that she had a confession to make and that I wouldn't like it. She said that there were always queues at the bar and that I'd have to be patient – she didn't want me to make a scene. I gave a look that left her in no doubt that I wasn't happy.

The cab pulled up outside and beeped to let us know he had landed. We both got into the back of the car and the driver said in a broad local accent, 'You and the rest of the country are going to Amphora's tonight. It's packed and they're queuing round the corner.' Emma gave me a look as I told the driver to make sure he pulled up right outside.

The queue was indeed a queue to be cherished. The cabbie did his job and pulled up right alongside the doors of Amphora's. I got out and Nathan clocked me – before I'd said a word he went to Emma's door and opened it and said hello. She was a little taken aback. I paid the driver and said I'd ring him later for the return journey. Nathan came over and shook my hand, unhooked the rope and led us into the bar. It was three-deep with punters waiting to be served. He beckoned the head barman over, who seemed a tad flustered, but when Nathan said, 'Mano, this is Joe. Can you please look after him and his missus?' he smiled and said it would be his pleasure. Nathan told me to have a good night: 'Anything you want, Joe, you know where I am.'

I could feel Emma staring at me, but she didn't utter a word. Mano introduced himself to both Emma and me, and asked us what we would like to drink. I ordered a bottle of Laurent-Perrier Rosé and gave him £100. He told us to try and find a table in the garden and that he'd get the drinks brought out to us. We made our way through the packed bar to an overcrowded decked area. Emma pinched my arm as we found a small bit of space next to a table. 'How the hell did you manage that? How do you know the bouncer, and why the five-star treatment with waiter service? I've been here four or so times and I've never been treated like that.'

I shrugged my shoulders. Before I could answer, a Laurent-Perrier ice bucket with two glasses was brought over, and the chilled bottle was opened and poured for us by another barman. He said, 'Mano said to tell you, anything else you want, just shout.'

I thanked him and gave him a tenner for his troubles. Emma looked at me and said, 'You certainly know how to make an impression – everyone in the queue, bar, and now the garden wants to know who you are.' I held out my glass and clinked hers, then took a long sip of the ice-cold bubbles of the champagne.

I looked around and took in all the faces in the garden without focusing on anyone in particular. When we first found the table, I'd noticed a couple of six-foot-plus black guys stood just behind us. They'd moved up onto a step to allow us some room but I purposely ignored them. I could feel their eyes burning a hole in the back of my head. We finished our first glass and I poured us both a second. As I did, I looked up at one of the black guys and said, 'Fuck me, mate, you're tall. You must be nearly seven foot!'

He looked at me, and in a very uncool way said, 'No, mate. I'm just over six but I'm stood on a step.'

The other guy nudged him and said, 'Don't be an idiot. The fella's taking the piss, he can see you're on a step.' He held out his hand. 'My name's Ricardo. I haven't seen you before, have I?'

'No, Ricardo, I don't think you have, mate – but it's nice to meet you.' I shook his hand, and I could tell he had purposely put that extra bit of squeeze into it, just to let me know that he could look after himself. I introduced him to Emma, but didn't tell him my name and made my excuses whilst I went to the Gents. I could see the horrified look on her face, but I ignored it and chuckled to myself as I passed through the buzz of the bar area.

The toilets had a unisex hand-washing area that you walked through to get to the urinals and three individual toilet cubicles. As I used the urinal, I noticed two middle-aged guys squeeze into one of the cubicles together, and I could hear the nervous rustling of paper as they were obviously laying out powder onto the cistern. After two loud sniffs and a reshuffling of paper, they exited the cubicle together. I looked at them both as they came out and shook my head. One of the two summoned up the courage to say, 'Have you got a problem, mate?'

I looked the two of them up and down, and paused whilst I washed and dried my hands. I then addressed the one who had posed me the question: 'No, mate, I haven't got a problem, but that's not cool' – I pointed to the cubicle – 'two up in there, not cool.' I finished drying my hands and said, 'You may want to take that rolled-up note from out of your top pocket as well.'

As I turned away and walked out, both men were apologising and thanking me at the same time, whilst the one with the £20 note was trying, discreetly, to unroll and straighten it out.

I made my way back to the garden, and Emma seemed pleased that I'd returned. The other man introduced himself as Johnny and said, 'You probably recognise me. I used to be a Premier League footballer.' I did actually recognise him, but I looked him up and down and said, 'I can't say I do, mate.' Without letting him explain who he was, I turned to Ricardo and said, 'You been looking after Emma?'

He smiled. 'She's been telling me all about you, Joe.'

I looked at her and said, 'Don't worry what she says about me – she's the clever one, the one that pays the bills and puts food on the table.' We then talked amongst the four of us about the business that Emma ran in town. Both men seemed interested, although Johnny didn't have the brain capacity to hold a meaningful conversation.

We ordered another bottle of champagne and two fresh glasses, and we shared the bottle and chatted and laughed together. Emma excused herself and went to the bathroom. As soon as she had disappeared out of earshot, Ricardo pulled me to one side. He said, 'Joe, I've not been long out of the shovel and I'm a grafter. I know what you are, it's obvious.'

I pulled him closer and said, 'Listen, Ricardo. I think you've got the wrong end of the stick, mate. I'm a straight-goer and I'm just out for a few drinks with my girl.'

'Whatever, Joe, you don't fool me. I'm not an idiot.'

'I never said you were, Ricardo.' I shook his hand just as Emma returned, and said, 'Was really nice to meet you and Tony. Emma and I are off.'

Ricardo had Emma's business card in his hand and shouted out, 'I'll ring you.'

Emma said, 'That bloke's called Johnny, not Tony.' I told her that I knew that, but he was a plum and I didn't want to acknowledge him.

I thanked Mano on the way out, and told him if Emma was ever in the bar without me, to make sure he looked after her for me. 'Joe, you have my word.' He shook my hand with both of his, and held on for a moment or two too long.

Nathan had a cab waiting for us, and opened the door for Emma to get in. Before I got into the back seat, I thanked Nathan. He said, 'Joe, I know you're no mug, but that Ricardo you were talking to is a right handful.' I thanked him for marking my card but said I'd been round the block a bit myself. As I got into the cab he said, 'You make sure I do see a lot more of you, Joe.'

Emma was a little tipsy, and she leant over to me and said, 'Thanks for a lovely evening. It's so nice having you around.' I looked at her and thought: *Could this actually be the place that we put down some roots? Could this be a proper home, a place for the two of us? Could this be our future?* For many reasons, it felt so right.

When we pulled up, I looked at the house the two of us shared. I was happy – the happiest I'd been for some time – and I knew Emma was too.

Eighteen

Emma was getting fed up with Ricardo ringing her and popping into the shop on the off chance that he would bump into me. I eventually rang him from her phone, and we met and had a few drinks together. He told me about his criminal 'standing' in the area; he made it clear to me that he was a bad boy, that he disliked the police and he knew everyone locally. It was as if he were trying to impress me, to big himself up.

Ricardo had already formed an impression of me. In his mind, he had no doubt that I was a villain, a wrong'un, a grafter, or whatever you want to call it. The more I told him that I wasn't, or that I'd put those days behind me, the stronger that opinion became. He asked me, hypothetically speaking, if I was 'still in the game', would I be interested in certain acts of criminality and ways of making money.

I told him that I liked him and I was happy to have a drink with him, but I didn't know him at all – we'd only just met. That maybe we would have that conversation again in the future, when we knew each other better. I did tell him that I'd be happy if whenever he was passing the shop, he popped his head in and made sure Emma was OK. Ricardo agreed to this but asked, in exchange, that I give him my number. He put his number into my phone and I missed-called him.

I received a call the following week from Ricardo. He said that there was someone that he'd like me to meet, a person that I'd get on with, and that he thought we had things in common. I was aware from the team that they were very interested in Ricardo – he was a decent local criminal and was well connected. I knew they were disappointed with my approach. They wanted me to bite his hand off, and their choice would have been for me to have told him I was a villain on that first meeting and see where it took us. I had different ideas, and thought that my approach would prove to be more tempting to Ricardo and the best way forward. I wanted him to chase me, and that's exactly what he had done. He asked that I meet him and his contact at a quiet local pub the following evening.

It was a particularly dark night, and I noticed that there was no moon to illuminate the evening's cloudless sky. I felt a little cold as I parked my car on the hill close to the pub, yet still far enough away that I could take in the surroundings on my short walk to the front door. From the number of cars I had noticed driving into the car park at the rear, the pub seemed very busy for a Thursday evening. I sucked in the night air, and as I exhaled I noticed that it was cold enough to see my breath in front of me.

As I strolled down the hill to the pub, I could hear the one-sided heated conversation of a man who was clearly speaking on the phone. As I got nearer, I saw that the voice belonged to a man who was dressed in a blue Barbour quilted jacket with the collar up. As I passed him and deliberately paid him no attention, I knew that this would be the man that I was about to meet.

The pub was packed, and unbeknown to me it was the very popular weekly quiz night. It didn't take me long to establish that it was being taken very seriously. My presence, as I surveyed the bar for Ricardo, was an unwelcome disturbance to their concentration. Particularly when he shouted over to me above the voice of the quizmaster: 'Over here, Joe. In the snug away from this boring mob.'

I heard a few muttered tuts and sighs, but I knew that no one would be brave enough to say a word to Ricardo. I squeezed past the packed tables and chairs of the enthusiastic quiz teams, and joined him in the snug. It was like a secret room – a lovely, warm, inviting place to while away the hours, just big enough to squeeze about twelve people into.

I shut the door behind me, and along with it the commotion of the quiz. There was a wood burner sat against one of the walls, with its panelled glass doors open and a couple of huge logs gently crackling in the heat of the embers. There were only two other men, aged about seventy years old and sat at a table playing 'crib', not taking a blind bit of notice of Ricardo or me. He gave me a huge affectionate slap on the back and shook my hand. He was in dialogue with the barmaid as to whether they had any Stone's ginger wine. She pulled a green bottle off the top shelf and poured it into three tumblers, which already contained large measures of what looked like brandy or scotch.

We chose to sit in a tiny corner alcove; it had a curved wooden bench seat with embroidered cushions sat on top. It was private and intimate, an ideal place for a subtle conversation. Ricardo told me that his mate, Ray, had arrived but was making a couple of phone calls and wouldn't be long. I asked him what we were drinking as he handed me the large tumbler. He explained it was a Courvoisier and Stone's – he described it as a 'knock out'. A few minutes later, the guy I recognised from outside crashed through the door, cursing as he sat down opposite me. 'Some people really take the piss.' He took no notice of me as he spoke to Ricardo. He grabbed his tumbler and swirled the three cubes of ice around in the glass before taking a swig. 'Fuck me, that's got a kick.' He then looked at me, and with a huge grin on his face, held his hand out across the table and said, 'I'm Ray, and you must be Joe. Good to meet you.'

Without hesitation, Ray went straight into a sales pitch. I listened to his offers of coke, 'Mum and Dad', 'green jackets' and 'trainers'. It was a little surreal, and I wondered what Ricardo had told him before the meeting for him to be so upfront about his activities. I knew immediately that I liked Ray. He was a warm, open and interesting person, and I knew that I'd get on with him. I let Ray finish what he had to say, and then I looked from him to Ricardo, and back to Ray. I then said, 'Can we slow down a bit? There must be something in the air here because we don't know each other. You seem spot on and Ricardo speaks highly of you, but can we have a drink and get to know each other before we jump into bed together?'

There was a brief silence before Ray said, 'You're right, that was a bit full on for a first meet.' He chinked my glass. 'Here's to getting to know each other. Let's call it a bit of foreplay.' He then laughed out loud at his own joke.

Ray and I talked and joked and laughed and enjoyed each other's company. Ricardo was a spectator for most of the evening, but had achieved what he had planned to do. He had 'intro'd' Ray to me, and I felt it had all the hallmarks of a long relationship.

Nineteen

Ray and I wasted no time getting to know each other. It was a fact that the two of us got on really well; we both liked each other instantly. We spent most of the weekend after we met in each other's company, much to the disgust of Emma. We went to a number of pubs together and talked about many different things. I knew that Ray had been in prison before, and also that he'd been a successful legitimate businessman, selling houses. He now earned his money as a full-time criminal, however. He had no legal form of income and led a very comfortable lifestyle. He lived in a decent three-bedroom house with his partner, Chloe, and their children, and they had the appearance of normal, happy family. He was about my height, in his mid-thirties and in reasonable shape, although he wasn't a gym-goer. Ray liked a drink and was a very sociable character – he was a happy person, or at least he was when we were in each other's company. I knew that he took cocaine, as he apologised for his runny nose and was always asking for tissues or pulling a scrap of toilet paper from his pocket to wipe it. He was embarrassed about this.

Ray knew everyone, and his phone never stopped ringing. When we were out, he would constantly take people to one side for a private conversation. I let him get on with it, and never asked any questions about what his business was. I had no doubt that Ray was a busy criminal and had his fingers in many pies, but I had made a conscious decision that I would wait until Ray brought up criminality. He knew from our conversation in the snug that I thought he had been a bit full-on with his approach to me. I wondered in my head how long it would take him to offer me a trade or a commodity. I also knew that he was dying to ask me a bucketful of questions.

The following Thursday, a week after our first meeting, I was dropping Ray off at his house. Just as he was getting out of the passenger seat of my car, he got back in and shut the door. He slumped back into the seat, sighed, shook his head and said, 'My pal's getting a nice bit of sniff tomorrow. I wondered whether you fancied coming in with me on it?' I could see that he was stressed about asking me, so I didn't want to prolong my reply.

'Ray, how much are we talking about, and do you trust the fella?'

A huge smile spread across his cheeky face. He vouched for the guy, who he said lived just around the corner, and we agreed for the first trade that I'd buy an ounce for £1,600. I could see how relieved he was. We said that we'd meet the following evening, at the pub at the end of Ray's road at 7 p.m.

The next night, Emma and I drove up to the pub, which was very modern and sat on the edge of a private housing estate. It had a happy balance between families enjoying a meal and the customary Friday-evening drinkers. Emma grabbed some seats while I went to the bar and ordered drinks. Ray came into the pub with his phone squashed to his ear as he shook a few people's hands. I ordered another pint of lager without asking him, and as I walked over to join Emma, he told me the fella would be ten minutes. We all sat down, and Ray was genuinely interested in Emma and the shop and told her that Chloe was dying to meet her.

I said to Emma that Ray and I needed to pop out for five minutes to speak to someone. She was expecting this and said she needed to ring her mum anyway, so she'd make the most of the time. I felt bad leaving her alone in the pub, and explained that to Ray on the way to my car. He directed me to a block of brand new flats that sat on the perimeter of the estate. We parked the car and I told Ray that I didn't want to meet any new faces just now, so I'd wait at the door whilst he went in. We were buzzed into a ground-floor flat, and Ray told me that the fella wanted this done in the next ten minutes as his ex-wife was dropping off their son for him to look after for the weekend.

The trade was done in seconds, and once back in my car Ray showed me two identical plastic bags, each with a solid block of white powder in. He held both up and asked me to choose which one I wanted. I told him I didn't mind, so he handed me the closest one. Ray said that he wanted me to let him know what my thoughts were on the gear. I told him that if it was shit gear, it would be the first and last trade we'd be doing together.

I dropped him at home, thanked him, and then rang Emma and told her that I'd pick her up outside the pub. Ray and I had just completed our first criminal transaction together. I hoped it would be the first of many.

Emma and I spent the weekend visiting many of the bars that she had struggled to visit on her own. It was a lovely area, and the people were so much friendlier than the Londoners I was used to. We made sure lots of people saw us together, and she couldn't understand how I managed to talk to anyone and everyone, wherever we visited. I wanted people to know about Emma's shop and the fact that she was open for business. We also visited a number of local estate agents and registered our interest in purchasing an executive house in the area.

On the following Monday, I met up with Ray and we chatted about the quality of the gear. He told me that people couldn't get enough of it locally and he'd had repeat customers. I explained that I thought it was OK but nothing to get too excited about – at best a six out of ten. But Ray didn't dwell on the quality of the cocaine for a second. He had a more pressing matter, and asked me if I fancied some 'Mum and Dad'. I knew that there was plenty of MDMA powder about at the time, but people were uncomfortable with it. Criminals weren't sure what price to knock it out at, how severely to cut it, and how best to take it. There were also varying qualities – some quite dirty in colour and probably from home-style labs. Others came as a clean white powder. However, the best quality I had seen was a brownish crystal, a bit like amber, that formed a white powder when you crushed it.

I asked what Ray thought about Mum and Dad. He said he preferred to stick to the bestsellers, but that there was a new market for this. He told me that the guy who had it was an eccentric academic, and he'd phoned him last night to say he had some new gear that was 'the bollocks'. I agreed to go around and see the fella with Ray later on.

That evening, we met for a quick pint before Ray directed me to a Victorian terraced house. We went down a side alley that led to the back of the house, and walked through a small, gated courtyard. We climbed three or four concrete steps leading to a green wooden back door that was ajar.

As we got to the top step, a tall, skinny, bare-chested man in his early thirties jumped out. He had a plastic-handled carving knife in his right hand, and he made a very loud growling noise in an attempt to scare the two of us. His eyes were like saucers, and he had a number of tattoos across his chest and stomach. I couldn't help noticing that it looked like there was chocolate spread dripping off the knife. He was convinced that he'd scared the two of us and couldn't stop laughing. Then he opened the door wide to let us into the chaos of his kitchen. He went to shake my hand, but I pulled it away to allow him to lick the chocolate sauce off his two middle fingers. I settled for a nod of my head instead, and 'Alright, mate.'

We walked through the kitchen into a dining room, where the man asked us to sit at the table. I could see piles of music books stacked on an armchair in the corner. I watched the bare-chested man, who said his name was Jeremy, walk back through the kitchen to a room I presumed was the bathroom. He came out holding a Tupperware box that had a red elastic band round its outside. As he placed it on the table I could see that it contained what looked like large amber bath salts. He shook the box and said, 'Ray, you have to have a go on this, it will fuck you up proper.'

Jeremy was enthusiastic about his merchandise. He grabbed a clean spoon and took one of the crystals out of box and crushed it into a virgin white powder. He asked us both to give it a go. In unison, we declined. I knew that this looked like 'top end' gear, so I asked Jeremy to sort me out an ounce. He grabbed a set of scales and carefully weighed out twenty-eight grams. He then got a clear bag, cut off the corner to form a triangle, placed the crystals inside and knotted the end. He handed me the bag and asked for £800 in exchange, which I gave him.

He pointed down to the white crushed powder from his demonstration and said, 'Gentleman, can I tempt you?' Again, both of us declined. Jeremy continued: 'Under those circumstances, it seems a shame to waste it.' He took a cut straw from his jeans pocket and snorted the powder. Then he told us it was a pleasure doing business, and Ray and I went to walk out together. As we got to the kitchen door, Ray said he'd see me in the car, as he wanted a quick chat with Jeremy.

I had a little smile on my face as I walked down the steps and through the yard; I knew Ray would be taking a 'cut' off Jeremy for the introduction to me. I sat in the car a few minutes until he returned to inform me that there was as much of the Mum and Dad as I could move. He also asked if I was going to 'see him right' for making the introduction. I laughed at him, and he said, 'What now?'

I told him to open the glovebox, and watched the smile on his face as he took a hundred pounds in £20 notes and put them in his jacket pocket. I was pleased with the evening's work, and I had no doubt that I'd just bought a very high-purity ounce of crystal MDMA.

Twenty

Emma locked up, and we linked arms and walked the short distance from the shop to the café. She talked non-stop about the customers that had stepped into the shop throughout the day. She was excited and enthusiastically described each and every character that she had met during the day. Her face beamed and she could not get her words out quick enough.

I looked at her and tried to concentrate on her every word, but it was difficult for me to take it all in. If I was honest, I was more interested in the reason that Ray wanted to meet me at the café. He had phoned me earlier in the day and asked to meet me there at 6.30 p.m. It was now 6.10 and I only had a few minutes to explain the situation to Emma.

I squeezed her hand and told her what a fantastic job I thought she was doing. I truly meant it – she was so natural at what she did. I told her that Ray was coming at 6.30 and I wasn't sure what he wanted to talk about. I asked her to go to the ladies after about ten minutes, as Ray was unlikely to discuss business in front of her. I also said that if I asked her if she'd got the DVDs for me, that was the time for her to say she'd left them in the shop and to leave Ray and me alone for fifteen minutes.

Emma understood this, and recognised the importance of my relationship with Ray. It was in no way a slur on her, it was the way Ray and I conducted our business. I'd told Ray that Emma thought I was back on the straight and narrow and that she didn't want me going back to my old ways. I'd told him that I wanted her to believe that I was a straight-goer now, and that if he was ever asked by her, he would confirm that I was behaving myself. I had said that Emma saw this as a new start, a clean slate, an opportunity for the two of us to build a future together. Ray knew the script, and if Emma was with me, he was very discreet in his conversations. But he also knew that she wasn't stupid, and he was almost schoolboy in his responses when she would say, 'I hope you two aren't up to no good?' I could see he had lies written all over his face when he answered her. Emma understood, and she played her part to perfection. I knew Ray liked her, and he was always courteous and polite around her.

At 6.30, he bounced through the café door with a huge beam on his face; he was one of life's happy people. He greeted

Emma and gave her a big kiss, joking that this must be my idea of taking her for a romantic meal.

Everyone in the café knew that Ray was there, as his voice was always that little bit louder than everyone else's. I think he thrived on being the centre of attention – this was his personality, it was in his make-up. He sat down opposite the two of us. Emma was holding my hand on the table in front of him, and I saw him glance down at this and then straight into my eyes. We made small talk and arranged that we would – together with Ray's missus, Chloe – all go out on Saturday evening for a meal and a few drinks.

Emma took this as her cue to excuse herself. I laughed to myself as she walked towards the ladies. I knew there was no chance whatsoever that she would allow herself to sit on the toilet seat in there, not in a million years. She would have to wash her hands over and over, and pray that no one else needed to use it.

Ray used the time wisely: 'I didn't want to say anything in front of her. But I wanted to know if you'd be interested in a bit of metalwork.' He held his hand on the table in front of me in a gun shape. 'I'm meeting the fella that's got it at seven thirty.'

I said I was definitely interested but that he should only ring me when he actually had it in his lap, and then I'd come and meet him later to collect it. Ray told me it had a 'shusher' and it came with seven or eight bits of 'food'. He said that I knew the fella that he was meeting, and we could sort the 'paperwork' out later. Sorting out the money was always the critical part. He said it would be about two and half bags.

I told him to say when Emma came back that maybe me and him could have a pint down the 'office' about nine o'clock, but that he shouldn't ring me unless he definitely had the 'thing' with him.

Emma rejoined us, and as she went to sit down Ray made his excuses and got up from the table. As he went to walk out, he turned around and said he'd call me later for a pint down 'the office'. Whenever Ray and I spoke on the phone about meeting at our pub, we referred to it as 'the office'. It was a pub we had made our own – a place we felt safe in, somewhere we discussed our 'business' together.

In the most unsubtle way, he then winked at me, and with a smile on his face bounced out of the café. Emma and I both looked at each other and giggled. I asked her how the toilet was, knowing she would go into a rant about hygiene in public bathrooms. And she didn't disappoint me; I felt I knew each and every contour of the toilet by the time she had finished.

I paid the bill, and as we walked to Emma's car I explained the purpose of Ray's meeting and the meaning of his exaggerated wink. I knew Emma didn't like guns, and I could see in her face that she was apprehensive about me buying this one.

I wanted to take her mind off the business of buying guns so I looked at her and said, 'Please, not sausage pasta again for supper!' She was good at many, many things, but her culinary skills were not at the top of her list of talents. I agreed that I would cook tonight, and said I'd meet her at home after she'd been to see Dave and the team.

I waved Emma off, and then phoned Dave as I walked into town to get some decent food so that I could cook dinner. As

I was talking to Dave, I received a text from Ray reading: *Not until 8, ring you later*. I replied: *Done*. I explained to Dave the details of my meeting, and that Ray had arranged to see someone that I apparently knew to collect a gun with a silencer and seven or eight bullets at 8 p.m. It would cost £2,500.

I could sense that Dave was excited but nervous at the same time. He started explaining that he'd have to let the bosses know, because it was a gun. I could feel myself getting angry: 'Dave, it's just a commodity . . . whether it's a gun or a kilo of coke, it's just a commodity, no need to panic. Trust me. Play it low-key, it's simple.' I could tell that Dave understood my thoughts, but I was unsure whether the people above him would see it that way. I told him that I'd let him know any news.

I tried to put the irritation I felt towards senior officers to one side. The sheer mention of a gun in senior police circles transcends into panic stations. They have no concept that this is just a business transaction between two consenting parties – it's a financial agreement and the commodity happens to be a gun.

I managed to forget the senior officers as I selected some fresh penne, basil and pancetta, and a rustic baguette and vine tomatoes. I was quite happy that I would have a lovely meal on the table when Emma returned home. But before I had started to create my magic in the kitchen and cook our meal, my phone rang. It was Ray, his voice loud and clear but very panicky. He said, 'Listen, I'm parked in the middle of a field off a country lane. They're all over me like a rash, I'm switching my phone off.' The line then went dead.

I tried to call him back immediately but it went straight to voicemail. I didn't bother leaving a message. I knew that this was genuine; I knew that Ray was in a corner and I'd heard worry in his voice. He was letting me know there was a problem, marking my card. He had done the right thing.

I picked up the phone and spoke with Dave, explaining the bizarre phone call I'd just had from Ray. I could hear Dave's other phone ringing in the background, and he said he'd call me back if he got any news. I knew Dave had a lot going on with this job at the moment, and it was taking up all his time. I couldn't think about cooking and I didn't want to second-guess what may have happened to Ray. There was only one thing I knew for certain: I wouldn't be buying a gun with a silencer and bullets tonight.

I left Emma a note saying that I'd popped out and I'd be back to cook her a lovely meal. Then I drove out of town, not really knowing where to look. It was more a gesture than anything else. If I could find him and help him out, then that would be a massive bonus.

I phoned Chloe and explained what had happened this evening. I was careful not to tell her too much, but enough to let her know I was concerned. I wanted her to know that I was out trying to find him. Ray and Chloe had an open relationship – that's to say she knew exactly how he earned his money. She knew where he got the money to pay the mortgage, she knew how he paid for their food and clothing, and she was happy for that to continue. The one thing she couldn't contemplate happening was Ray getting nicked.

Chloe wasn't overly concerned about his current predicament, and told me that she would ring me with any news but she was sure all would be well in the morning. As I was about to hang up, she told me that she was really looking forward to us all going out on Saturday night.

I liked Chloe – she was a strong lady, a good mum, and she kept a good home for her kids. She was pregnant again, and this meant there would soon be another mouth to feed. She wore the trousers in that house, no matter what Ray said.

Chloe's calmness was infectious, and I put the CD player on in the car as I drove through the country lanes. I relaxed and took in the words of Oasis as I blasted out 'Champagne Supernova': As Liam was singing about getting high, I was enjoying the tranquillity of the countryside, and Ray's troubles now seemed a long way away. I was sure that things would be fine – they always looked better the next morning. I phoned Emma and told her I'd be home in fifteen minutes, and I enjoyed the peacefulness of the journey home.

Twenty-one

My phone rang, and I could immediately sense that there was something wrong, before Ray had even breathed a word.

'I need to see you now, for a face to face, where are you?' I detected severe panic in his voice, and uncertainty. He was uncomfortable and I knew it. But I didn't show any concern in my voice when I replied, 'I'm just jumping in the shower, where d'ya want to meet?'

He said he was down the Spanish coffee shop, and to hurry up and not to tell anyone we were meeting. I said I'd see him in half an hour. I hung up, and sat in silence pondering what had happened the previous evening: why the panic in his voice, why the urgency? This was not the Ray I'd spent time getting to know. Not the man who had already sold me cocaine,

Mum and Dad, and offered me a gun and silencer. Ray was a reliable villain, who moved reasonable amounts of powder and earned his living this way. He did his utmost to avoid the Old Bill. He'd introduced me to people who only traded with those they knew and trusted, and I was now amongst them, talking to them on equal terms.

I had little time to dwell on things. I jumped in the shower, and the power of the water and the cracked-black-pepper shower gel concentrated my mind. I looked in the mirror and realised that the amount of money I had paid to Molton Brown over the years wasn't really reaping its rewards. Then my thoughts turned back to the previous evening and my meeting with Ray in the café. I had been very casual with him after he'd offered me the handgun and silencer, telling him to ring me only when he had it with him.

As I was getting dressed, I phoned Dave and outlined my brief conversation with Ray. I could tell from his reaction that he was apprehensive about me meeting him. However, he said he'd go along with whatever I thought. He asked me if I wanted a team to back me up, to cover my back in case it all went wrong. I told him I'd rather be on my own, but if he hadn't heard from me in an hour and a half from now, I may have a problem. He went quiet, and said, 'Don't say that.' I told him I was joking, that it would be fine and I'd ring him when I was done. He paused and said, 'Be careful. I mean it.'

'Don't be a lesbian,' I said, and ended the call.

I knew he was worried, and it was often the case that it was far more stressful for the other person than for me in these situations. They were in the dark, isolated, sat waiting and not knowing what was happening, going over and over in their mind whether they should've sent a backup team. Staring at the phone, praying that it'll ring or a text will come through saying all is well.

I couldn't worry about Dave; I had a job to do. I jumped into my car and put Elbow on at full blast. The word 'gun' seemed to linger, seemed to hold my attention.

I parked my car and strolled casually into the coffee shop. The smell of the freshly baked *pasteis de nata* and the strong ground coffee was soothing. I ordered a double espresso, and turned from the counter to see Ray sat in the corner on his own. He didn't look well. There was no colour in his face, his lips were dry and it looked like he'd been up all night. He looked like shit, like he had the weight of the world on his shoulders. I sat down opposite him and studied his face. His eyes were red, like he'd been crying. I wanted to try and gauge how serious this problem was.

He didn't wait for me to speak. 'I'm just going to say it. I've been told you're Old Bill.' His lip was quivering as he said the words.

I held his gaze, and I laughed out loud and said, 'Thank fuck for that. I really thought something terrible had happened. Is that it?'

Ray didn't think it was funny; he said he'd been sat in his car in the middle of a field last night for four hours. He'd had the 'filth' all over him once he'd left me to collect the metalwork, and then he'd had a call to say I was Old Bill.

I stirred a tiny bit of sugar into my espresso; I wanted to drink it whilst it was still hot, to show Ray I wasn't fazed by what he'd said. That at that moment the coffee was more important than his bombshell disclosure. I sipped the coffee and it felt good, just enough sweetness to complement the bitter strong taste.

Before I could speak, he said, 'I don't want to believe it – it can't be true, otherwise I'm fucked, I'm gone . . . I'll be in the shovel for a long time.'

I looked at him and said calmly, 'Listen to yourself . . . listen to what you're saying. Get a grip, will you? It makes no sense. How many times have I told you to slow down, to stop introducing me to new people, to stop middling deals with people we don't need to know or need to meet. I've told you over and over to be sensible otherwise you'll get us both nicked.'

He said, 'You're right. I know you have. You've warned me to be careful, but I've been told.' There was colour back in his cheeks. My calmness and balanced argument was definitely winning him over.

I asked him who had told him, said to ring them and get them here now. I was taking control of the situation. I didn't want to antagonise things or go overboard with denials, so I told him I wanted the person to look me in the eyes and say it in front of Ray.

He dialled the number and I immediately recognised the voice. It was Ricardo. He was tall, well built and not shy of inflicting violence; he had a particularly nasty reputation. A career criminal, who had spent long stretches of time at Her Majesty's pleasure.

Undercover

When Ray hung up, he said Ricardo was down the road but had just ordered rice and peas. 'Fuck his rice and peas! I'm going to see him now.' I didn't shout, I didn't scream, but Ray had known me long enough to know I wasn't happy. I wanted to sort this bollocks out now.

I saw him sat with two other guys in the window of the Chicken Shack. I went in, and told him to come outside and tell me to my face what he'd told Ray. He was reluctant to get up, so I took his knife and fork off him and told him I'd buy him a fresh plate if it went cold.

Ricardo towered above me, and as I looked up at him he had a piece of rice on his moustache. It was annoying me, so I told him and he brushed it off with his hand. It was only at that moment I noticed the size of his hands. He was a big, powerful man – an intimidating man to most normal people, and physically much stronger than me.

'Go on. What have you got to say, Ricardo?'

'Look, I've been told by someone I trust that you're Old Bill. He told me to tell Ray and that's what I've done.'

'For a geezer that's traded with me and intro'd me to Ray, you don't seem too bothered.'

'Let me make this clear. If you are Old Bill, you're dead. You're gone.'

I looked up at him and poked my finger into his chest. 'Ricardo, if that's what you believe, stay the fuck out of my way.'

I didn't wait for a reply; I turned and walked back to Ray, who was waiting outside. He had a bounce back in his step, the colour was back in his cheeks, and he was like the old

Ray – the Ray I liked, the Ray I considered my mate. I'd spent more time with him in the last three months than any of my family or friends.

Ray *was* my friend.

Before I could tell him about my conversation with Ricardo, he pulled me close to him and said, 'Joe, I don't want us to speak about this again. It's dealt with, it's over.' He held out his hand and I gripped it firmly and shook it.

I said, 'It's up to you, Ray. I'll walk away now if you believe him.'

He grabbed the lapels of my coat and said, 'What did I just say? It's dealt with. We never talk about it again.' He paused. 'There's a lovely bit of chisel on offer, but it's a drive this afternoon. Meet me at two thirty at the back of the Mercedes dealership and we'll go and see the fella.' He gave me a big hug and said, 'You know I love you, Joe. Let's make loads of money.'

I walked slowly back to my car, trying to digest what had just happened, the bizarre turn of events. I had a strong feeling in my stomach that this wasn't yet over.

I didn't know it right then, but this was going to be a long, long day.

Twenty-two

As I pulled onto the driveway, I looked up at the house and felt calm, content and happy. It was a comfort to know I was home. I could see Emma looking out of the window; it was as if she had been waiting for me. I knew she would've been worried. I had told her before I'd left that I'd had a phone call from Ray and there was something wrong. Emma knew me well, and I didn't keep secrets from her. She knew Ray and I had been in the middle of negotiating the purchase of a gun and ammunition. She was aware of the potential dangers that he posed to me and to her.

I could see the worry etched on her face. I smiled at her and the worry seemed to fade away.

At that moment, my phone rang. It was Dave. He was agitated and his words were rushed: 'You need to come and see me now, I've got things I need to tell you.'

I asked him if they could wait, as I'd just pulled up at home after my meeting with Ray and run-in with Ricardo. But he demanded that he see me straight away. Without getting out of the car or explaining to Emma, I reversed off the drive and started on the twenty-minute journey into the countryside. I could see the confused look on Emma's face as I backed out of the drive. I would ignore her phone calls until I had something concrete to tell her after seeing Dave.

I relaxed on the journey, and let my mind drift off to another place. When I arrived at the long lane that led to Dave's house, it was if the last twenty minutes hadn't happened; I couldn't remember anything about the journey. Dave was waiting outside with his black Labrador at his side. The house was his pride and joy; recently painted a subtle pastel blue, it was like a picture-postcard cottage.

'Joe, we need to talk. The bosses haven't been giving me the full picture and I'm not happy.' Dave was angry and disappointed, and I could tell he was worried.

We went into his cosy kitchen, where he had hops hanging from the beams, and a beautiful cream Aga with a matching Le Creuset steam kettle sat on the hotplate. This was a tranquil, peaceful room; I could smell toast, and imagined happy family meals taking place at the large antique pine dining table where I sat.

Undercover

Dave handed me a mug of hot tea and passed me a cracked Cornishware sugar bowl, with a spoon that was caked in sugar. I found myself staring at the grains of coffee that were scattered amongst the white granules. Dave grabbed my full attention when he said, 'Joe, last night there was a big problem with the surveillance team. Ray used a pal of his who took out two foot-surveillance officers and one of the surveillance cars.'

I looked at him. 'No one told me there was a surveillance team on the job, Dave. What the fuck's going on?'

He said that he wasn't told, that the bosses had got nervous I was buying a gun and they had insisted that there was a surveillance team used. I told him that he could thank his bosses, but their naive decision could've got me killed.

I took a long sip of the strong tea as Dave said, 'Joe, that's not the worst bit. The pal of his is an ex-policeman. He knows this world and he has knowledge of surveillance. Last night he tapped two of the surveillance team on the shoulder and asked them who they were following.' Dave went on to say that the surveillance team were so embarrassed about their performance that there'd been a closed-door debrief. This went on for four hours, and the team leader decided it was too late to tell anyone what had happened that same night. He'd made the disclosure this morning.

I was fuming. I hated using surveillance teams, and there was always a risk that the team would 'show out'. If they did, it could put me in a very difficult position – could put me at considerable risk.

141

What was the reason for using a team? All I was doing was buying a gun, silencer and ammunition. Who had made the decision, and who was the team leader who'd gone to bed rather than tell someone that his team had been 'burnt to cinders'?

All these questions needing answering, but my biggest worry was who this ex–Old Bill was. What threat did he pose to me, and was he the reason for my grilling from Ray earlier?

Dave looked at me and said, 'What do you want to do, Joe? I'd understand if you want to throw the towel in.'

'Dave, don't be a plum. This situation isn't good, but I'm supposed to be meeting Ray in an hour and a half to buy some coke from a new fella.' Dave said that he'd been told by his bosses to say that they'd understand if I wanted out. 'Dave, tell your bosses to stick to organising speed bumps on busy roads, and I'll stick to what I'm paid to do.'

Dave showed me a picture of the ex-policeman, and asked if I'd seen him before. He said that a few years ago Ray and this guy had been very close, but intelligence said they'd had a fall out. The policeman had resigned from the force following an investigation into his criminal connections. The reality was, he'd jumped before he was pushed.

I didn't recognise the face in the picture, but wanted to ensure it was ingrained in my mind. I knew it would only be a matter of time before the two of us met face to face.

Dave was really concerned about the predicament we were in. He told me in confidence that he knew this guy well, that he'd worked with him. As with so many corrupt officers, he'd sailed close to the wind. He'd been a good thief-taker and people had liked him. He'd had good informants, and was often used by the bosses to get good 'clear up' figures. These were the 'write offs' that burglars would admit to – under no danger of further sentence – and they resulted in favourable crime figures. The bosses didn't want to know how they were obtained, but were grateful when they were. 'Noble cause corruption', as it was called.

Dave said it was much deeper than that; this guy was a criminal who had carried a warrant card for many years. He was aware of all the tactics available to the police, and had experience in undercover operations. He was bent from head to toe, a 'proper wrong'un'.

I got up from my seat at the table, opened the top of the stable door and looked out to the open fields in the distance. I sucked in the air; it smelt of the countryside, of fresh sheets, of holidays as a kid camping in a farmer's field in Cornwall. It was so tranquil, a million miles away from guns and drugs, corrupt policemen and villains – a world apart.

I turned to Dave. 'We are where we are, Dave. I see it as a bonus that I know this now. I've got his "boat" in my mind and I'll be on my toes from this moment on. I want to do this trade this afternoon. It may settle Ray down. I'm gonna go back, get the money for the coke, and fill Emma in as to what's happening.'

Dave said he'd already had Emma on the phone as I was driving over. He'd brought her up to speed and he thought she was worried for me. I told him I'd settle her down. I put my mug in the Belfast sink and turned back to him. 'No more secrets, Dave. Tell your bosses that. And keep the surveillance team away from me.' I shook his hand. 'If anything ever happens to me, bury me under that cherry blossom.' I pointed to a beautiful mature tree that sat to the side of his cottage; it had an old-fashioned wooden swing on it that was blowing gently in the wind.

Twenty-three

As I drove up I expected to see Emma's car, but it was gone. I walked round the back of the house and over the raised decking area, and opened the patio doors into the kitchen. A note was attached to a fresh bunch of lilies that had been carefully arranged in an old cream-enamel jug. The note read: *He's told me everything, don't do anything stupid. Emma xxx*

I looked at the flowers and remembered my granny telling me that they signify the purity of the soul and the return of innocence after death. At that moment, I saw myself standing in Dave's garden, watching the wooden swing blowing gently under the old cherry tree. I wasn't the sentimental type, and hadn't given my granny a thought for many years. She had died when I was young, before we'd had sufficient time to build a close bond, but I remembered those words.

Today had been a whirlwind of revelations and bad news, of information and situations that made my job so much harder to do. I now knew that I couldn't have totally convinced Ray I was OK, especially if he had his ex-policeman friend filling his head with information. I knew I had to stay calm, to focus on what was in front of me.

My phone vibrated on the worktop and danced across the marble surface. It was a text from Ray: *230 at back of Asda superstore by recycling*. That gave me an hour until we were due to meet, and it was about a twenty-five-minute drive away. I rang Dave and told him the arrangements before I replied to the text: *Done*.

Then I removed two tubes of Pringles from the cupboard above the sink. I popped the tops and removed £5,000 from one tube and £2,500 from the other. I counted out the money, and rewrapped it into seven £1,000 bundles and one £500. I placed them in a pair of Loake shoes, put the shoes into their dust bags and into their dark-blue shoebox. Then I wrote on the back of Emma's note: *Lilies, thanks!!! See you tonight. xxx*.

I walked to my car and placed the shoebox inside my sports bag in the boot. I pulled out of the driveway and felt a tad excited about what the afternoon was to hold for me. All I knew at this moment was that Ray was taking me somewhere to meet someone and buy some cocaine.

I don't know why but I wasn't worried, I wasn't nervous, I wasn't even apprehensive. I'm sure my psychologist had warned me in the past that these were alarm signals for someone that's on self-destruct or out of control. But I couldn't help how I was feeling.

I pulled into the car park, which was busy with Friday-afternoon customers doing their weekly shop to fill their ordinary fridges in their normal houses, where their normal families would be sharing a special meal together at home. I parked my car close to the recycling and watched a lovely couple in their seventies lock the door of their pristine 1956 Rover 75. They were holding hands, and he stopped for a moment to turn the collar of her coat down gently. This was what I thought love should be – couples that couldn't live without each other. I imagined that they'd probably never spent a night apart in their lives.

My mind was brought back to reality when Ricardo knocked heavily on my passenger-door window. I pressed the central locking and he squeezed his huge frame into the cream leather seat. I looked at him, waiting for him to say something. He was close enough to smell the fact he'd had a brandy or two before he met me. He broke the silence and said, 'I introduced you to Ray, so that's why I'm here. We're all in this together.' He told me to follow Ray's Range Rover.

I looked at him. 'Ricardo, if you think I'm a dirty Old Bill then that's you and me done – I don't want you anywhere near me.'

We sat in silence for a while as we drove out of the main town and onto the roads that led into the countryside .The car was full of anxiety and uncertainty. I could feel Ricardo's fear. He pointed at the Range Rover in front; I could see Ray with his mobile squashed to his ear. 'Do you know who he's on the phone to, Joe?' He paused. 'His best mate, who's Old Bill, and he's telling Ray what to do to you if you are the filth.' He spat the last word out; he made it feel a dirty word to me.

I knew Ricardo was praying it wasn't true, because he and I had done things together that would put him behind bars for many years. He was a worried man, and that made him dangerous to me.

The roads became narrower and windy as we headed towards the coast. I had been subtly looking in my mirror to see if anyone was following, and to my horror I'd seen the same Skoda Octavia a number of times. It was now about three cars behind me. This meant one of two things: Ray had some of his heavies who were going to join us, or there was a surveillance team following me. I could see the car had two people in it.

I wanted to keep Ricardo's attention focused on the bumper of Ray's Range Rover, I didn't want him to get an eyeful of the Skoda. So I handed him my phone and said, 'Ring Emma and tell her what you think I am.' I wanted to get a message to her. I wanted to somehow let her know that all wasn't fine. I knew Ricardo liked Emma; he'd spent time with her and I'd asked him to keep an eye on her when I wasn't about. He'd done that for me and I knew he'd enjoyed it.

He dialled the number and I could hear her voice. She was surprised to hear Ricardo on my phone. I could hear her say, 'Where's Joe?'

Ricardo told her, 'We're taking a drive to the seaside, nothing to worry about.' I knew that the last four words he used would alarm her. He didn't say anything else and hung up. I was confident that Emma knew I'd done that for a reason.

I looked at him and said, 'Listen, Ricardo, until you apologise to me I've got nothing to say to you, so it's gonna be a quiet journey.' I knew he had a million questions he wanted to ask me, and I was sure Ray would've given him instructions about what to quiz me on. For some reason, Ricardo wasn't using his time with me wisely. He was a big man, and I knew the damage he could do to me, but at this moment I could feel and smell his fear.

As we took a couple of left and right turns, I was left in no doubt that the Skoda following us was indeed a surveillance car. It was getting closer and more obvious by the minute.

It was getting dark as we drove through a tiny village with a few shops and houses, smoke coming from the chimneys. I saw a split in the road with a brightly lit fish and chip restaurant in the centre acting like a keep left/keep right bollard. I could see that to the left was a sign to a car park and to the right a sign to the creek.

I followed Ray to the right, to what appeared to be a harbour. I could see an old building with a sign that read *Cinque Ports Board of Trade, Wreck Warehouse*. Ray turned his car around, as did I, and we parked perilously close to what appeared to be the harbour wall. Ricardo got out of the car first and spoke to Ray. I got out of the car, as I wanted to see exactly what was beyond the wall. The evening sky lit up an extremely muddy creek or inlet; the mud looked wet, thick and deep. All I could think was that if it was my only escape route, I'd get stuck in the mud and be an easy target for some-one who wanted to shoot me.

I walked over to Ray and said, 'What's going on, Ray? Where are we?' He pointed to a newly built block of flats that had a very nautical look to them. 'Ray Winstone's got one of them gaffs. I bet it's the penthouse.' I looked at him and said sarcastically, 'Nice.' Ray said, 'Let's go and have a cuppa tea. We need a chat.'

We made our way to the fish and chip restaurant and I ordered drinks, but Ricardo said he was hungry and wanted to eat. I'd decided if I wasn't talking to him, there was no way I was buying his dinner. I took my cup of tea and Ray's hot chocolate over to the table. Both were in polystyrene cups. I don't know if they did it on purpose to intimidate me, but Ray and Ricardo both sat opposite me, looking out onto the split in the road where we had driven in and turned right. I was fac-ing the counter and the windows that looked out onto the car park at the rear of the restaurant.

Ricardo got the biggest plate of cod and chips I had seen for some time, and his culinary class had seen him order a side plate of three oversized pickled eggs. Ricardo ate like a pig at the best of times, and I wasn't looking forward to sitting opposite him for the next ten minutes. I looked out the window as I sipped my tea, and as clear as I could see the shiny skin of the pickled eggs, I saw two men standing at the side of the Skoda. They were looking into the restaurant as I looked at them. The two surveillance officers were doing all they could to expose themselves to the two villains that I was sitting with.

Ricardo was stuffing his face full of cod, chips and pickled eggs. As he asked me to pass the vinegar, he spat out a combination of all three. I felt a bit land on my face, and I immediately got up from my seat and said, 'I can't sit opposite him when he's spitting his food everywhere.' I called Ricardo a pig and said, 'I'm having a slash.' I didn't need the bathroom, nor was I overly bothered by Ricardo and his eating habits. But I had to get rid of the surveillance team before it was too late.

I went into the Gents, and whilst stood at the freezing cold urinal I frantically texted Dave: *get rid of the 2 gimps in the Skoda before they get me hurt.* I hoped that neither Ricardo nor Ray had followed me in and caught me in the act of sending it. It was a judgement call, and luckily I managed to send and clear it before returning to the table.

Ray leant over the table and said, 'The fella coming is a proper face. Don't fuck him about.' Ray said he wanted me and him to split a 'German', and it would be seven and half bags each.

'Why the fuck have we brought Ainsley Harriott with us' – I pointed at Ricardo – 'I didn't know this was a beano.'

Ray said that a lot had happened over the last twenty-four hours, and he and Ricardo needed to be sure about me. I asked him if they were, and he said, 'Not yet.'

In my mind, I knew that Ray needed me for this trade. I didn't think this 'face' we were meeting would serve up less than a quarter of kilo of cocaine at a time, and Ray didn't have £15,000 today to trade on his own. I know he wanted this trade to happen, and he needed my half.

Ray's phone rang and he went outside to take the call. Ricardo was now wiping the remnants of food from his face. He looked at me and said, 'This ain't over yet, Joe.'

'Thank fuck that is,' I said, pointing at his plate. Then I got up and joined Ray in the doorway of the restaurant. He pointed to another Range Rover parked in front of his. I could see two large men inside, both smoking.

Ray asked for my money. I told him he could have my money from the boot of my motor once I'd seen the gear. I told him I wasn't having my pants pulled down in the middle of nowhere. Ray wasn't happy, but I walked over to my car and popped the boot. The vanity light lit up the darkness, and I could hear the noise of the creek filling up to my left and a squelching as the water slowly covered the mud. I could sense someone directly behind me; it was Ricardo. 'Ray wants the readies. Give me the money.'

I took one look at him and said, 'Fuck off out of my face, Ricardo. This is Ray's and my trade.'

This was the point I was at my most vulnerable – there were four of them and I was on my own – but I was sticking to my guns. It seemed like an eternity before Ray came to the boot. He wasn't happy as he said, 'I've had to weigh that in the back of the motor.' He handed me a Sainsbury's bag, and inside was a clear bag with a block of white powder. I could smell the distinct smell of cocaine. Ray said, 'It looks proper – I've just had a go and it's bang on.'

I looked at him. 'Is it spot on the weight?'

Ray nodded his head. 'If it's light I'll sort you the difference later.'

Undercover

I wasn't about to weigh it in public in the boot of my car; I'd do that when I was home. I had taken the money out of the shoebox and I now handed it to Ray. As I did, a new face appeared by the boot.

'Everything sweet, fellas?' He was a big man; he had a big head with bulging veins the size of hosepipes pumping across his forehead. It was clear to see he was on steroids. He held out his hand and said, 'Dazza – nice one.'

I shook his hand. 'Nice to meet you, Dazza. If you gentlemen don't mind, I'm a long way from home and I've got people waiting on this.' This was the moment – if they were going to make a move on me, it would be now. Dazza had had no need to come to my car. No reason to put himself there.

I needed to get into my car and away.

I shut the boot with the gear safely inside, but as I went to get in my car Ricardo grabbed my arm. I turned – almost too quickly – ready to confront him, ready to fight as best I could. I was in a vulnerable situation, surrounded by dangerous men. He held my arm tightly and said, 'Don't call me a pig. My old man used to, all the time, and I hated him.'

I pulled my arm away, and as I got into the car I said, 'Well, don't eat like one then.'

I didn't wait to hear his reply.

Twenty-four

I was so relieved to shut the door of my car. I knew I was safe now. My initial thought as I went to pull away from the murky quayside was to drive as fast as I could away from this place. To put as much distance as I could between myself and this inlet of the Essex coast, a place I didn't want to visit again.

Instead, I memorised the registration of the other Range Rover and pulled slowly away, leaving behind the silhouettes of the three men standing on the quayside. I could see the embers of their cigarettes light up two of their faces as they watched me. I passed the fish and chip restaurant where Ricardo had gorged like a pig, and drove quietly and anonymously out of the village.

It had been a long, testing and dangerous day. I turned the CD player on, turning the volume control on the steering wheel to near its maximum I sang along at the top of my voice. It was my favourite song. I sang along in a world of my own, and by now I was clear of the place I never wanted to return to.

I pulled off the main road into a service lane that sat behind a line of thick conifers. I could see there was a middle-aged couple in a Belgian-registered motorhome making a hot drink on their Primus stove. I picked up my phone and called Emma, and it seemed like she picked up the phone before it had even rung.

'Where are you? Are you OK – what's happened?' I could hear, in her voice, the fear and worry and genuine concern for my safety.

'Emms, I'm fine, I promise you. Do me a favour. Ring Dave, tell him I'm safe and that I've got half a German in the boot. I'll tell you everything when I get home.' She paused, then said, 'I've been so worried.' I apologised and said I'd see her soon.

As I pulled back onto the main road, my phone rang and it was Dave: 'Fuck me I'm pleased to hear your voice. What happened?'

I went through the sequence of events since we'd shared a cup of tea earlier that day. He listened without interrupting, which was a great talent in itself. When I'd finished, he took a deep breath and said, 'I don't know how you've managed to turn that around. I know one thing, I need a drink.' I told him that it would probably take me over an hour to drive to him and we could share a glass together then. Before he ended the call, he said quietly, ' Well done, mate. You did real good.'

I think it was more of a relief for Dave – a weight had been released off his shoulders. For the time being, he hadn't lost an undercover officer on his watch.

As I drove to meet Dave at the office, I pictured his chocolate-box cottage. I could see the wooden swing under the cherry tree and I imagined me pushing my daughter gently in the sunshine. She was shouting 'higher' and screeching with laughter.

It was at moments like this that I regretted the times I wasn't there for the people I loved, the ones that needed my protection and guidance. Did it really matter that I'd just bought a chunk of cocaine off some Essex gangster? I knew my little girl wouldn't care, was too young to understand. All she wanted was her dad to be there at bedtime to read her a story and kiss her goodnight. To make her breakfast in the morning, and walk hand in hand with her to school. Surely that wasn't a lot for a little girl to ask of her dad?

I fought with issues like this in my own head. I never shared them with anyone; I kept them inside, I battled with them alone. Why was I working undercover, anyway – who was I doing it for?

I knew the answers, but I didn't want to admit them. I buried my head in the sand, said I'd make it up to my little girl one day: put it right, make amends for all the times I wasn't there for her. If I kept telling myself that, it must come true.

Thankfully, my sad thoughts were interrupted by a text from Dave: *glass of Peroni here for you, how long you gonna be?* I was only ten minutes away, so I didn't bother responding.

Undercover

I pulled into the underground car park and could see Emma's car parked. I wasn't expecting her to be there. I got the lift up to the office, where it appeared the whole team was awaiting my arrival. 'What are you lot doing here on a Friday evening?'

The sharpest young lad from the support team, Carl, quipped, 'Waiting for you – what took you so long?' The rest of the team laughed, as did I. He brought me a glass of ice-cold Peroni, and I could tell they had all sunk one or two already.

Then Emma came over and sneakily gave my hand a squeeze. 'I've been beside myself. Don't do that again.'

We dealt with all the formalities of the operation, and then Dave took me into a side office and shut the door behind him. We stood close to each other and he told me that he was sorry that I'd been put in the position I had today. He said that most of the bosses wanted to shut the job down. He said it had taken balls to go to that meet today and to tough it out. He was really pleased, and he said he just wanted to say thank you. I looked at him and said, 'Shut up. When did you go all lesbian on me?'

He laughed and, as I opened the door, said, 'I mean it.'

We went back into the main office, where Carl was sat at the table with three mobiles lined up on the desk in front of him. The rest of the team was gathered round watching his impression of Dave throughout the afternoon and evening. He kept repeating in Dave's local accent: 'I knew this was a bad idea, and who's arse is on the line when it goes wrong? Mine.' The team was laughing, and Carl looked at me. 'Honestly, if he said that once he said it a hundred times.'

Carl then lifted his glass and said, 'Can we agree now, never to deploy on Friday the thirteenth again.' I wasn't superstitious in the slightest, but I could see from some of the team that they clearly were and it wouldn't happen again.

We tidied things up in the office, and Emma and I left before the rest of the team. She followed me back home, where I was so relieved just to lie back on the sofa and sink into the sumptuous cushions. I knew she would have a thousand questions for me, but I shut my eyes tightly, breathed in the aroma of the Molton Brown candles that were flickering on the mantelpiece, and forgot about everything that had happened that day.

Twenty-five

I was driving up the Dirty Dozen far too fast to stay anywhere near the speed limit, in an attempt to make up for time lost and the terrible journey I'd had to endure on the M25. The loudness of my *Kill Bill* ringtone interrupted the soothing Scottish voice of Alan Brazil waxing lyrical about the raw talent of Wayne Rooney. The call provided the perfect reason to turn the radio off. It was Dave, who asked me where I was. When I told him, he said not to go straight to my house, but to pull off the A12 and meet him at a very discreet café.

I liked meeting at this particular café, which was a beautiful converted stables. It was a stone's throw away from the main thoroughfare to London, yet it could have been miles away, in the middle of the countryside.

I drove around the horseshoe driveway just as Dave was getting out of his car. I loved the sight of the vast cedar trees that surrounded the stables. I got out of my car and sucked in the smell of the cedars. I could hear the sound of the wind blowing gently through their branches, and I could see that the lawns had just been cut to a pristine standard any golf course would've been proud of. Dave was already on his way into the coffee shop, and I knew the reason why.

Over the last eight months, Dave had shed a lot of weight – he now realised that it was possible to see his toes when naked and no longer needed assistance with putting his socks on. He had even started running. It was a tremendous achievement, but Dave didn't always see it that way. Dave loved his food, and he really missed cooked breakfasts, Chinese takeaways and sit-down Ruby's. But most of all, he missed cake – my God, did he go on about cake – and I knew he would be gutted that I'd just pulled in, because he would've been hoping to attack a vast slice of carrot cake before I got there.

I pushed open the stable door, and the chime of the bell echoed around the vaulted ceiling. Dave looked over from the counter at me and said, 'I've ordered your usual with an extra shot, and I remembered, not in a poncy glass.' He was overkeen for me to find a table and he said he'd bring the drinks over. I sat down in the corner and looked out through the gleaming floor-to-ceiling windows, admiring the garden. I heard the local twang of the lady serving saying, 'That'll be nine pounds, eighty pence please, sir.' I purposely didn't look over at Dave, but it didn't take a mathematician to work out that a cup of tea and a cappuccino wasn't that price. I chuckled to myself, knowing that he had paid for a slice of the freshest, sweetest cake for him to take away once I'd left.

It was always good to see Dave, but he seemed to have the weight of the world on his shoulders. His glass was often half empty, and he was a worrier. We worked well together because I never really worried about anything, but he took on worrying for the two of us. Dave was in a difficult position because he was responsible for the operation. From a policing point of view, the buck stopped with him, and he knew that. He said that he had been offered another pair of hands to come and help me on the operation. I explained that this was all very sudden, and I questioned whether we needed anyone else. I said that Emma was doing a brilliant job in the shop, and my side of things was expanding every day.

Dave said that he felt the job was moving so quickly that someone helping me with the drugs side had to be of benefit. He wanted to attack the lower-level dealers and that certainly wasn't my style. Before our discussion went any further, a battered Berlingo van pulled into the driveway and carefully parked next to my car. A skinny, long-haired man got out and stopped to roll a cigarette. I could see that his jeans were saggy at the back, as if someone had made off with his arse. He looked like he needed a good meal. At that moment, I was slightly worried that I hadn't locked my car and this fella would nick something out of it. I stared at the man as he pulled on his roll-up, then got up from my seat and went even closer.

It was only then I recognised him – it was Freddie, a guy I hadn't seen for many years. I liked Freddie, and he was good at his job; his profile was very different to mine, but it was unique and I would be glad to have him on board.

I went outside and shouted, 'Oi, mate! Keep your filthy hands off my motor.' He looked over at me and was about to shout abuse back when I saw a big smile break out across his face.

'Fuck me, if I knew it was working with you, I'd have hired a Boss suit.' He walked over to me and we hugged each other. It must have been at least four years since we had seen each other.

I said, 'Don't worry, Freddie. You won't be needing a whistle – in fact you're dressed just fine as you are. Once a smackhead, always a smackhead. You'll go down a treat.'

As Freddie and I chatted non-stop, I saw Dave walking to his car hoping that we hadn't noticed him or the white cake box he had concealed behind his back. He got to his car, and was just placing the box onto the passenger seat, when I shouted out, 'I take it that's a pressie for her indoors, is it, Dave?'

He looked at me and said, 'Do you know what – life's too short. How can a slice of chocolate cake do that much damage . . . I'm gonna savour every bite.' He said he'd leave Freddie and me to chat things through, but that he'd sorted the paperwork for Freddie to start from next week.

We both shook Dave's hand and I thanked him for the coffee. I knew that he would be pulling into the first available lay-by and devouring the chocolate cake in no more than four mouthfuls.

Freddie and I used our time wisely. I brought him up to date with where I was at with the job, and how Emma had been running the shop on her own and had done a great job. We agreed that I would paint the picture that Freddie was a thief and a recovering heroin addict who now wanted to make some money. I would say that I'd known him many years and wanted to give him a second chance, as I trusted him. I would also say that Emma had a soft spot for him and wanted me to help him get back on his feet. There was no need for Freddie to know who the bad guys were: if he didn't then he could react naturally when he met them.

It had been so good to see Freddie again, and I was looking forward to seeing how he fitted in with Emma and me. My only disappointment was that Emma hadn't been part of this meeting, as it was her who had started the whole job in the beginning. Freddie smoked another roll-up and we agreed that I would meet him with Emma first thing next week, and then get him started on the job. We shook hands, and as he walked away I called out: 'Freddie, this is going really well. Whatever you do, don't fuck it up.'

He laughed a little nervously and replied, 'No pressure then.'

It is fair to say that Ray was more than pleased when I spoke to him about our trip to the Essex coast the previous day. He said that Dazza had plenty of work for us, and that he was working for a good firm. He said the gear would be regular and good quality. I had differing feelings about our 'little trip to the coast' – it had not been my favourite seaside memory, but I knew it would stay with me for a long time.

We were having coffee together at the Spanish café in town, and the atmosphere was considerably different from the last time we had sat opposite each other. Ray had his usual beam on his face and upbeat outlook on life. He had colour in his cheeks, and life seemed good for him.

I thought I would test the water and asked him why Ricardo had come on our outing yesterday. He said that it was only right that he did under the circumstances, as he'd intro'd me to him. 'Anyway, like I said yesterday, that's dealt with and we won't talk about it ever again.'

I said that I didn't like Ricardo's attitude and I was sure that he hadn't 'buried' it like Ray had. He explained that it was up to Ricardo what he did with me, but as far as Ray was concerned, him and I would make lots of money together. I was happy to drink to that, and I tapped his cup of cappuccino with my latte and toasted those words.

I told Ray that Emma was going to join us for a coffee and that she might ask what we were doing at the seaside yesterday, as she had spoken to Ricardo on the phone. I said to tell her that we had been to see a car that he wanted to buy, and Ricardo had come along for the trip. Ray laughed and said he hoped she didn't ask any difficult questions. I was hoping she did ask a few questions, and I'd let Ray squirm his way out on his own.

Twenty-six

I travelled up the M6, looking in awe at the huge red kites as they circled gracefully in the skies above the motorway. It had been a whistlestop visit home that had probably caused more damage, not repaired things as I'd hoped it would. How did I think one night at home would do anything but aggravate a developing situation, one that needed my full attention? I should have dropped everything to put right what I had allowed to happen in my marriage. My wife had not done a single thing wrong. To me, Sarah was the perfect mother: a loving, caring and nurturing mum. I could never have chosen anyone better to have children with or to bring them up in the best possible way. I didn't understand why I was allowing all of that to crumble in front of my eyes. It was my fault, my responsibility, and it was in my court to put things right.

I was driving with a set of headphones plugged into a laptop that I had on the passenger seat next to me. I was making use of the five-hour journey to review some of the conversations I'd had about a 'contract killing' that I had deployed on. I shouldn't have been doing this, other than under secure conditions, but I had been so busy that it was now a necessity. I listened to a man calmly telling me that he wanted his wife and the mother of his two young children murdered. He was emotionless and matter of fact, and was more concerned about how quickly he could raise the money to take her life away. I had purported to be the person who would kill his wife, the cold-blooded murderer capable of taking the life of another human being for money. It was surreal listening to such a conversation with thoughts of my own family spinning around in my head. It was hard to comprehend the contrast between the two separate lives I was leading.

I was driving to Manchester to help with the national undercover course. I was looking forward to seeing many of the friends I had in the north. Good undercover officers that I had done many operations with over the years.

My best mate Don was also observing the course, so tonight would be a great opportunity to catch up with him. The course was professional and tough, and an incredible challenge for prospective undercover officers. At the time, it was run by a number of my really good friends. They had a massive amount of pride in the course; it took months to organise, and dedication and commitment to deliver it. I was glad that I could help them.

The sergeant who ran the course ran it very well. He was a good motivator and an even better delegator; this man had a great talent for getting people to happily do his work for him. In actual fact, many would volunteer to do things on his behalf. I called him PK (or 'Parker Knoll'), as he was always so laid-back about everything.

At the time, there were two undercover courses running annually in the country. There was this one in Manchester and another in London. I had been involved in running the London one for ten years. Both sets of staff were very proud of the reputation of their respective courses, which were run by the most experienced operatives. This was not textbook learning – it was very hands-on, with the students dealing with live situations.

As I drove up the M6 listening to the conversation through my headphones, it dawned on me that it seemed such a long time ago, and my thoughts had been on more recent events with Ray. I felt that having got through the aborted gun purchase, the compromise of the surveillance team and my trip to the Essex coast, maybe I had settled Ray and Co. down. In any case, I was glad of the break from them for a few days. It would give me a chance to clear my head and to plan ahead.

I was desperate for the toilet and saw the sign for Corley services. At the last minute I decided to pull in, rather than pressing on and waiting until I arrived in Manchester. Against my better judgement, I left the laptop in the footwell of the passenger seat with the headphones still attached. I parked as close as I could to the service station and made a dash for the Gents. I ran past an RAC man touting for new customers, and nipped ahead of a coach full of Welsh pensioners who were slowly making their way towards the toilets. I did what I had to, and then marvelled at the power of the Dyson dryer as I watched a teenager drying his hands.

I came out into the food hall, and the waft of KFC tempted my taste buds. I found myself arguing in my head about the pros and cons of grabbing a takeaway. The end result was that I decided I needed something in my stomach. I ordered and paid for two pieces of chicken, fries and a Diet Coke, and grabbed a handful of hand wipes and serviettes and a straw before heading outside. I held the paper KFC bag in one hand and my car keys in the other as I strode towards the exit.

As I looked up, ten feet from me in a row of three was Ray, his mate Mario and the biggest skunk dealer in the area – a guy I referred to as 'Amnesia', due to the strain of skunk he sold by the kilo and smoked like a train. All four of us stopped in our tracks and the three of them stared at me.

Ray broke the silence: 'What the fuck are you doing here, Joe?' I was calm, but the main focus of my attention was the laptop that I'd left in my car. I looked at Ray and replied, 'I was about to ask you the same.' Mario and Amnesia just stared at me. I could smell the skunk that clung to the green duffle coat that Amnesia never took off.

I had met him on a number of occasions previously, but he had never uttered a word to me. He reminded of the character from the Ready Brek TV advert in the 1980s. It featured

a schoolboy walking to school in the winter, a red glow surrounding his body after eating a bowl of Ready Brek. The
slogan was 'Central heating for kids'. Well, Amnesia walked
around with a permanent green glow surrounding his body,
from all the skunk that he smoked. He appeared to be constantly on a different planet and slightly unhinged. He made
me feel a little uncomfortable.

I told them that I was on my way to Manchester, but the
name of the city had barely left my mouth when Ray replied
that so were they. There was a long pause before I said, 'I'm
just gonna grab my "dog and bone", and I'll come back and
eat this with you.' I raised my KFC bag in the air to indicate
what I meant.

I didn't look back until I got to the boot of my car, which
afforded me a clear view to see if anyone had followed me. I
left the boot up, quickly opened the passenger door, grabbed
the laptop, and threw it in the boot under my overnight bag.
I shut the boot and took my phone from my pocket, then
locked the car and walked back to the services. I knew that
the next ten minutes were going to be uncomfortable for me,
but I needed to face the three of them.

What were the chances of bumping into those three, at that
time, at that place? Of all the service stations in the country,
how did we both happen to stop there at the same time? I
didn't believe in coincidences, but I had one to deal with now.

The three of them were next to each other on a raised
wooden table and bench. They were just opening their KFC
bags as I sat on my own opposite them. I could sense that
they had already had a conversation about me, and that it

hadn't quite been concluded. I started to tuck into my first bit of chicken, and Amnesia's eyes were concentrated totally on my face. I didn't want to be too interested in where they were going, so purposely didn't ask any questions. But Ray asked me what I was doing in Manchester. I explained that I was going to see a pal I hadn't seen for a while, who had just come back from Spain. I didn't want to expand any further, and I asked what they were going to Manchester for. Ray looked at the other two before answering: 'Just a bit of business.'

It was pointless me staying any longer, as they were yet to make up their minds whether this was just a coincidence or something else. I felt that nothing I said at that moment would help them make up their minds. 'Nice as it is seeing you boys, I'm running a bit late and the KFC isn't doing it for me.' I looked at Ray and said, 'Ring me if you need anything up there.' Neither Mario nor Amnesia said a word.

I left my KFC on the table and walked slowly to my car. As I drove out of the car park, I saw Ray standing in the doorway of the services watching me go. I felt so relieved that I was using the same car that Ray always saw me in.

I now wondered whether, following this encounter, the suspicions that Ray had about me would have increased. The only thing I was pleased about was the fact that I had already been in the service station when they arrived. If it had been the other way round, they may have thought that I was following them. It was a small consolation, but one that I would hold onto.

Once I was back on the motorway and knew that the three of them weren't following me, I phoned Dave to explain the downside of having a KFC lunch at Corley services. At first he didn't believe a word I said, but I was insistent, though he still found it hard to comprehend what the chances of that happening were. I left out the small detail of the laptop.

We both second-guessed what the fallout of this encounter would be for the operation. Just as we thought we had settled suspicions down, everything had been thrown off balance. We would just have to wait and see. It was out of our hands.

I continued on the journey to Manchester and arrived about teatime. I sat and had a brew with the training staff, and we caught up on the course and all the operations. It was great to see the boys again. I was told that I had a four-hour window starting at 8 a.m. to deliver my lecture. It was one that I had delivered many times, and so I had nothing I needed to prepare for it.

As we were chatting away, my phone rang and it was Ray. I told the boys it was a work call and they understood that they shouldn't say anything stupid. Ray asked me where I was and I told him I was sat with my pal having a cuppa, and I asked him, 'Why?' He explained that they had a bit of a problem. They were sat in a pub in Salford waiting to 'back' some gear to a firm from up here, but the gear couldn't be collected until the morning. He said that the three of them had come up in one van and the other two had to get back tonight. He asked if he could stay with me.

I pondered Ray's request and asked him the name of the pub he was at, and told him that I'd be there in an hour and a half. He thanked me and said he'd sit tight with the other two until I got there, as the pub was a complete shithole. The guys who I was with knew the place well, and told me that I couldn't have chosen a worse pub in Manchester. There had been a number of shootings there, and it was mainly used by criminals.

I grabbed Don, who was sat quite comfortably, enjoying the prospect of a few days observing the course. I told him he was coming out to work with me tonight. I filled him in on the background of the operation and the sequence of events that had led up to this evening's meeting. He wasn't overly enthusiastic about the deployment, but as we were so close, he said he'd help me out. I explained that I had told Ray that Don had just got back from Spain, and that was the reason I was in Manchester. Don was as South London as anyone could possibly be, and what he knew about Manchester was minimal. We agreed that we'd tell Ray that Don's girlfriend lived here and that she didn't like me. That would be a reason for me not to be staying with Don.

We were both very relaxed about things as we drove to Salford. The pub was indeed a shithole, and as I pulled up outside, three or four faces came from the side of the pub to check out who we were. I rang Ray and told him that I was parked outside. A few minutes later, Amnesia, Mario and him walked out of the pub. Ray was pleased to see us, but the other two didn't even acknowledge we were there. All three of them went to a white Transit van that was parked under a lean-to at the side of the pub. Ray came away from the passenger side carrying a weighted Sainsbury's bag in his right hand. The Transit van pulled away, with Amnesia doing his best to stare me down as he drove away.

Undercover

Ray walked over to the driver's door of my car and I put down the window. I introduced him to Don, and I could sense that he was relieved that I had arrived. It was just getting dark and the area was becoming more eerie by the minute.

Ray held up the Sainsbury's bag, leant through my window and said, 'This is my responsibility.' Don and I both laughed and said, almost in harmony, 'Fucking right it is.' I popped the boot and told him to stick it in the compartment with the spare wheel.

He climbed into the back of the car and sat in the gap between the two front seats, then leant forwards to explain his predicament to us both. They had bought some base amphetamine that was supposed to be the bollocks. It hadn't turned out to be the quality that they'd expected and Ray had got a number of complaints from his customers. He had four kilos in the bag in the boot that the firm had said he could back, but no one could take it off his hands until tomorrow morning. We had a discussion about Amnesia, and I asked Ray what his problem was with me. He told me that Amnesia was the same with everyone, psychotic and completely paranoid, but he was the best skunk farmer and dealer in the area. The problem was he had never adhered to the rule 'Don't get high on your own supply', and he was permanently off his nut.

I drove straight to the car park of the Malmaison hotel and asked Don to take Ray into the bar area to the left of reception. I booked two separate rooms for Ray and myself, and then joined the two of them in the bar. Conversation was really relaxed, and we spoke openly about criminality. Then one of the fellas from a local band came over to our table and was a little worse for wear. Ray said he couldn't understand a word he said. We sent him on his way when he started slagging off cockneys.

Later, we went by taxi to Chinatown and the three of us enjoyed a huge table of food together. It was the only thing I'd eaten all day apart from the one or two bites of KFC at Corley services. That seemed a lifetime ago.

Don left the two of us in the restaurant and I promised to see him early the next morning for a breakfast meet. He apologised for me having to stay at the hotel, but I told him I'd rather that than having my ear bitten off by his missus, and in any case I'd give him the bill at breakfast tomorrow. Ray shook Don's hand and the restaurant owner showed him to his cab. I saw Don give the owner a wedge of money to cover the meal and a hefty tip.

As we sat there, Ray told me how much he liked Don. I explained that we'd known each other all our lives, and our dads had grafted together back in the day. We were offered a free taxi back to our hotel, which we accepted; it was lazy really, but I didn't fancy the walk.

We went straight to my car in the car park and I removed my overnight bag, and I told Ray to grab his Sainsbury's bag. I handed him the paper wallet containing the key card for his room. He was a happy man, that's for sure. We walked into reception, and I was just about to say goodnight when Ray sheepishly said, 'I know you've done me a massive favour, but I've got no wash stuff for the morning.' I told him not to worry, I would be up and away before he had even thought about getting up, so I'd leave my washbag outside his room in the morning. He was so grateful and said, 'Thanks for everything today, mate, you're a lifesaver.' He disappeared clutching the rolled-up Sainsbury's bag with both his hands into his chest.

The rooms at the Malmaison were always sumptuous and decadent, and the beds were so comfortable. As I set my alarm for 6.30 a.m., it pained me that I was to spend so little time making the most of this bed.

Before I knew it, I was up and in the shower and scrubbing the tiredness out of my body. I dried myself and put on fresh clothes, then brushed my teeth, carefully folded my dirty clothes and placed everything neatly back in my overnight bag. I used the stairs to drop down one floor and left my washbag outside Ray's room. I settled the bill at reception, and walked to my car.

I drove back to where the course was being held, parked my car and was escorted into the training team's office. The guys were keen to know exactly what had developed overnight. They all agreed that you couldn't make something like this up, and it would be a brilliant scenario to give the students once the operation was concluded. I had a cup of tea with the team, and Don came and joined us. I gave him £75 in cash back for the meal he had paid for last night, and £20 for his cab fare. He told me to leave him in peace from now on, and that he was quite happy stepping aside and leaving it to the 'new kids on the block'.

Don and I went for a quiet chat alone about our meeting last night. I was keen to get his opinion, as a fresh set of eyes and ears always helped. Don told me he thought that there was a lot of respect from Ray towards me. He said that he hadn't sensed or noticed a single thing that pointed to Ray being suspicious. He said if I hadn't told him to the contrary, he would have thought Ray and I had known each other for many years. There was no doubt in his mind that Ray liked and trusted me very much. I respected Don's opinion; he had the experience and depth of knowledge to make very sound judgements. I felt that the previous day had concluded in a very positive way. I laughed to myself thinking that Ray would be lying in his king-size bed, with four kilos of base amphetamine under the duck-feather pillows. Then PK interrupted us and said, 'Enough about real operations – you've got a lecture to deliver, now get on with it.'

I spent the next four hours giving an interactive lecture on drugs operations. The students realised that this would be the bread and butter of many of their future operations, and took part throughout. The time flew past and there were constant questions. My motto in such lectures was to never tell the students anything that I had not done myself or witnessed with my own eyes. I had seen too many people over the years say things that were untrue or that had never happened, just to make themselves look better in the eyes of the students.

I thanked all of the students for their input, and wished them all success in passing the course. PK then thanked me and asked if I had any expenses. Just then, my phone rang again and it was Ray. PK shook his head in amazement. Ray told me that he was on his way to Haydock and asked if I could pick him up at the petrol station just off the motorway.

I told him I was just having a cup of tea with someone, but would see him within the hour. PK looked at me and said, 'Are you winding me up – does he know the timetable of the course or what?' He gave me directions to Haydock and said it was about a thirty-five-minute drive. We shook hands, and he told me to be careful and – as he always said – to 'keep it real'.

I hadn't had the chance to fill Dave in on the previous evening's events, but I utilised the next half an hour to bring him right up to speed. He was really happy with the outcome of the previous day.

I now had a five-hour journey to look forward to with Ray. I arrived quicker than expected, and Ray was sat in the rear of a blacked-out Range Rover. I chuckled at the obvious look of the drug dealer's car as he got out of the back. There were no big handshakes; all Ray had in his hand was my Louis Vuitton washbag. The Range Rover drove off, and Ray climbed in the passenger seat of my car and said, 'Good to see a friendly face. Fucking scousers, I hate them – they're messers.'

Ray explained that it really had been a long morning. He had sat in the hotel until about eleven o'clock, but he'd got proper paranoid and was sure there were a couple of plain-clothes coppers watching him. So he'd left the hotel to kill an hour before the Scousers were supposed to pick him up. He said that was when the deep paranoia set in. He was convinced that the base was illuminating the bag from the inside and that the four-kilo blocks could be clearly seen through the bag. He even went and bought a thick fifty-pence bag from

Tesco to put the Sainsbury's bag in. He looked at me and said that he'd never been so glad to see the back of four kilos of anything before in his life.

I told him to relax and enjoy the journey; there was nothing for him to worry about now. He then gave a full and comprehensive review of his hotel room and raved about it. When he paused for breath and there was silence in the car, he patted me on the shoulder and said, 'Joe, do you know what – you're a proper mate, and I mean that.'

Twenty-seven

The journey back with Ray was arduous and testing to say the least, as we talked for the entire journey. I cannot recall a single awkward silence or a pause for breath. The conversation was continuous and the vast proportion of things we talked about were nothing to do with criminality – in fact I would say only about 10 per cent related to anything other than innocent chat.

This is the type of situation where your skills are tested to the extreme. I find it far easier to deal with direct confrontation than having to carefully recall minute details of forgettable conversations that took place over a protracted period of time. It's the subtle conversations and harmless questions and spontaneous replies that can lead you into danger. You have to remember exactly what you have said at previous meetings and during innocent conversations.

I dropped Ray off at his house and Chloe came out to say hello. He thanked me and told me that he owed me proper for the last couple of days. He said he'd ring me tomorrow. I drove off but stopped in the car park of the first pub I saw. I felt drained by the journey. It seems crazy to say, but five hours of non-stop chatting when you are pretending to be someone you're not is exhausting. I just wanted to enjoy five minutes' peace and quiet before I got home and had to tell Emma everything. For some reason, as I closed my eyes, my mind focused on a job that I had done many years before.

It was the 1990s and I was meeting a lovely East End villain in the Cumberland Hotel in Marble Arch. He was about sixty years old and he had a twinkle in his eye. He was already sat close to the huge piano that was the centrepiece of the bar. He had a pint of light and bitter in front of him, and a copy of *Sporting Life*. His name was Billy, and he was smartly dressed, with a spotted handkerchief in the pocket of his burgundy blazer. He had an open-neck black shirt on, and a huge gold belcher chain with a heavy pair of gold boxing gloves hanging from it. He had been expecting me, and he stood up and shook my hand, and insisted on me sitting down whilst he went to the bar and got me a drink.

I looked at the *Sporting Life* that was open at the greyhound-racing pages. He brought my drink back and asked me if I liked a flutter. He then educated me about the dogs for at least half an hour. He advised me never to bet on anything other than the longest dog races. He explained that even the best dogs can get bumped on the first two bends, but in the longer races there are enough bends for the best dogs to survive a bump and come through and win. I loved a bet, but stuck with the horses unless I had a tip. Billy concluded this conversation by saying, 'Anyway, there's far more money to be made on this project.'

He leant forwards, and in his deep, gravelly East London accent he explained that the people he represented had a large amount of isosafrole. He told me that this was the main ingredient needed to make Ecstasy. His people had a large amount of the compound, but did not have the knowledge to convert it into the rave drug. I knew they needed a chemist, and the potential earnings from this project were huge. Pills were the most popular drug at that moment, and every weekend huge raves were being organised, where people spent the night in a dancey, happy place after popping a decent E or two. People wanted good quality E, and were prepared to pay top money for it.

I leant back in my chair and said, 'Hypothetically speaking, if I did know a chemist that was willing to help, what's the plan?' Billy explained that they would find a suitable place to set up the lab and would pay for all the necessary stock to get it up and running. I said I took those requirements for granted in a project like this, but I was more interested in the payday at the end. Billy threw it back in my court and asked what I wanted out of it. I liked his style.

I said if I provided the 'chef', I wanted either a third of the profit from the completed commodity or a third of the merchandise. Billy said it was him and two others in on this bit of work. He said he would have to meet with the two of them and put my proposal to them. He knew they would want to meet me and my chef, and he asked if I would be available to go to his gaff later in the week. I said I'd give it some thought and I'd phone him tomorrow, so Billy gave me his home phone number and asked me to ring between 10 and 10.15 in the morning.

I shook Billy's hand and left him sat there, studying form whilst sipping his pint. He was an interesting character and I liked him. He was a gentleman villain; he knew all the faces and gangsters from the 1960s and had spent considerable time in prison with them. He was trusted, and had been given the job of putting this bit of work together. But I knew that there must be a bigger player who sat above Billy and actually had control of these chemicals.

I had done my research through the precursor unit at the Yard, and I knew that isosafrole was mainly used in the perfume industry and had a fragrance of anise or liquorice. It required a permit to buy, and as such was monitored. It was also one of the main chemicals that could be converted to MDMA or Ecstasy. It was clear that this firm could smell the money, if they could just find a chemist with the talent and balls to convert it for them. Without the chemist, they could achieve very little. All the advice I was getting said that the whole process was extremely dangerous, as isosafrole was highly volatile. We would have to be very careful as we progressed with the operation.

The first issue was to find a chemist, or at least someone who had the intellect to pretend to be one. I knew exactly who

I wanted, and I telephoned his office at the Yard to ask him to meet for a coffee at the Broadway Café, very close by.

James was a truly nice man; he was a very experienced detective and competent UC who had been doing the work far longer than I had. He spoke very well, with a Home Counties accent, like a middle-aged man who had been privately educated. He didn't look like a typical policeman, and could easily have passed as a university lecturer or a vet. I asked him directly if he fancied being my chemist. I was portraying a South London drug dealer, and he would be the chemist who had the knowledge to convert isosafrole to MDMA.

James looked at me and said he'd love to do it; he thought it was a real challenge and different to most jobs he'd done before. I explained that the guy I had met represented two other villains from East London. I thought that once I introduced James to Billy as the chemist, then the operation would open up. I told James how I'd like him to dress for the meeting, and begrudgingly he agreed. Then I gave him the contact details of the precursor unit staff, who could help to educate him in respect to the chemical process. James was keen as mustard and I really enjoyed his company. I asked him to keep Friday free, as I knew he had a really busy day job. He was very humble and thanked me for asking him to help, and he said he was looking forward to it.

I phoned Billy the next day and he answered politely and business-like. He said he'd see me and my mate on Friday at 11 a.m. in the Wimpy at Barking train station. Once he heard me acknowledge the appointment, he hung up. I confirmed with James that he was available and we agreed to meet early

Friday morning for breakfast before we travelled to Barking together. In the 1990s, we were required on certain operations to record conversations in order that our evidence could be accepted in court. If you can imagine the size of the first mobile phones, which were like house bricks, then this was mirrored in relation to recording devices. I had to wear a huge recorder, which had been designed by the Polish inventor Stefan Kudelski. It had revolutionised sound recording for television and radio, as it allowed directors to record outside the confines of a studio. The device was the size of an A6 diary, and as thick as a deck of cards. It had two reel-to-reel spools that you had to manually wind the tape onto. I used to wear it on the small of my back, and there were leads as thick as phone chargers that I had to wear over my shoulders. These leads had microphones on the ends and I would tape these to my chest. It was hugely cumbersome and not in any way safe to wear, and it was virtually impossible to conceal. But those were the rules back then, so I had to wear the device on this occasion.

James and I made our way to Barking station, and when we arrived Billy was waiting for us. He shook my hand and nodded at James. I was expecting him to lead us into the Wimpy restaurant, but instead we walked past and he said he would make us a cup of tea at his place. We walked in virtual silence for the next five minutes until we arrived at a small block of council flats. Billy took a set of keys out of his Crombie coat, and unlocked an iron gate that protected a small tiled area leading to a front door. I could see a camera to the left of the door, facing the metal gate. All three of us were now between the gate and the door, and Billy locked us in no man's land before unlocking three locks on the front door. I could see that he was protecting something, or just paranoid about security.

Billy used two keys to secure deadbolts in the door so that we were safely locked in. He winked at me and said, 'Save anyone disturbing us.' There was a long corridor that led to a closed door at the end. Billy took his Crombie off and hung it on a coat rail in the hallway, I noticed a baseball bat and a large machete neatly positioned behind the door. Both James and I waited for Billy to lead the way. He opened the door at the end of the hall and told us to join him.

As we both stepped into the room, I tried to take in all my surroundings. To my left was a raised area almost like a stage, with an organ on it, spotlights, and a bar area with two stools. There were optics behind the bar, and West Ham merchandise covered the walls. There was a framed 1975 FA Cup Final programme – West Ham versus Fulham – that caught my eye.

I looked to my right; sat on a green chesterfield sofa were two white men around the sixty-year mark. Both spoke with East London accents, and one wore a black roll-neck sweater underneath a black silk blouson. The other had a Gabicci striped black cardigan on, with black Farah trousers and black oxford shoes. Both men were smoking, and there was a large glass ashtray on the coffee table in front of them that was full of half-smoked cigarettes. The curtains were pulled shut, and the only illumination was from the lights on the stage. I noticed that there were two dining room chairs on the other side of the coffee table, facing the two men. The roll-neck man beckoned us both to sit down. My first thought was that there wasn't a dining room table in the room; these men had strategically placed the chairs there pending our arrival.

Roll-neck man introduced himself by his full name and explained in a very aggressive manner that I could go down the East End or into Essex and ask anyone his name and people would reference him. He went on to say that he'd spent over eighteen years in prison, and then rattled off a number of names of gangsters that he knew well. He then introduced Gabicci by his first name and said, 'Gary has a similar pedigree as me.' He took a long tug on his cigarette, held it for a moment, and then exhaled and said, 'Now, who the fuck are you?'

This was a classic, 'old school' sit-down to get to know each other. We were locked in a flat with three career criminals who wanted to know exactly who we were before they decided to do any business with us. This had the potential to go horribly wrong, and although these were older guys, they were used to violence and would think nothing of harming us. Add to that the fact I had a 'ghetto blaster' strapped to my back, and the situation was very volatile.

I knew that I had to take control of things before they got out of hand. I looked straight at roll-neck, and then turned to James and said, 'Do you mind waiting in the corridor while I have a chat with these gentlemen, please?' I could see the bemusement on his face, but he nodded and sheepishly got up. Then he slowly walked to the door, after awkwardly picking up his tatty rucksack from under his chair on the second attempt. I waited for the door to close behind him, leaving the four of us in the room alone.

I then leant forwards and said in a very calm and quiet voice, 'Don't ever pull a stunt like that again. I've spent the last forty-eight hours convincing the chef to help us with our project. He was worried, as he isn't like us four, he's made of different stuff – he isn't a villain, he's an educated man. You're scaring him half to death, I could feel him shaking sat next to me. Ask what you like of me, but if you want me to keep him on board, treat him with a bit of respect. Be nice to him.'

The two men on the sofa looked at each other, and roll-neck acknowledged that his approach was completely wrong as he apologised to me. So did Gabicci, who then asked, 'Do you think we've naused this up?'

I ignored him and said, 'We need him more than he needs us, that's for sure. Are you gentleman with me on this one?' All three agreed and apologised again. I asked them to give me five minutes with him in the corridor, and I'd try and bring him back in.

James was down at the front door keeping an eye on the baseball bat and machete. I walked over to him, and he whispered that he hadn't been expecting the reception party. I explained what I'd just said to the men, and James had a little chuckle. I told him that if they asked him a direct question, to look at me before he answered and I would give him the nod. We walked back into the room, and roll-neck took control. He was like a different man, and he explained to James that he was really grateful that James had come to this meeting. He apologised for the misunderstanding earlier and said he was looking forward to getting this 'thing' underway. He paused for a minute and then said, 'I've only got one question for you – can you make us the product we want with twenty litres of isosafrole?'

James looked sideways at me and I nodded. He replied in a clear but quiet, eloquent voice: 'Yes I can, and I will do my utmost to get the maximum product for Joe.'

Roll-neck and Gabicci stood up at the same time, shook James's hand and thanked him for coming. I asked James to give us a minute. Again, he walked out of the room. I looked at the three men and asked if we were all happy. They had smiles on their faces and shook my hand. Gabicci said he was thankful that I'd squared things up, and the men agreed that it wouldn't happen again. I told them that I'd get my fella to come up with calculations for the amount of possible end-commodity and a list of requirements. We agreed that we'd meet again the following Tuesday in the West End.

Billy walked us to the door, and unlocked all the bolts and the security gate. He thanked me again and whispered to me, 'I could tell he was a scientist – the jumbo cords were a give-away.' Then he winked at me.

As James and I made our way back to Barking station, he said out of the side of his mouth, 'I've been to strange meetings in my time, but that ranks at the top.' I told him that the one thing that had won the day for us was the fact that he was wearing jumbo cords as I had requested last week. We both laughed out loud.

Twenty-eight

Billy and I had spent the next three weeks together, mostly driving around in the dodgiest Luton van he could've chosen. We looked like one of the rag-and-bone vans that used to call door to door and take away anything that people didn't want. Billy really was a character. He loved to sing and play the piano and organ, and we had many a sing-song in his Barking flat. He'd told me that he'd been asked to do the music for the 'Mad' Frankie Fraser film.

We had also had meetings, where we agreed that there would be a four-way split on the commodity at the conclusion of the chef's work. The other three's thought process behind this was that it was in my best interests for the chemist to be on the button with his work. The better he was at his job, the more MDMA would be produced, making more profits for the four of us, who would split the pills four ways.

At the time, MDMA was sold in pill form and the bestsellers were mitsis, doves and double doves, hens and speckled hens. The dilemma that we had as a group of four criminals was the fact that we would end up with MDMA in powder form at the conclusion of the chemical process, but the demand from all the customers was for a pill with one of the most popular motifs on. There were two choices: place powder into capsules or convert it into solid pill form. The decision of the East London firm was to convert to pills. This required a pill-making machine, where the powder or paste is fed in one end, and the mechanisms within cut and round the tablets. However, a separate machine was then required to stamp the pills with the chosen motif.

The first job for Billy and me was to find a suitable property to use as a lab to make the Ecstasy. I had read up a lot on this, and in my head I pictured a secluded cottage deep in the English countryside, with smoke coming from a chimney. Away from any prying eyes, curtain-twitchers or nosy neighbours. There had been a number of well-documented explosions in such places, due to the necessity of heating highly volatile chemicals, and so our choice of premises was particularly important. After viewing many properties, the firm decided on a fifth-floor council flat in the heart of East London. The thinking behind this was that people in the area minded their own business and were highly unlikely to call the police. It would be easy to come and go freely.

Undercover

There were two bedrooms in the flat, which was completely and utterly unfurnished. One of the most important issues was to install a good extraction system to ensure that all the fumes safely left the flat without poisoning anyone, inside or outside.

I had one final meeting at Billy's flat with the three East London men. In the lead-up to the meeting, Billy had said that the other two were happy with the progress we were making, but wanted a final sit-down to discuss the specific details of the project. As usual, I was locked in the flat with the other three. Billy made cups of tea for us all, and had bought a packet of ginger nut biscuits especially for this meet.

The roll-neck man, Jimmy, was clearly sat at the top of this criminal organisation. I was expecting a calm and relaxed chat amongst the three of us, but Jimmy clearly had different plans. He looked me up and down from the comfort of the chesterfield, and quietly said, 'Gary and I were just having a natter before you arrived, and the truth of the matter is we know very little about you.'

I was much younger than these men, but I had seen their criminal records and the intelligence on their criminal activities, and I knew what they were capable of. I was on their 'manor', and was locked in the flat with no real way of escape. If I took these three men on, I wouldn't come out the winner.

I needed to nip this in the bud and deal with it head-on, so I looked at Jimmy and said, 'Do you know what, Jimmy – you're right. You don't know me, and I only know you through Billy. Like my old man told me once or twice, if you're not happy with someone or it doesn't feel right, walk away. So now is the time to make that decision, because I came here today to tell you gents that the chef has booked three days off from his day job to complete our project. And that's next Wednesday to Friday – only a week away. So tell me now if you want to walk away, fellas, so we don't waste any more of each other's time.' I took a ginger nut from the packet, dipped it in my mug of tea, and broke the soft half off in my mouth.

I could see Jimmy taking in what I had just said. I knew Gary would go along with him, but I was certain Billy was on my side because we had already done so much work towards setting up the flat. I was nervous, and inside I was praying that they would see how close the pound notes were.

I needed to tempt them further. I'd asked James to make some calculations as to the potential yield, and so I took these out of my jacket pocket. The precursor unit had confirmed these figures, and the numbers were reliable. I placed the notes on the coffee table and purposely slid the ashtray closer to them. 'If the cook goes exactly to plan, there should be over one million tablets . . . that makes a split of 250,000 pills each. Single tablets are selling for between five and ten pounds at the moment. That's a nice payday for us all.'

I could almost see pound signs in their eyes; the payday was so close and they knew they had to do very little to earn it. Jimmy took the bait completely, and there was excitement in his voice when he said, 'Gary and I will do security on the place for the three days.' He insisted that from the moment the chef arrived at the flat, it would be on lockdown until the process was complete. He said that the flat needed to be self-sufficient, and he dictated a list of requirements to Billy that included two 'put me up' camping beds with sleeping bags – for Gary and him – a fully stocked fridge and endless toilet rolls. They knew that the project was in its final stages. For the next hour, we discussed the logistics of what would happen next.

I had hired a lock-up, where I had stored all the glassware and barrels of other chemicals that would be required for the cooking process. Jimmy insisted that, on the Tuesday, all the glasswork should be set up during the day. In the evening, Billy and I would collect the remaining chemicals required from my lock-up, and at that stage he would bring the isosafrole. Jimmy had also managed to get his hands on an industrial extractor fan, which would ensure all fumes safely left the flat and didn't kill anyone inside.

Jimmy handed Billy a wad of money to pay for his shopping list, and we all agreed that Billy and I would meet again on Monday to complete the final stages of the lab set-up. Before I left the three men, I reminded them that the chef would also have to sleep, but he would need a proper mattress with a duvet and pillows. There was no point having a tired chemist who messed up the cooking. Billy put these further requirements on his list, and Jimmy counted a few hundred pounds more off the wad he had in his pocket.

I knew that we had got lots of evidence against the three men for conspiracy to manufacture MDMA, but it was crucial that we recovered all the isosafrole. This would be the vital piece of evidence, as without that one chemical it was impossible to manufacture MDMA, and we needed to prove they had possession of that key ingredient. I had worked hard on this job to convince the two old lags that I was what I said I was, and Jimmy had been a particularly hard nut to crack.

As we were now so close to the end of the job, I needed to go and see James to bring him up to speed with where we were. James always reminded me of a scruffy public schoolboy. His clothes were well made but also well worn, and his shirt always seemed to be untucked. He worked under chaotic conditions in his office, and I wondered how he ever got anything done.

He had just poured boiling water out of the kettle from the next-door office into a cafetière. I could see one polystyrene cup left on a tray in the corner of his office so I grabbed it, as there was no way I was going to drink from any of the filthy china ones. James poured me a full cup of coffee, and sat down and demanded to know where we were at with the operation. I explained everything to him and requested his attendance next Tuesday evening, when everyone would be at the flat ready to go into production the following morning. I told him it would be good if he got the train out to East London as if he'd finished his day job, and to bring an overnight bag to look like he was staying for three days. This would be the time that everyone would be arrested – once Jimmy and Gary had brought the isosafrole to the flat. For all his years as a detective and as a UC, James was thoroughly impressed with the operation and said he was looking forward to Tuesday. I ensured he knew exactly where he needed to be and, of course, told him to put his 'lucky' jumbo cords on.

I spent all day Monday with Billy transporting the camp beds, sleeping bags, mattress and fridge, as well as tray after tray of lager – and almost as much toilet roll – to the flat.

Billy checked all the lighting, heating and gas to make sure it was working, and we collected the industrial extractor fan from one of Jimmy's lock-ups in Bethnal Green. We stopped at Kelly's on the Roman Road for double pie and mash with liquor, and Billy had some hot eels. A tummy full of pie and mash always makes you feel better.

We did one more shopping trip to Tesco to buy three days' food and then deposited this at the flat. Billy wanted to spend the evening in the bookies, so he dropped me at the train station and we agreed to meet at 10 a.m. the next day.

I was up bright and breezy the next morning, as we had a full briefing with the drugs squad and precursor unit. There were a number of staff that would be working on the operation today – from surveillance, arrest and search teams to the laboratory staff, who would ensure the flat was dismantled safely. I knew that I would be under surveillance for the duration of the day, starting with me getting picked up at ten at Barking train station. I was also told that there would be staff filming us picking up the glassware and chemical barrels from my storage premises just off the North Circular Road, near Neasden. At the conclusion of the meeting, everyone understood his or her role. I agreed with the detective in overall charge of the operation that I would only go and pick James up from the train station if the isosafrole had been brought to the flat and all the bad guys were present.

I knew it was going to be a long and tiring day. It was already really warm, and I wasn't looking forward to spending the day in and out of a Luton van with a house brick strapped to my back. I travelled from Central London out to

Barking, and Billy was waiting for me outside the station in the van. He said he was starving and wanted to grab a bacon roll and a cup of tea at the café round the corner. We decided that, as the weather was so nice, we would sit outside on one of the two picnic benches that were perched on the pavement.

Billy had a scruffy white T-shirt on and a pair of jeans that he really didn't look comfortable in. I knew that I'd have to spend the next ten minutes listening to him telling me how close he'd been to winning a small fortune last night on the dogs, only to be let down by one dog. I pinned my ears back and listened to his sob story whilst I ate my bacon roll.

We finished our breakfast, and Billy made a brief stop at a call box to phone Jimmy to say that he and I were on our way to my storage facility. Billy didn't know where the lock-up was, so I directed him around the North Circular. We pulled in at the storage facility as the midday sun was at its height. It was a balmy London summer's afternoon and the roads were busy and hot; there was no air conditioning in the van, so both our windows were wound down. To get as close as possible to my storage unit, it required the van to be reversed under roll shutters and this was a little tricky. I jumped out of the passenger side, and stopped briefly to adjust myself to ensure the house brick hadn't dislodged from my back. The storage facility had modern offices on either side that were completely glass-fronted. As I looked up at the second floor of the offices to my left, I could see as clear as crystal a tripod holding a camera, and two men, one of whom was talking into a radio. It was the observation team. They may as well have been standing in broad daylight in front of us.

Undercover

I prayed that Billy hadn't seen them, otherwise I was in a lot of trouble and the whole operation would be blown. I quickly shouted at Billy to watch his side as he reversed and I would make sure the passenger side was clear. There was nothing I could do to make those officers get out of sight. If I gestured to them, Billy would wonder what on earth I was doing. So I just had to pray that Billy didn't see them.

It was absolutely painful and I was completely unable to alter the situation. However, I decided in my head that if Billy got out of the car and walked around his side of the van to join me at the back, I would have about five seconds to get their attention.

I was shouting directions at him as he reversed the van, and then I told him that he'd come far enough and to stick the handbrake on and turn the ignition off. Now was my chance; I needed him to get out and walk around the side of the van, not around the front, so he was out of sight of the observation team. He jumped out, and as I heard the door slam I made the decision to gesticulate like a mad man at the two observation officers. I waved my hand down, indicating them to lie down, then waved the flat of my hand across my neck a number of times to tell them to stop or finish. I saw them both look at each other and drop to the floor, but the tripod and camera were still stood there, like a mounted machine gun pointing at us. I needed to stop Billy coming out from the area at the back of the van; I wanted him to remain out of sight.

I unhinged the loading ramp and pressed the button to lower the heavy metal ramp to the floor. I then took the keys for my storage unit out of my pocket and threw them to Billy. I said to him, 'F11, ground floor, just round to the right, mate.' He caught the keys and started walking towards the lock-up and out of view. I immediately turned, and with both hands gestured for them to go away. I also made a triangle sign and a camera motion, as if I was playing charades. I must have looked like a complete idiot to anyone watching me but it seemed to have the desired effect, as the next thing I saw was the two officers crawling out of sight, one of them carrying the tripod with him. I gave a deep sigh of relief as I walked into the darkness of the storage facility, thinking to myself that I really didn't need this added pressure.

Billy and I loaded up the blue barrels. I had painstakingly marked them with the relevant chemical names to ensure authenticity, but Billy didn't take a blind bit of notice. We then carefully placed all the individually wrapped pieces of glassware into plastic storage boxes before putting them in the van. There were also some trestle tables and free-standing three-speed fans, which we put on board. We were both sweating from the manual work on such a hot day. It had probably taken us about an hour to load the van, and now we needed to get back on the road and set everything up back in East London. We stopped at the first petrol station, and I bought some cold drinks whilst Billy used a payphone to call Jimmy and tell him we were on our way back to the flat.

We were getting close to the endgame now. I hoped that Billy's phone call would be the trigger for Jimmy to travel to wherever he had the isosafrole stashed. Once Jimmy, Gary and the isosafrole were with Billy and me in the flat, that would be the perfect moment to bring this whole operation to its conclusion.

Billy and I got back about 3.30, and we started carrying the barrels and glassware up to the flat. I had a diagram that James had allegedly given me with the correct layout of the tables and glassware. Billy and I followed this carefully, and by about 4.15 we had it all laid out as per the diagram. There was then a loud knock on the door and Billy, very reluctantly and nervously, opened it a small amount, his foot blocking the possibility of it opening any further. I heard the loud, gruff voice of Jimmy: 'Stop fucking about and come down and help carry these things in.'

We both left the flat and went down to Jimmy's car. Gary was sat in the passenger seat, and Jimmy told him to get out and open the boot. All four of us stood there as Gary opened it to reveal two white barrels that sat underneath a tartan blanket. Billy and I took one each, Gary grabbed two sports bags that were on the back seat of the car, and we all walked to the block of flats. We squeezed into the lift; I could smell alcohol on Jimmy's breath. No one said a word until we got into the flat and locked the door. We put the barrels down underneath a trestle table.

Jimmy showed his approval of what we had set up so far, then stopped in the middle of the room. He sucked in deep through his nose and said, 'Can you smell that?' He took another deep intake of breath. Billy looked bemused, and he too tried to smell what Jimmy could smell. Jimmy then said, 'That, gentleman, is the smell of money.' He gave out a huge laugh, and as usual, Gary joined in. I didn't want to stop their fun or curb their enthusiasm, but I needed to know for definite that we had everything in the flat. I looked at Jimmy and said that the chef was on his way, but once he arrived he wanted the door locked and no one to leave until his job was complete. So I needed to know now that we had everything that was necessary. I went through a checklist, and when it came to the two barrels that Billy and I had carried in, Jimmy confirmed it was the isosafrole.

I gave them a talk as to how they should treat the chef, and said that I didn't want them to put him under any pressure, but leave him to do what he was best at doing. Jimmy agreed to all my demands, and asked if I wanted him to come with me to collect James. I told him I'd rather go alone in case the chef had anything he wanted to ask me, away from the three of them. Billy threw me the keys of the Luton van and I said that I'd be back just after five o'clock. I pointed down to the car park, and showed them where I would park the van when I got back with the chef. I said I wanted to know that it was safe to bring him up, so I would beep the horn three times when I returned, and if it was OK for us to come up, then someone should open the curtains in the small bedroom. Jimmy took it upon himself to take charge of this task, and confirmed that if he opened the curtains, all was fine for us both to come up.

As I left the flat and walked to the van, I had a strange feeling come over me. I knew that each of the three men was thinking in their heads that they were so close to earning over a million pounds each from this criminal enterprise. In their minds, I was on my way to collect the key that was going to open the door to that fortune. There had been a quiet buzz of excitement in the room when I left, as this would be a huge payday for these men, and I'm sure they had extravagant plans to spend the money. I felt a little bit guilty, particularly for Billy as I'd grown to like him. He was a nice man – yes he was a criminal, but we got on really well and I'd miss our chats and his singing and his stories of 'the good old days'.

I knew that the team understood that if I went to the train station to collect James, then all the pieces of the jigsaw were in place. He was waiting outside the station with his rucksack, cagoule, scruffy long-sleeved shirt and green jumbo cords. His trousers were slightly short for him and he wore muddy walking boots on his feet. He did look like a proper boffin – there was no doubt about that.

James climbed into the van and I filled him in on the events of the past couple of days. I explained that we would park the van at the block of flats and on a signal from Jimmy that it was safe, we would go up to the flat. James knew exactly what I expected of him and he was keen to get to the flat. Sure enough, Jimmy opened the curtains and it was time for us to leave the van. I grabbed James by the arm and held on for a moment. I said to him, 'Is it right that I feel a tad guilty right now, James? Billy and the boys are going away for a long time because of me, and I'd be lying if I wasn't a little bit sad about that.' James held my arm and said, 'They're called feelings, Joe, and it's how we deal with them that makes us who we are. Now come on, you have a job to finish.'

We made our way up to the flat and Billy let us in. Jimmy was over-the-top nice to James and he was offered a cup of tea, which he declined. He took his cagoule and rucksack off and put them on his mattress, and he rolled up the sleeves of his open-necked shirt. Billy, James and I went through the diagram that he had 'given' us to ensure we had set up the glassware correctly. Jimmy wanted to go through the potential yield directly with James, as if he wanted to hear from the horse's mouth how rich he was soon to be.

At that exact moment, the front door of the flat came crashing in; it was smashed to pieces as uniform police in boiler suits and riot helmets came through the door. We were all thrown to the floor before a question was asked. Two of the officers then sat on the small of my back and handcuffed me with plastic cuffs. I was trussed up like a Christmas turkey.

As we lay face down on the floor, we were all informed that we were being arrested for conspiracy to manufacture MDMA. I looked at Billy as I lay on the floor; he was about five feet away from me. I could see the enormity of the situation hit him – he closed his eyes as he lay there and more than one teardrop rolled down his cheek. I could have cried with him, but I was unceremoniously yanked to my feet and taken out of the flat. As the officers led me down the stairs, the detective inspector in charge of the operation stopped them. He held both my shoulders and said, 'Fantastic work, Joe.'

I didn't reply to him because, at that moment, I didn't feel so great about myself. I was taken to the back of a police van and locked in the cage; I sat there alone, with only my thoughts to keep me company.

Twenty-nine

I must have drifted off to sleep, because I was woken by the sound of my ringtone. The engine was still running and it was really warm in the car. I looked up to see the sign for the pub and realised I was sat in its car park, and I wasn't sure how long I had been there. I saw Emma's name illuminate the screen of my phone and I answered. She said that she'd been worried and then asked where I was. I explained that I had just dropped Ray off at his place and I'd be home in ten minutes. I asked her if she minded running me a bath with some cracked-black-pepper bubble bath. She told me that Dave wanted me to ring him when I got back. Instead, I used the journey time to bring Dave up to speed with the current situation, and we agreed that Emma, myself and the team would meet up the following morning at eleven to work out the way forwards.

I stopped briefly at Marks and Spencer and grabbed a bottle of house champagne and a pizza and some garlic bread. The thought of Emma doing her very best to knock up a meal worried me slightly, and of course I was thinking of her when I made the decision, as she was busy enough without having to slave at the stove. At least that's what I'd tell her.

I came in the back door, handed her the bag of shopping and told her to get some ice for the fizz. She said I shouldn't have bothered, as she was just about to start cooking. 'Well, I thought I'd save you the time. It'll be cooked by the time I'm out of the bath.'

I had a lovely, relaxing, ten-minute bath as I listened to Cat Stevens's *Tea for the Tillerman*. I loved the words of his songs and the emotion in his voice, which was interrupted by Emma telling me to come and join her for supper. I sat in a T-shirt, shorts and flip-flops as we both enjoyed a perfectly cooked pizza and garlic bread, and a few glasses of bubbles.

Emma filled me in on her day, blow by blow. She was very descriptive in explaining to me all the characters who were coming into the shop. She had been very busy and really was doing a great job; she was running the shop on her own and was managing to keep on top of all the bookkeeping and relevant paperwork. I thought to myself that I was very proud of what she was doing; not many, if anyone at all, could have achieved what she had so far. She was a mother and a wife, but her commitment to this operation was truly commendable.

Undercover

The next morning Emma wasn't opening up the shop, but instead of us having a lie-in before the meeting, I dragged her out of the house at eight o'clock to go to the gym together. She really was a misery in the mornings, and without her caffeine intake, even grumpier. It annoyed her that I was so lively from the moment I was awake. But we had a good workout and I finished with a lovely steam, which Emma skipped so she could grab a coffee for herself.

We travelled in separate cars to meet the team. I saw in my mirror that Emma stopped at her favourite delicatessen, so I arrived before her. The team was all gathered together, and there were two new faces I had never met before. I was introduced to the two of them by Carl. One was like a character from *Countryfile*; he was about forty years old, and wore a tweed jacket and a shirt that had seen better days around the collar. He was called Adrian and he spoke with a broad Norfolk accent. Adrian looked like he spent a lot of time working outdoors; he had a weathered face, and a strong handshake without trying. He was a real jovial character, and said he was really glad he'd been chosen by Dave to join the team. The second one had a mop of ginger hair; he was fresh-faced and had a huge beaming smile on his face. He was good friends with Carl, who had recommended him for the role. His name was Cameron, and he had a great knowledge of IT and technical systems so would be a good asset to the team. He said that he'd heard a lot about me.

Emma came through the door holding two white cakeboxes in front of her. Before she could say a word, Carl shouted out, 'At least someone appreciates the work we do, Joe.' She placed the boxes on the table, and opened them carefully to reveal eight gorgeous-looking cakes and french fancies.

It was true what he'd said – I was so absorbed in my own little world that I didn't appreciate the people who were important in my life. I didn't mean the team, but my wife, my children, my loved ones. I couldn't remember the last time I'd phoned my mum. I had to rack my brains to remember the last time I'd told her that I loved her, and sadly I couldn't. I loved my family dearly, but I hadn't phoned my wife or spoken to the children since I'd popped home at the weekend. I was in the middle of a room full of happy people, but all of a sudden I was overcome with sadness. What was I doing here – pretending to be a successful gangster, laughing and joking with my colleagues – when my real life was far from perfect?

I had a real desire to quietly walk out of the door and drive home. I imagined myself waiting for my daughter at the school gates to surprise her. She would run across the playground and I would kneel down as she threw herself into my arms. As she wrapped her arms around me and kissed me, I'd hold her tight until she told me I was squeezing her. We would walk home hand in hand together. In my mind, I could see the huge smile on her face as I carried her schoolbag and she chattered nonstop about the day, the week or the month that I had missed in her life. How could I make this up to her –could I put it right?

Emma came over to me and asked, 'What on earth is the matter, Joe? You look like you've seen a ghost.' I told her that I thought I'd lost a load of money, but I'd just remembered it was still in my overnight bag at home. We all sat around the table and discussed the next stage of the operation. Everyone on the team knew their role and what was expected from them. Dave said that it was going to be a very busy few months, and he demanded 100 per cent commitment from the team. He stressed the importance of secrecy and told them if he caught anyone talking about the operation to anyone other than the other members of the team, they would be off the job instantly.

Dave took Emma and me into his office and thanked us for our efforts, saying he understood that we both had families and that it must be taking its toll. I told Dave that if it hadn't been for Emma setting the job up so well, we wouldn't be in the position we were now. We laughed about the fact that it was only by default that I'd come on the job in the first place. He asked us both if we were happy with the plans, and said that the top boss wanted to come over and meet us.

We waited for about ten minutes before we were joined by the head of crime for the force, who was a genuinely nice man. He was a career detective, and fully up to speed with the operation. The first thing he did, after introducing himself to the two of us, was to apologise for the compromise on the evening of the gun purchase. He assured us that it wouldn't happen again and that he understood the dangers it had placed us in. He knew that we'd overcome a number of challenges and very difficult situations. He said that he was really pleased with where the operation was at, and hoped that we could both progress it further. I had listened to a lot of bosses over the years giving similar speeches and many of them were simply paying lip service. This one was different, and he meant it. I felt that he was on our side and wanted us to succeed.

We finished our meeting, and Emma and I left Dave and the boss alone in the office. I told Emma that I'd see her later, after she'd closed the shop, and we agreed that we'd go out for a few drinks at the wine bar later that evening. I had a lot of things to catch up on at home, and there were a few matters to put right in my personal life. But I hadn't even reached the house before my phone rang. It was Ray. He asked where I was and said he wanted to meet up, and could I come and pick him up as Chloe had his car. I agreed I would collect him, but I said I wouldn't be with him for at least an hour.

I wanted at least half an hour to myself; I wanted a bit of peace and calm and quietness. I opened the patio doors at the back of the house, and sat on the bench seat looking out onto the garden. I could see a grey squirrel holding a nut in his two hands, greedily munching on it in a very apprehensive manner. I thought to myself that it must be a nightmare to be a squirrel; they seemed to be permanently on edge and nervous. My thoughts were confirmed as the squirrel scuttled away and out of sight on hearing the sound of my neighbour opening her kitchen window. I didn't move from the dining table, but the solitude of the moment was disturbed by the annoying tick of the second hand of the huge clock that hung on the wall behind me. It seemed to be getting louder and louder, and it was enough for me to grab some money and head straight back out the door.

I drove to Ray's house and rang him as I sat in the car outside. As usual, he was happy as a sandboy and wore his customary huge smile on his face. He told me that he had some paperwork to collect, and asked if I minded calling at a few places where the fella might be. He said that the guy had been ignoring his calls, and he didn't want him taking the piss. He pulled out a steel-and-gold Rolex Submariner from his pocket and handed it to me. He explained that he had been given it by the fella until he could pay his debt, but he'd had the watch checked out and it was a fake. I asked how much the geezer owed him and he said it was only a 'bag of sand', but it was the principle. He also said that he needed the money to put into something that I might be interested in.

We drove to a couple of places before we found the fella outside a house that he was in the throes of decorating. As we pulled up, he was bizarrely eating a bowl of cornflakes. He looked at us as I parked the car, and if I had a million pounds to bet on the first words to come out of his mouth, I would have done so. Ray got out of the car and walked over to him with a bit of a swagger that I hadn't witnessed before. I stayed in the driver's seat but had my window down to listen to the conversation. The fella put the spoon into the bowl, and as Ray got within five feet of him, I clearly heard him say, 'I was just going to ring you.' I laughed aloud and thought about me collecting my winnings.

Ray then took the watch from his pocket and threw it at him, saying, 'Where's my money?' The watch hit the man on the chest and landed at the man's feet on the grass verge where he was standing. I thought that the man's next reply would decide what Ray did next.

Ray didn't walk any closer, but stood his ground and waited for the man's answer. The fella replied, 'I've got your money in my car.' Well, I was now pondering whether I should put my huge winnings from my last bet into a 50-50 bet. Did this man have a thousand pounds in his car, and was he about to give it to Ray or not?

Ray allowed him to walk to the car on his own. I watched the man put his bowl of cereal on top of the estate and climb into the driver's seat. I expected the car to start up and roar away – well, as much as an old Rover estate was capable of roaring. Within seconds, the fella was back out of his car and holding a tattered white envelope in his hand. He walked over to Ray, and casually bent down and picked up the watch on the way. He stood two feet away from him, face to face, and counted out what appeared to be half the contents of the envelope. Ray put it straight into his pocket, and without even saying thank you, turned away from the man and walked back to the car.

He waited until I pulled out of sight of the man before he burst out laughing. 'Fuck me, Joe. I thought there was more chance of meeting Beyoncé in the office tonight than him giving me my money.' Ray was a thoroughly happy man, and he had a thousand pounds in his pocket that I knew he would want to 'put to work'. He looked over at me, but before he could speak I said, 'Whatever you're going to say, can't it wait until we've had something to eat?'

I drove the short distance to the Spanish café and parked the car. I wanted a full stomach to listen to Ray's next proposition.

Thirty

I sat with Ray and Ricardo in our usual corner table in the office. The pub was our little haven – a cosy, warm and safe place. We were having a few drinks, and I was trying to convince Ray to go back to his legitimate job. I told him that he was a great salesman, that he was charming and polite and I thought he could sell ice to the Eskimos. Why didn't he end this villainy and be a straight-goer? I told him I wished I could do it. There was nothing I'd like more than to say to my daughter that I was an accountant or teacher, or anything that made her proud of me. I didn't want her to grow up knowing that her dad earned his living by doing 'this and that'.

I told Ray that I wasn't proud of what I did, and if I had my way again things would be different. Ricardo started to laugh. 'Fuck me, I'm welling up here. Ray, get me a tissue.' I told Ricardo to fuck off and said I should've realised I was wasting my time on the two of them.

I knew that Ricardo would slip away shortly, and I wanted a proper chat with Ray. There was no doubt that he was a good villain. He had contacts for every commodity you could imagine. He was a placer: he could put two people in contact with each other, knowing that one had a product that the other wanted to buy. He was very good at this, though there wasn't a huge profit in introductions. But he was introducing me to many people.

Ricardo finished his drink and said goodbye; he had his beloved Jamaican rice and peas to get home for. I looked at Ray as Ricardo left the office, and said, 'A tenner says he goes home to toad in the hole or shepherd's pie.' Ray laughed out loud and asked me if I fancied another Courvoisier and Stone's ginger. Of course I wanted another. Ray returned with two heavy crystal tumblers, half full of the lethal combination. I moved seats so I could be a tad closer. We clinked glasses and I said, 'This time next year, Ray.' We both laughed.

I said to Ray that he had been a good friend to me and that I trusted him. I told him that I needed a favour, but I had been waiting for Ricardo to go before I asked him. In the morning I was meeting a fella who was collecting twenty-five bags from me for a bit of graft. I was meeting him at the train station, and it would be a short meet before he got the first train back into Liverpool Street with my money. I told Ray that my old man had grafted with this fella's uncle back in the day, but I'd never done any graft with him myself. I wasn't worried about the fella, but I was going to tell Emma that Ray and I were going to look at a house together. I explained to him that I wanted him to tell Chloe the same, in case Emma checked with her. I said that he needed to make himself scarce between 10.00 a.m. and 11.30 and I'd meet him at the Spanish café at 11.30, once I'd done what I needed to do. I told him not to tell a soul about my meet, and all being well, we would have a 'nice little drink' tomorrow evening together.

Ray said it stood to reason he would not say a word to anyone. Then he said, 'As we are on favours, you can do me one back.' He went on to explain that he had a lovely young girl who was bothering him about spending the night together. He had arranged to see her Friday evening, and was going to tell Chloe at the last minute that he was staying with me. He asked me if I was OK with that. I took a long sip on my drink, and held it in the back of my mouth before I gulped it down and felt the heat of the drink warm my throat as I swallowed. I said, 'What colour is the duvet in my spare room?'

He looked perplexed. 'What are you on about?'

'How many pillows are on the bed and what's the wallpaper like?'

I could see the confusion spread across his forehead. 'Fuck me, where are you going with this, Joe?'

I took another mouthful of the Stone's combo, realising that a few more of these and I'd struggle to hold a meaningful conversation. I then explained to Ray that these were the questions that I was asked when I last did exactly what he was intending to do on Friday night. I didn't know the answers as

I'd been staying in a plush hotel with young attractive company, and it came back to bite me on the arse.

Ray started shaking his head. 'Fuck, I'd never have thought about that, mate, that's genius. Is Emma home, or can we pop round now and have a butcher's?' The two of us finished our drinks and drove the short distance to my house.

Ray was like a kid running to his bedroom after school to open a present. He took two stairs at a time, and as he reached the landing, I shouted up, 'It's the one next to the office – give your eyes a treat.' I could hear him plodding around the bedroom and opening a few drawers. 'Keep your hands in your pockets, Ray. I know what's in them drawers, you tea leaf.' I could hear him laugh to himself. A few minutes later, he joined me in the kitchen. He sat on the bench seat at the large antique pine table, and with a beam on his face said, 'Go on, pretend you're Chloe and ask me anything.'

I handed him a Le Creuset mug of steaming-hot tea, and a bowl of sugar for the four spoons he'd heap into the mug. He was confident now, and I sat in the big pine seat at the head of the table, I put my mug down on a coaster and flicked one across the table for him to use. My first question caught him off guard: 'What blinds do they have in their spare room, Ray?' Straight away, he was out of his seat and bounding back up the stairs. I could hear him pulling the blackout blinds down and then drawing the curtains shut and opening them again.

'This ain't straightforward, is it, Joe?' he said as he sat back down. We continued the interrogation, and Ray only returned upstairs once more to look at the colour of the towels in the bathroom that he'd have used after he showered. He was quite pleased with himself.

His smugness was only interrupted by the sound of Emma pulling up in the driveway. He went to get up and leave, but I told him to sit down and say hello to her. I wanted to use her arrival to my advantage.

She came through the back door laden with shopping bags, and Ray got up like a gentleman and helped her. I gave her a kiss and said it was lovely to see her so early. She asked what Ray and I were plotting and planning; I explained that Ray had a mate that had a couple of houses that weren't yet on the market, and he and I were going to look at them tomorrow morning. I told her that if they were nice, me and her would go at the weekend before they went on the open market next Monday. Emma looked at us both and said, 'And there's me thinking you two were up to no good!'

I could see from Ray's face that he wanted to get out of there before he got asked any difficult questions. He said goodbye to Emma, and I walked him out to his car. I held his door open and told him not to forget to make himself scarce in the morning from ten o'clock. I'd meet him at the Spanish café at 11.30, all being well. Ray looked up at me and thanked me; he told me he was really glad he'd done his homework on my spare bedroom. As he pulled away, he shouted out the window, 'Cracked-black-pepper handwash in the bathroom, check me out!'

I went inside and listened to Emma telling me about her day as we put away the shopping together. I had seen a recipe for quinoa left in one of the drawers, so I grasped the moment, quickly saying that I fancied a Ruby's takeaway and it would save Emma cooking after a busy day. I'm fairly sure Emma knew that I couldn't face pretending to enjoy another one of her meals. You could never ever fault her effort in trying to create a dish worthy of eating, but unfortunately, apart from sausage pasta, none was edible.

Emma rolled her eyes and agreed with my suggestion. Before she could change her mind I threw her a copy of the menu, though I already knew exactly what she would order. She always spent three or four minutes peering at the menu and then said, 'I know it's boring, but chicken korma, pilau rice and a garlic naan.'

I laughed to myself as I phoned the order in. I could've had it delivered, but I loved to spend ten minutes chatting with the owner of the curry house whilst having two spicy popadoms, some chutney and a Cobra beer. It was the best part of every Ruby's meal by a country mile.

I ran into Dave on the way back from the curry house, and arranged to collect £25,000 from him at 8 a.m. I told him that I'd just picked up a curry to avoid being poisoned by Emma, as I had found a recipe for quinoa. Dave laughed and said that his missus had made him eat that as part of his diet. I said she'd have me living barefoot in a tree house drinking nettle tea by next month.

Emma had made the house all cosy, and there were candles in the front room and kitchen. She had laid the table and poured us each a tall glass of ice-cold beer. She had really made this house feel like a home. She had good taste, and an eye for interior design. We were never quite sure when we would get a knock on the door or an unannounced visit, and we always had to be prepared for that eventuality. But she had created an oasis – a place we could spend time together. It was a loving, warm and comfortable home, and we were both in a happy place.

Emma was a great talker and I suppose I was a good listener; I was always interested in what she had to say. She started telling me about Ricardo, and how whenever he came into the shop, a string of wrong'uns normally followed after he left. Every time he came in he would tell her, 'I made a promise to Joe that I'd look out for you and that's what I'm doing.' She said he would sit and chat and have a cup of tea with her. She told me that he really liked me and was genuinely looking out for her.

I finished my meal but, as usual, Emma had eaten very little of hers. She always said the same: 'I'll freeze this and it'll save me ordering anything next time.' Of course, there were already three or four boxes of leftover korma sat in the freezer, awaiting further use, so I put the contents of hers in the bin. I blew out all the candles, and we went to bed.

Thirty-one

I was up with the larks and singing to myself as I filled the espresso pot with Illy coffee and water before placing it on the gas hob. I'm a morning person, and from the moment I wake up I'm full of beans. I've always wanted the ability to lie in, but it's a talent that's evaded me all my adult life. I have sleep envy towards those people who can sleep in until lunchtime. Once I'm awake, that's me up for the day. And obviously, the rule is that once I'm up, I see no reason why everyone else should not also be awake.

I prepared the warm milk for my coffee in a separate saucepan and took Emma's bone china cup and saucer out of the dishwasher, ready to pour her Americano. I noticed that Emma had bought some of Marks and Spencer's finest croissants and so I heated them under the grill. I knew that it wouldn't be long before the lovely aromas of buttery croissants and fresh coffee would tempt Emma down the stairs. And before I had finished pouring the hot milk into my cup, there she was at the table. She held her frizzy bedhead hair in her hands as she yawned and said, 'How come you're always so happy in the morning – how do you do it?'

I ignored her question and passed her the cup and saucer full of hot coffee, together with a croissant covered in lashings of proper butter. I looked at her and said, 'At this point you say, "Thank you, Joe, you're the best."' I sat with her at the table and tried to make conversation, but I knew her well enough; until she finished her coffee I had no chance of lengthy responses. And she sipped her coffee so slowly that I didn't have the time to wait. I kissed her on the top of the head, held my nose and said, 'A little bit of shampoo wouldn't go amiss on that barnet.' I laughed and went upstairs to brush my teeth. By the time I came back down, she had moved to the sofa. She was sat with her feet tucked up underneath her, and I caught her sniffing the ends of her hair.

I grabbed my keys and told her that I'd see her tonight, but that if she even thought about cooking quinoa, I wasn't coming home. She giggled as I shouted, 'Don't you forget to have a shower!'

It felt like I had been up for hours. I was wearing a crisp white shirt I'd ironed with starch that morning, as well as a smart pair of Seven jeans and a pair of polished brogues. I waved at the neighbour opposite; he was always out early, busying himself in his immaculate front garden. I thought that there was very little on our road that he didn't know about. I wasn't quite sure what he made of me, but I was always very polite to him, and I'd once helped his wife up the drive with her shopping and I think he was grateful for that.

It was a toss-up between Alan Brazil on talkSPORT, or me listening to a compilation CD. I plumped for the CD, and the first track was The Verve's 'The Drugs Don't Work'. I waited until I got to the end of my street before I turned the volume right up. When I was stuck in traffic and I looked over at a fellow driver singing at the top of their voice, I often wondered what song they were singing along to. There was no way of telling, but it was a therapeutic way of losing yourself in the confines of your own car. I made sure I sang every word and missed every note, but it certainly livened me up on my journey.

I drove off the main road and onto the windy country lane that led to Dave's cottage. He was just waving his wife and kids off on the school run. I pulled up alongside his wife's driver's side and said hello to Elaine. I told her that she looked great and that she'd done a top job keeping Dave off the take-aways and out of the pubs. I said I'd just read an excellent article stating how fantastic quinoa was in a diet. She thanked me and said she'd give it a go. I laughed to myself, thinking of poor old Dave.

I shook Dave's hand and removed a Loake shoebox from the boot of my car. We walked through the kitchen to a cupboard under the stairs, where I saw a huge antique Samuel Withers safe. It was a proper old-fashioned safe, with a big mounted manufacturer's crest on the green-patterned front. There was a single keyhole in the middle of the door, and a handle that was shaped like a fist holding a small metal rod. Dave put the key into the keyhole and turned it, and with his other hand twisted the handle and slowly opened the heavy door. There was a loud creak as the weight of the door opened to reveal the contents.

He quickly pulled out a Sainsbury's carrier bag – the more expensive type, the ones that you have to pay for at the check-out. He handed it to me and then couldn't close the door or turn the key quick enough so as to get me out of that cup-board. He clearly didn't want me to see the specifics of the secrets that sat in the safe. I looked at him in the hallway with-out saying a word. 'What!?' he blurted out with a contorted half-smile on his face. I shook my head and said to him, 'You're a dark horse, young David, aren't you?'

I went to the kitchen table and turned out the contents of the bag, taking my time to count it all. There was £25,000 in £10 and £20 notes. I had brought some thin rubber bands, and I wrapped the money in twenty-five rolled-up £1,000 bundles and placed a rubber band around each of them to keep them in place. Dave looked at me and said, 'It's like watching a pro-fessional in action.' I ignored him and placed the twenty-five rolls into a dust bag and then into the shoebox.

My work was done with Dave. I told him that his secret was safe with me, and I promised not to break into his house and steal whatever the contents of his safe were. He chuckled and said, 'Whatever you do, don't get yourself arrested with all that money.'

It was my intention to park in the train station car park and wait for the 10.05 train to arrive from Liverpool Street.

But I didn't want to sit there too long, drawing attention to myself. I had half an hour to kill, so I stopped at a Costa coffee and reloaded on caffeine. I had placed the shoebox under the passenger seat of the car and it was hidden from view. I pulled into the station slightly after 9.55 a.m., and parked away from the cab rank but close enough to be seen by someone exiting the station. Just after 10 a.m., two cars pulled into the car park. They had police written all over them. One had three burly white men inside, and the other had four similar-looking males. Instinctively, I didn't give them time to focus their attention too much on me and I drove out of the station. However, I wasn't quick enough, and I noticed that one of the rear-seat passengers had spotted me. I could see him pointing to my car as I drove off.

I went through the first set of lights with the intention of casually driving to my gym, which was nearby. I noticed that both of the cars had joined the same line of traffic as me, about four cars behind. The journey to the large car park in front of the gym only took about four minutes. The two cars followed my every turn, and as I pulled into the car park, so did they. One car pulled alongside my driver's side, and the other parked directly behind me. All seven men were out of the two cars before I'd switched off the music.

One of them knocked on my window and said my surname. I thought this was very strange. I took my time putting the window down and said, 'What did you say – my music was playing.'

I was instructed to step out of the car and put my hands on top of my head. I was then told to kneel down, plastic cuffs were placed very tightly around my wrists, and two of them carried out a physical search. This spectacle was taking place right outside the gym, and a small group of people had gathered to watch my humiliation. A young girl in her training kit who I recognised asked if I was OK. I told her I was fine. The detectives were firing a number of questions at me, about where I had been, where I lived and so on. I didn't answer a single question.

They pulled me up off my knees and took me around to the passenger door, which was open. Sitting on the passenger seat was the Loake shoebox, with the lid off and the dust bag wide open to reveal the rolled-up £1,000 bundles. I was then arrested for money laundering and cautioned. I was asked if I had any comment to make; I didn't even respond to the question.

The shoebox was placed in a large see-through evidence bag, and I was put in the back of one of the unmarked cars, with an officer either side of me. Both of them were doing their best to convince me I was in a whole heap of trouble. They said they knew who I was and that they didn't need a 'wannabe' or 'has-been' gangster in their area.

We arrived at the gates of the police station without me having uttered a single word. The plastic cuffs that were behind my back had been done up so tight by the detective that they were cutting into the skin of my wrists, but I wasn't going to let them know that they were causing me pain. I was pulled out of the back of the police car and led through a metal cage into the custody suite, where all arrested persons are processed. It was at this stage, in front of the uniform sergeant, that one of the officers had to give the reasons for my arrest. He said that I had been observed acting suspiciously this morning in the vicinity of the train station. I had been furtive and evasive and had driven off. When stopped, a large amount of cash had been found underneath the passenger seat of my car.

The sergeant asked me if that was correct, but I made no comment. The sergeant was then shown the contents of the exhibit bag. He instructed the other officers to count the contents in my presence once I had gone through the administration of being booked in. I gave the sergeant all the standard information: my name, address, date of birth. I declined a solicitor and had to sign to confirm the fact that I had been offered one. The plastic cuffs were kept on me, although the sergeant had instructed the officers to cut them off. This they only did once every note of the £25,000 had been counted. My right wrist had started to bleed by this stage, but I ignored it. I was allowed one phone call, and I phoned Emma on her mobile to let her know the situation. I told her not to worry, that I'd done nothing wrong and I'd be home for dinner.

The detective who appeared to be taking charge of the situation returned to the charge room and slammed the exhibit bag onto the sergeant's raised desk. He blurted out in a cocky voice: 'Twenty-five thousand pounds, Sarge, in used ten- and twenty-pound notes – just what we all keep under our passenger seat when we pop out to the shops.' Two of his colleagues laughed but I just stared at him, emotionless. There were two men in their twenties sat on the bench behind me waiting to be booked in, with a couple of uniform police officers alongside them. I heard one of the two say, 'Fuck me, did you see all that dough?'

Undercover

I was asked to sign to say that the money had been taken from my car, which I willingly did. I told the sergeant that I wanted every penny back as it was my legitimate money. To further my degradation and humiliation, my belt and shoelaces were removed to prevent me harming myself. I was placed into cell number three and the heavy metal door was slammed behind me. The noise reverberated around the cell for a few moments.

I stood about a foot inside the cell and took in my surroundings. There was a wicket in the middle of the cell door – these can be opened from the outside so that officers can pass your food through and check on your welfare. To my left was a metal toilet that had suffered a few dents and scratches and smelt of urine. I knew there was no way in the world I'd be sitting on it. There was a buzzer on the wall to get the attention of the gaoler or sergeant. A blue, plastic single mattress sat on a wooden bench opposite the door, and a manky blue woollen blanket was at the end of the mattress.

I took a deep breath and the smell of the urine stayed in the back of my throat. I unravelled the blanket, took my shoes off and lay on my back on the mattress, with the blanket laid carefully over my front to ensure it went nowhere near my face. I looked up at the ceiling, where '0800555111' was painted alongside the word 'Crimestoppers'. The fact it was perhaps a tad too late for me to ring them, now that I was lying in a cell minus a phone, was not lost on me though it could have been genius if they'd actually a phone with a direct link to the Crimestoppers office. I'm sure many a trapped man would've dialled the number in a moment of despair, and shared a few

225

criminal secrets and shopped a few people to get out of a sticky situation.

My pattern was always the same when arrested: never eat or drink anything whilst in police custody; never talk to anyone through the cell wicket; and never engage in banter, shouting or conversations with any other prisoners in the cells next to me. I was always polite but not friendly, and I would sleep or try to for as many hours as I could.

About two hours after I had been placed in my cell, I was woken by the sound of the wicket being opened. I could hear a soft female voice that sounded South African, an accent that I hated. I'd rather listen to a broad Brummie accent than South African. She apologised for waking me and asked me to come up to the door to speak with her. I sat up and swung my legs around. I was now sat looking directly at two dark eyes and a mop of dark brown hair. The lady, who I would've guessed was about thirty years old, told me that she was a drug counsellor and said that I could talk with her in confidence about any drug addictions I had. She would be able to help, whilst I was at the police station and also if I was released or remanded into prison. I let her finish her speech, and paused before I said, 'No, thank you.' Then I turned and faced the wall, and covered myself with the blanket. She continued offering assistance but I gave no response, and I heard the sound of the shutter and bolt closing.

I soon knew the Crimestoppers phone number backwards: 1115550080. I had numerous visits from the gaoler; I was offered breakfast and cups of tea but I refused every offer. I was woken from another sleep by the gaoler opening my cell door and telling me that I was going to be interviewed. I was walked down the cell passage to the bright lights of the custody suite. I looked up at the large black numbers on the plain white face of the clock above the sergeant's head. It was 2.10. I found myself staring at the clock, trying to establish in my head what make it was, but there was no name on it. The sergeant interrupted my mundane thoughts to inform me that two detectives were taking me to interview. He asked me if I wanted to be represented by a solicitor during the interview. He also commented that I hadn't eaten or drunk anything since I had been arrested and he offered both again. I politely declined all offers.

I was taken into a soundproofed interview room by the sarcastic detective, and his awkward-looking partner. I looked around the room whilst he explained the procedure to me. I could see there was a camera in the corner of the room, and the awkward detective was clumsily trying to take the plastic wrapper off one of the interview tapes. It was really bugging me, and I had to stop myself grabbing both tapes from him and opening them myself. Eventually, he found the brown strip that was clearly visible, and used it to break the plastic seal.

Two tapes were placed in an outdated black recording device that sat on the battered table. He pressed two buttons on the machine, and a buzzer sounded for about five seconds and then stopped. On the desk in front of the two detectives was a plastic-coated guide to the interview procedure. I could see that they were reading from this sheet.

The first one introduced himself as DC Gables, and his awkward colleague as DC French. I was asked to state my name, which I did. I was then cautioned and told the reason for my arrest, and asked if I wished to make a comment. I said, 'All the money that was taken off me today is legitimate money. I can account for every single penny, and I will be getting it back.' For the next forty-five minutes, I didn't answer another question put to me by either of the detectives.

At the conclusion of the interview, I was returned to the custody office. There was a new sergeant on duty, together with an extremely fresh-faced inspector, who was very well spoken. Both of them introduced themselves, then they told me that my detention was authorised, so the detectives could investigate my arrest for money-laundering offences. Again I remained passive and polite, and showed no emotion. I was led back to my cell and remained there until 7.30 p.m., my only interruption being the concerned gaoler continuing his offers of food and drink.

Eventually I was told that I was being released from the police station, but that I had to return in six weeks' time, when all enquiries by the detectives would be complete. I was informed that my money would be retained until its legitimacy was clarified. I was given my mobile phone and personal belongings back, together with my Hermès belt and shoelaces.

They then buzzed me out of the custody area and into the public waiting area. I looked at my reflection in the window as I switched my mobile phone back on; I could see bits of blue wool from the blanket stuck in the stubble on my face.

I stepped outside and rang Emma. I heard her voice immediately. I told her I was out of the police station and asked her to pick me up. She said she'd been sat in her car, parked around the corner, since five o'clock. Before I'd even hung up, she pulled around the corner and I jumped in the passenger seat. The car smelt clean and welcoming, and it was lovely and warm inside. Emma gave me a big hug and a kiss and said she was so pleased to see me. I looked at her and said, 'Let's go home, I need a shower.'

Emma asked me question after question on the drive home, getting very little in response. As we pulled up on the drive, I looked at her and said, 'Ems, let me have a hot shower. You put the kettle on and we can sit and I'll tell you everything.'

Thirty-two

I undressed in the hallway and let all my clothes fall onto the oatmeal carpeted floor. There were many flecks of blue wool that had attached themselves to my clothes, and the contrasting colour was evident as they nestled amongst the carpet fibres. I picked my clothes up, and lifted the hinged lid of the vintage teak sea trunk we used to store our dirty washing in. I could barely see the fading words of the import company on the front of the trunk, and I wondered what treasures it had stored whilst at sea.

I closed the lid and walked into the bathroom. I grabbed a clean white towel and held it to my face with both hands, breathing in the freshness as deeply as I could. I loved the smell of the fabric softener. I put the shower on full blast and stood under it for an age before I started scrubbing the grubbiness of the police station out of my skin and hair. For a brief moment, I sat down in the shower and let the power of the hot water pound my head.

I felt clean and refreshed as I dried myself with the fluffy towel. I put on a pair of plain grey Ralph jogging trousers and a plain white Ralph sweatshirt, and a pair of pristine Stan Smiths on my feet. I went downstairs to find Emma had made me two rounds of cheese on toast and a huge mug of tea. I would never have asked for this to eat, but it was absolutely delicious. She said that Dave had phoned and wanted to speak with me.

Emma and I chatted about the events of the day and she told me that Ray had popped into the shop to see her. He said he'd been expecting to meet me at 11.30 at the Spanish café opposite the shop, but I obviously hadn't shown. She had told him I'd been arrested and was at the police station, but that she didn't know what for. She said that he didn't hang around, but asked her to call him if she heard any news.

I told Emma that I needed to borrow her phone to ring Ray. I took his number out of my phone and tapped the digits into hers and dialled the number. Ray answered, and I told him who it was and that I needed to see him straight away at the office. He said he'd be there in fifteen minutes. I put the phone down without saying goodbye.

I asked Emma if she minded dropping me down the office, and explained to her exactly why I wanted to see Ray. She understood and told me to call her when I was done. I grabbed my Aquascutum scarf and the two of us jumped in the car.

Emma pulled up outside the front of the pub. I thanked her, and told her that I'd text her from Ray's phone when I was done as I didn't have mine with me.

I paused outside the doors to the pub and watched Emma drive away; she was looking in her mirror and waving at me. I stepped through the doorway into the warmth inside. There was a lovely, open log fire burning, and the aroma and crackling of the seasoned cedar wood filled the small snug area. I ordered two large Courvoisier and Stone's, and positioned myself out of sight at our usual table. I sat and stared out the bowed window of the pub, my mind drifting as I watched a dad holding his daughter's hand as they crossed the road together. She was oblivious to the potential danger of the traffic as she skipped across the street, chattering away as she looked up at her dad. She knew that she was safe because he had hold of her hand; she knew that he would never let her come to any harm.

I asked myself why I was sat in this pub at this time waiting for Ray to arrive, after spending eight hours in a police cell? Why was I not hundreds of miles away, feeling the warmth and softness of my own daughter's hand in mine? Making sure she was safe and happy, and listening to stories of her day. Telling her how much I loved her and that I'd always be there for her, no matter what. What was wrong with me – why did I choose to be here instead? After all, it was my choice.

As I was mulling over these dark thoughts, Ray startled me back to reality. I had to do a double take before it registered who it was. He was wearing the blue padded Barbour jacket that he always wore, with the collar up and his hands thrust deep into the side pockets. He told me that he'd been calling over to me from the bar, but I was staring into the darkness outside the window.

He asked if I was OK as he sat down opposite me. I didn't say a word as I slid the second drink across the width of the table to him. I watched him closely as he picked up the tumbler and put it to his mouth. I was annoyed by the fact that his lips looked really dry and needed some Vaseline or Carmex.

I lifted my own glass up and looked through the crystal of the tumbler at Ray. 'There is no point fannying around this, Ray. Two people knew what I was doing today and where I would be. One of them I'm looking at now. I end up being jumped on by the plod, and when they nicked me they knew my surname. The copper called me by my fucking surname as he knocked on my window.' I said this last sentence slowly and clearly. I finished off by saying, 'That means they were expecting me, so it was either you or the fella from London who served me up to them . . . which one was it?'

I could see that Ray was taking in the magnitude of this situation. I wasn't calling him a grass, but under the circumstances it was either him or the other fella. I told him not to answer yet. I explained that they had seized my £25,000 and I wasn't a bit happy, but I told him my biggest issue was that I was now on the radar of the local filth.

Ray took a huge gulp of his drink and didn't hesitate before he took another. He looked at me and said, 'He's got to go – that fella has to go.' He told me he hadn't uttered a word to anyone, and he'd been waiting for me at 11.30 as I'd told him to. He took a long look at me and said, 'On my baby's life, I had nothing to do with it. You have my word.'

I emptied my drink and said, 'I believe you, but you're right – that no good piece of shit has to go.' I left Ray sat at the table, walked to the bar and asked the young emo-looking barmaid for a reload of the same drinks. She didn't even need to ask what they were, and poured them into fresh tumblers.

I thanked her, paid for the drinks and returned to sit opposite Ray. He poured the contents of the new glass into what remained of his first drink. He thanked me for the drink and said he was really sorry about the Old Bill nicking my dough. I clinked his glass and said, 'You're right, the fella has to go, but I need one of them' – I held my right hand in a gun shape – 'I could go to the Smoke, but I don't want anyone that end knowing I'm after one.'

Ray said, 'Don't worry about that. It's best you have a shusher for that type of work, and I'll sort that.'

I took another sip, clinked his glass again, and thanked him. 'That's one less thing for me to worry about.' I could see in Ray's face he felt gutted for me, but knowing that he was helping me to get rid of a grass was a consolation. He said he'd sort it for me as soon as he could.

I told him that I was going to finish this drink and then call Emma to come and pick me up. I explained that I had played everything down and told her they'd pinched five grand off me as I didn't have receipts for the money. I asked if he could text her to pick me up, which he did. He then said, 'Joe, before you go – what was the name of the copper that nicked you?' I told him his name was DC Gables. Ray then explained that he had a mate who would be able to do some digging on him, and he'd let me know what he found out.

I downed the rest of my drink, and as I got up to go, Ray said, 'I feel bad saying this, but don't forget tomorrow night I'm with you.' He did one of his over-exaggerated winks. He told me it would be really handy if I could have a few early drinks with him, and then he'd slip away and do what he needed to do. I told him that wasn't a problem and we'd have a meet-up tomorrow. I reminded him that if he wanted to get hold of me, he'd have to ring Emma's phone. I said I'd get a new phone tomorrow and I'd get my number to him.

He stood up and gave me a big hug. 'You're doing the right thing, mate. The fella has to go.' I said goodbye to the bar-maid, and the cold air hit me as I stepped out from the warmth and cosiness of the bar. I thought a walk would do me good, but as I looked up Emma pulled alongside me. I jumped in the car, and leant over and kissed her on the cheek and thanked her. I rested my head on the plush leather of the interior and closed my eyes, just for a moment.

Thirty-three

I wasn't quite ready to sleep when Emma and I got home, so we chatted on the sofa whilst she sipped on a tall iced Bacardi and Diet Coke she had made for herself. I didn't fancy another drink but was quite happy to sit and listen to Emma telling me about her day. The shop was getting busier and she was doing well to deal with the number of customers through the door. She described the type of characters wandering into her little world within the four walls of the shop. She liked the diversity of people and their greed for money, and she noted the amount of people who tried their very best – but failed miserably – to 'have her over'.

I was getting tired now, and I was looking forward to sleeping in a proper bed, with Egyptian cotton sheets rather than a rough, dirty blue woollen blanket on a blue plastic mattress. I brushed my teeth and slid into bed, and as my head touched the pillow I was asleep, happy that I'd wake to a new day.

I was up and at 'em the following morning. Downstairs in the kitchen, I looked out onto the back garden through the patio doors as the rain bounced off the decking. There was an old-fashioned clothes line with a pole, made to hold the drying clothing aloft in the wind. Today was not a day for hanging clothing out to dry. I put the espresso pot on and found myself staring at two starlings bathing themselves in a small pool of rainfall that had formed on the path that meandered through the garden. I knew I needed a decent cup of coffee to concentrate my thoughts. I phoned Dave and we agreed to meet for breakfast in half an hour – just enough time for me to finish my coffee and drive to the Stables café. I left a note for Emma saying that I was meeting Dave and that I'd call her after. I grabbed my Henri Lloyd jacket and locked the patio doors behind me.

I drove through the rain listening to my favourite sports presenter Alan Brazil; the man had a melodic voice and I loved his sense of humour and fun. The fella could certainly tell a story and I loved the fact that he liked a drink. I often thought that he and I would have a really good night out together. The banter between Brazil and Mike Parry on talkSPORT kept me entertained all the way to my breakfast meeting.

The rain was still lashing down as I held my jacket over my head and ran for the comfort of the café. Dave was already sat in the corner, his hair was wet and there was condensation on his glasses. This didn't bother him, as he was devouring the second triangle of a lovely toasted sausage and bacon sandwich. There was a slow trickle of brown sauce oozing out of one end of the sandwich and onto the stubble of his chin. It took him three wipes with a paper napkin to ensure his chin was sauce-free. He looked up and said that he'd paid for my usual coffee for me.

I walked over to the counter and ordered two eggs on brown toast, which I paid for, and the lady poured me the coffee that Dave had already bought. I took my coffee over and sat opposite Dave. I was happy to see that his sandwich was gone and his face was devoid of sauce. He was wiping the condensation from his glasses.

Dave said that he was really pleased with the way the past few days had gone. He said that, unbeknown to me, Ray had already made contact with his pal the ex-policeman, who in turn had made a couple of discreet calls to old pals of his in the force trying to find out about my arrest. He said the calls were casual and not in any way corrupt, but the ex-policeman had confirmed someone had been nicked with a lot of cash. Dave also commented that he was happy that Ray had now offered me a gun to deal with the person who Ray believed was a grass. He was honest enough to say that he hadn't been convinced the plan would work, but he was now very confident we would secure the weapon.

I looked at Dave and told him that there had been plenty of talk about guns, and I wasn't going to get too excited until I actually had it in my lap. I also told him that I wasn't having the circus that had surrounded the aborted purchase. The panic of the senior officers in using a surveillance team had put myself, Emma and the whole operation at serious risk. I said I wasn't going to let it happen again, and if Ray came up with the gun, I was going to keep things very low-key.

I could see that Dave saw my point of view, but I wasn't convinced that he believed anything would change in 'their' approach to the next potential purchase. I knew Dave was caught in the middle and his position was a little awkward, having to keep me keen and also keep the bosses well informed in order to make decisions.

My breakfast arrived, and Dave and I spoke more about the ex-policeman, who was named Frank. He explained that the fella had split the opinion of the people he used to work with. Half thought he'd been excellent Old Bill, and the other half thought he was the complete opposite and shouldn't have been in the police. Dave said that Frank was well versed in many techniques, and had knowledge of surveillance. The research they'd done had revealed that Ray and him had been very close and clearly still were. Frank had left the police after some discipline issues, and Dave told me that I really needed to be on my guard if I came across him.

I told Dave that Ray had mentioned him yesterday evening – not by name, but he'd said he had a pal that might be able to do some digging. He'd asked me for the name of the arresting officer, and I had given him the name of Gables. Dave said we all had to tread carefully with Frank, as he could really cause us some problems. I'd left a triangle of toast on my plate, and Dave looked at it and said, 'Do you mind?' He had it en route to his mouth before I'd acknowledged it was his for the eating.

The rain had just ceased, and we walked out to our cars together. I told Dave that Ray and I were having a few early drinks this evening and that he'd asked me to cover for him as he was seeing another bird for the night. Dave laughed and commented that he wouldn't like to be in Ray's shoes if Chloe found out. I explained that he'd had a good look around the spare room in case Chloe sat him down and questioned him about his sleepover. As we were discussing this, my phone rang. I looked at the screen and said, 'Talk of the devil.' I answered, and Ray said he wanted to see me. We agreed to meet at a garden centre on the outskirts of town.

Dave and I agreed we would speak after my meeting with Ray. As I pulled away, I rang Emma to check that everything was OK. She seemed in a really bubbly mood, and said that the shop had been busy this morning. She said she'd like to go out for dinner tonight, and I agreed that she should choose somewhere to eat and to book a table for after eight.

I pulled into the garden centre, which was in an elevated position overlooking a picturesque river. The parking spaces in the car park were neatly marked out, and the whole place had a feeling of money and a touch of class. Ray only ever drove at one speed, and he pulled into the car park as I was stood next to my open driver's door moisturising my hands. Parking was like a pit stop in a Grand Prix to him, and he was oblivious to the presence of normal people going about their daily business. He pulled his car alongside mine and jumped out. 'What's that shit you're putting on your hands?' I looked at him and said, 'Don't knock it until you've tried it.'

Undercover

He shook my hand and we walked together across the car park. I looked at the quality of the cars parked close to mine. This was a pretty upmarket place to buy a few bedding plants. Huge glass windows were set in the timber-clad exterior of what looked like a huge barn. We strolled through the home and garden section, and past the food hall, looking at the fresh produce at the fishmonger's and the array of olives and cheeses in the delicatessen. I could smell the freshly baked cakes in the bakery. It was like a mini version of Harrods Food Hall, and the aromas that drifted through the air were enough to tempt the most earnest of dieters.

We found our way to the café at the side of a formal restaurant, which had pictures of recent weddings that had taken place there displayed on an easel. I ordered coffee for myself and Ray, and he grabbed a slice of rocky road that the enthusiastic young assistant said had just been baked. As usual, we positioned ourselves at the most remote table, out of earshot of the good and decent people that were enjoying a lovely shopping trip. We sat opposite each other next to a huge window. Ray dipped the tip of his rocky road into the froth of his cappuccino, and he momentarily closed his eyes as he savoured the flavours before saying, 'Fucking lovely.' I shook my head and said, 'Greg Wallace's job on *MasterChef* is under threat with comments like that. You missed your vocation in life.' He ignored my comments, and continued munching on the rocky road.

After he swallowed the last mouthful, he leant across the table and explained to me that his mate, the ex-policeman, had done some digging on the copper who had nicked me. DC

Gables was on a special squad at the moment, and Ray's mate thought that maybe the squad could be looking at me and for me to be careful. He said his mate had his finger on the pulse with the local Old Bill, and that I should keep my eyes on my rear-view mirror. I took in what Ray was telling me, and said to him that it didn't sit right with me that his friend was an ex-copper; it didn't feel comfortable to me. Ray said that he had known him a long time, and that they had done things together and that he was like one of 'us'.

I explained to him that my dad had told me many years before, 'Once a copper, always a copper.' I believed that to be true. He said that this fella was different and that I would change my mind when I met him. Ray seemed to think it was just a matter of time before the two of us met. I looked at Ray and said I would keep my head down for a bit, but I was always careful anyway. We finished our coffees, and I grabbed 250 grams of salami on the way out.

As we got to our cars, Ray said that he wanted to meet here again if we needed a quiet chat. He reminded me that he wanted to see me at the office tonight at seven. He showed me some of the text messages that the girl he was seeing later had sent him. He screwed up his face and said, 'She's going to get it tonight.' I told him to spare me the details and to clear the messages off his phone. He had a huge grin on his face as he climbed into his car. I followed him to the main road and we both went our separate ways.

Thirty-four

I drove straight home and thought I'd spend a little bit of time with Emma before I met Ray for a few drinks. She had told me on the phone that she was going to shut the shop early, as it was Friday and she'd already had quite a few customers that day. She told me that she had to meet with Dave and sort a few things, and then she'd be home.

I was quite happy in my own company, I was used to spending a lot of time on my own and it didn't faze me. I sat down in the front room in the huge, battered leather armchair and let the peacefulness of the house calm me. I put my head back onto the soft leather, and I couldn't help thinking how I had changed since the first day I was deployed as an undercover officer. My mind drifted back to my first job as a UC.

As I walked out of the briefing room at Snow Hill Police Station, I thought to myself that I was in the land of the giants. All the detectives were huge, and all bar one were male. The City of London Police was a busy, vibrant and demanding place to work as a detective, and they had a very successful and well-run undercover department. I was working for the Central Detective Unit (CDU), a team full of experienced detectives headed by a detective inspector who had been in charge of many similar operations over the years.

The briefing was very matter of fact, and there was a huge assumption on their part that I had an in-depth knowledge of 'bearer bonds'. I had never heard of them, let alone seen one. But as I looked around the briefing room, I made the decision that now was not the time to declare that I did not have a clue what they were talking about.

I was told there had been a theft of a significant amount of bearer bonds at one of the major financial institutions in the City. These bonds were worth millions of pounds to the holder. I would be meeting a man they believed was now in control of the bonds. I was shown a picture of the target and given his criminal history. He was recently released from prison, and had previously been a very successful amateur boxer who had turned professional. His career had been cut short by his keenness to rob security vans and a long spell in prison.

I was told to get £5,000 from the exhibits officer, which I did. My role was to negotiate with the man and buy up to

£5,000 of bonds as samples, and to confirm that he had control of all the bonds. The DI told me that there would be a surveillance team following me and he wanted them all to meet me. We walked a short distance down a flight of stairs into another briefing room, and I was shown to the team. I also gave them the registration of the Mercedes I would be driving.

The meeting with the ex-boxer was at 8 p.m. at Watney Market, which I was told was only a ten-minute drive away. The briefing room quickly emptied, and the DI looked at me and said, 'I'll see you back here when you're done. Don't lose my money.' I had £5,000 in my hand, my warrant card in my pocket, and my head was spinning with my ignorance about bearer bonds. This had disaster written all over it.

I managed to find my way out of the police station to where I had parked my car, which was at least a start. I hid my warrant card in the boot and put the cash under the driver's seat. I had come too far now to turn back, and this was now very, very real. I was nervous – but nervous that I would mess it up, rather than of the fact I was about to meet an ex–pro boxer who used to rob security vans.

I drove to Watney Market without too many issues. I now knew where the handbrake was and, more importantly, the release for it. I felt a million dollars driving this lovely car – leather throughout – but I was now feeling the nerves and was trying my very best to control them.

I pulled up at 7.55 and sat in my car waiting; it seemed an age before I got a knock on the window. There was a stocky male with a grey hood pulled over his head, and he was wearing a Lonsdale woollen hat. He climbed into the passenger seat and said, 'You must be Joe. Go down Lukin Street towards Shadwell.' I didn't know this part of East London particularly well, but didn't think I should tell him that. Our conversation consisted of him telling me he didn't want to go back to prison and asking me if I could move some 'puff', as one of his pals had a load of 'soaps' at the moment. I told him that I wanted to get this thing sorted first. He was directing me on a number of left and right turns in quick succession, and I wasn't really sure where I was.

After about ten minutes, he told me to pull over and park the car next to a old, red-brick block of flats that had about five floors. The passenger door was right alongside a wide concrete stairwell. He told me to wait in the car and that he'd only be five minutes. Because I was parked alongside the building, I couldn't see where he went once he leapt two by two up the steps and out of sight. It was just a matter of me sitting tight on a cold November evening in the dark. I remember a number of fireworks going off very close to me, which didn't help in calming my nerves.

I reached under my seat to feel if the money was still where I'd placed it. There was absolutely no reason that it wouldn't be there, and sure enough my hands felt it. I had not given the surveillance team a thought since I'd left their briefing room. I had no idea whether they were watching me at that moment or not. The fella came bounding down the stairs quicker than he had leapt up them. He sat next to me and told me to drive. I asked him if everything was OK and all he said was: 'Sweet.'

He said he'd taken me on a longer route to get to the flats, and there was a much quicker way back.

Sure enough, it wasn't long before I recognised the buildings of Watney Market. He told me to pull over near to where I had picked him up. I parked the car, but it was directly under a street light and he asked me to pull forwards a bit, which I did. He took an A4-sized envelope out of his pocket and asked me for the money. I reached under my seat and gave him the cash as I looked gingerly into the envelope. He counted all the money and then looked at me. I didn't say a word. He laughed and started nodding his head and said, 'I get it, come on, let's go and get the rest.'

I really didn't know what he meant, but I started the car and we went the most direct route back to the block of flats. As we drove, he said he realised it had been a test and that there had to be trust between us.

We were back at the tenement block in no time. He was up the stairs and back much quicker than the first visit. He handed me the same number of bearer bonds that he'd given me already in the envelope. He shook my hand and said, 'I like you. That was cute, giving me double the amount of dough to see if you could trust me.' He went on to say, 'You have them checked out and confirm they're pukka, and when you're happy we can trade the rest.' I really hadn't a clue what he was talking about, all I knew is that he seemed to be happy with what had just taken place and he was even offering me the remainder of the bonds.

I dropped him off at Watney Market and said I'd be in touch. I couldn't wait to get out of there. It dawned on me as

I drove back to Snow Hill station that I'd given him twice as much money as the bonds were worth, because I didn't have a clue what I was doing. I looked at the envelope and the additional bonds that sat on top, and wondered how I'd explain my inadequacies to the DI and the team. I felt that this might be my first and last deployment. It would surely rank as the shortest undercover career on record.

I must admit I wasn't looking forward to explaining myself. I parked a little away from the police station and retrieved my warrant card from the boot of the car. I had the bearer bonds tucked into the inside pocket of my coat.

I flashed my badge at the front counter and made my way sheepishly to the briefing room. There was a buzz of noise in the room as the surveillance team mingled and chatted with the detectives from the CDU. I sat down at a table and tried to avoid making any eye contact in the room.

I felt a tap on the shoulder and a very ordinary middle-aged man introduced himself as Mick, the DS of the surveillance team. He sat down next to me and shook my hand. He thanked me for my excellent work tonight and said he was glad that I'd realised the surveillance team had lost me and that I had come back to the place I'd picked the target up from. He said the team had waited there for me on the off chance I'd come back. He apologised, and said that on the second visit his team had managed to identify the flat that he went into. He shook my hand and thanked me again.

I was unsure whether he was winding me up or not, and I wondered if he saw the bemused look on my face. This was soon answered when the DI called me into his office and thanked me for getting the team out of the shit. He said that it had all worked out in the end, and asked to see the bearer bonds. I showed him them and explained that the fella had told me to check them out and then we could trade for the remainder. I could see him studying them closely – something I hadn't even bothered to do. He said that he was 99 per cent sure they were spot on. He stood up, gave me an overenthusiastic slap on the back – which caught me by surprise and winded me slightly – and said he owed me a pint and he'd see me in the bar.

I sat there for a while, confused, relieved and amazed that I had somehow come out of the evening's catastrophe smelling of roses. I watched the surveillance team leave the room, all of them acknowledging me and some of them congratulating me on their way out. Mick told me they were going to conduct their debrief and he was sure he'd see me again. The exhibits officer sat next to me and took possession of all the bearer bonds, and he told me he would get them officially authenticated in the morning.

I completed all the necessary paperwork and left it with the exhibits officer. I couldn't face going down to the bar, so made my excuses and told him to apologise to the boss. I said I had a long drive tonight and that I needed to be back in town by 7 a.m. He shook my hand and thanked me for all I'd done tonight.

I slipped out of the police station as quietly as I could, walked to my car and climbed inside. I thought I could really do with a drink, and I decided to stop on my way home to have an anonymous drink in a pub where nobody knew me.

The fact was that, although I got away with it tonight, I was a fraud to all those new colleagues of mine who thought I'd done such a great job. I'd even managed to blag my luck with the target. I knew I would never let that happen again.

That was to be a wake-up call for me – from then on, I would be more professional.

I looked up as the words 'I got away with it tonight' were whizzing through my head. Emma was stood in front of me with a huge smile on her face. I wasn't sure how long she'd been standing there, or whether I'd been asleep and had been dreaming. She said, 'Penny for your thoughts, Joe?' She laughed and asked me to come and help her carry some shopping in from the car. She said that she'd been knocking on the patio doors but I hadn't moved. I apologised, and stepped out into the fresh air to help carry the shopping into the kitchen.

My mind was now focused on today.

Thirty-five

A few days later, I was speaking quietly on the phone to Dave as I walked from the office, where I'd just had a Courvoisier and Stone's with Ray. I had known Ray for about six months now, and we spent most days together. Long periods of time in each other's company had brought us close – we knew each other, we relied on each other, we trusted each other, though that hadn't always been the case.

Ray was a popular guy, and people liked him. I liked him. I still thought to myself that he could have been anything in life. Whatever he wanted to be, he could've chosen whatever job he wanted. I knew he had been a very successful estate agent once upon a time – utilising his charm and charisma to a wholly societal end – but that wasn't the life he chose.

Ray confided in me, he spoke about things he hadn't talked about before, he asked me for advice. He also borrowed money from me, and when he was misbehaving he asked me to cover for him. In another life things would've been different. But this was now and he was a career criminal, and I had a trade to do.

I told Dave in a very matter of fact way that I'd just had a meet with Ray and I was walking back to my gaff to collect some money. I was meeting him again in half an hour at a nearby pub to buy a 9mm handgun with a shusher and eight bullets.

'I take it you're winding me up,' Dave said with just an inkling of hope in his voice. I explained that I was collecting £2,100 and then driving to The Railway pub to meet Ray and his associate called Pegg, who I thought had the gun.

Dave wasn't happy and didn't want me to go. He said I needed support and he knew the bosses would insist on an armed team backing me up. I told him to keep it low-key; I didn't want a big drama made out of it. I wanted to treat the trade as if it was any commodity I was buying. I told him I'd ring him just as I walked into the pub, and to start worrying if he hadn't heard from me in an hour. I could sense his nervousness and knew he had about a thousand questions he wanted to ask me, but I cut the call short.

I strode up the driveway to my house and let myself in, and went to the freezer in the kitchen. I removed £2,100 from £5,000 that I had hidden in a box of loose tea leaves. I opened the back door and took the four steps down to the lawn and dug up a handful of soil. I placed the cold earth amongst the

£10 and £20 notes and wrapped them all up in a Waitrose bag. I then placed this into a Mulberry leather-handled presentation gift bag, as if I'd just bought a designer handbag from New Bond Street.

I stepped into the bathroom and brushed my teeth, and when I was happy they were clean I picked up the Mulberry bag and locked up after myself. I pressed the boot release of my car and placed the bag inside; it was made of card and sat up proudly, so I laid it on its side. I got into the driver's seat and started the engine, then selected a track on the CD and turned the volume up. It was only a short journey to The Railway; there was a small sheltered car park at the back, and I squeezed my car next to an old Luton van that belonged to a local antiques dealer.

I made a quick phone call to Dave, but before I could speak, he said, 'You know, you should've given me more notice for this, Joe—'

I stopped him short. 'I'm here, Dave. I'll bell you when I'm done, for you to collect the thing. Stop worrying.'

Leaving the money in the boot of my car, I walked into the pub. Dave knew exactly why I hadn't given him notice. He knew that I'd dropped it on his toes so that the bosses couldn't mess it up this time.

The salon bar was dark – very dark – and it was only because of the sunlight that streamed through the door behind me that I could see anyone. The door stayed open long enough for me to see three figures on high-backed, dark wooden church benches. I recognised two as Ray and Pegg, who Ray was sat next to. I walked slowly over, taking in the surroundings. The third male was a man in a wheelchair. He was at the end of the table, to the right of them.

I sat down on the bench seat opposite Ray and Pegg. I couldn't see Pegg's eyes because of the dark glasses he had on, but Ray had a cheeky smile on his face. 'Who's he?' I said, as if the wheelchair man wasn't even there. Pegg told me not to worry about him, he was OK.

Pegg then looked straight at me. 'You give me the dough, and Ray and I will be about ten minutes and be back with it. The shusher isn't with it at the moment, but you can have that later.' I knew by the blasé way he was talking that he wasn't at all bothered or stressed by this deal, he just wanted it done. I sat back and felt the wood of the bench against my head. I didn't want to give Pegg my money. I wanted him to go and get the gun and bullets, bring it back to the boozer and we could swap the cash for the gun in the car park.

I didn't know Pegg that well; I hadn't previously traded with him, although I'd met him quite a while ago. What I did know about him didn't fill me with confidence. He was a thief from East London, and a slight man, but an extremely violent one. He'd stabbed a top Gypsy criminal repeatedly following a feud. It was known that recently he had fired two rounds through the door of a local drug dealer who wouldn't answer the door when Pegg went to collect a debt.

I said, 'I tell you what, you go and get the thing, bring it back here and we can do the trade right here or round the back at my motor. I ain't just giving you two bags to walk off with.'

'Joe, it ain't gonna work that way. I need the paperwork up front.'

Then Ray stepped in and said, 'Listen, Joe, I want this to happen, there's a drink in it for me. It's down to me – if this goes wrong I'll stand you two bags of sand.'

I looked over at him and nodded. 'It's against my better judgement, Ray, but this is down to you.' I knew how many previous trades Ray and I had done. I knew he'd grafted with Pegg before and he'd used Pegg to enforce debts for him.

Ray and I walked out of the pub to the car park, and I popped the boot and got out the Waitrose plastic bag and handed it to Ray. He looked through the bag and could see and feel the soil in his hand. A huge smile came over his face and he laughed out loud. 'You've been digging in that garden again, you dodgy fucker!' He took the bag and looked over his shoulder as I returned into the pub with the Mulberry carrier bag.

I asked the wheelchair man if he wanted a drink. He didn't hesitate, and asked for a double whisky and half a Stella. I looked at him and said, 'You're a cheeky fucker!' Then I walked to the bar and ordered my pint and his drinks.

I put the drinks down on the table and he said, 'Thanks, Joe, I've heard you're a good bloke to know.' I told him not to believe everything he was told. He reached forwards with his right hand and said, 'I'm Bertie. I used to be a wrong'un – I used to graft with Pegg. I was a hooligan, I loved a tear-up.' It was hard to put the words to this person sat opposite me in the wheelchair.

'What happened to your legs, Bert?'

He sipped his Stella as he said, very matter of factly, 'Someone set them alight 'cos I owed them a bullseye for crack. Poured petrol over them and watched me go up like

Guy Fawkes. I was so off my face I just sat and watched them burn till I passed out. Woke up in the hospital like this.' He pointed at his stubbed legs.

As far as I was concerned, this whole situation was fucked: the darkness of the pub, the story from Bertie. Something was amiss, and I wasn't happy that I wasn't with my money. It didn't feel right.

Bertie said he was going out the front for a fag. He wheeled himself away and I found myself alone in the dim light of the pub. I closed my eyes for an instant, but was jolted awake by the sickening sound of the pub door crashing open with a huge bang, which almost rended it from its hinges. I saw Pegg's silhouette against the sunlight behind him as he stayed there for a brief moment. No more than a second, but long enough for me to see he was wearing a single, black leather glove. Time stood still for me as I pictured a black gun recoiling in Pegg's gloved hand, painting the walls with claret and fragments of my skull. I sat rooted to the spot.

Some five metres from where I was sitting was a loaded 9mm held in the hand of a man capable of killing someone. I could see he had the hood of his jacket pulled over his head, and the dark lenses of his glasses broke up his face. I decided I wouldn't move an inch; I'd look straight at him. The eight strides he took towards me were purposeful, determined steps. And then he was in front of me, with his outstretched hand. He screeched with laughter and threw himself onto the seat opposite me, hiding the 9mm on his lap beneath the table. 'You thought I was gonna stick one in ya!' he shouted in his broad East London accent. He pulled down his hood, removed the black leather glove and said, 'I wouldn't do that to you, Joe.'

'Fuck off, Pegg, and next time take your raspberry mate with you.' I put the Mulberry bag on the table. 'Put the thing in there.'

'Put it under the table, Joe.' I moved the bag under the table, and Pegg reached under to drop the gun inside. There was an almighty bang as the gun hit the tiled floor through the bag. Pegg laughed. 'You're lucky you've still got your bollocks, Joe, 'cos there's one up the spout.' He handed me eight bullets wrapped in tissue paper.

I took one look at Pegg, picked up the bag, put the bullets inside and got up.

'Where you going, Joe – ain't you have a drink?'

'What d'ya think, Pegg? I'm going to plug this up, and I want the shusher later.'

I left the pub and bumped into Ray in the car park. I shouted over to him that I wanted to get shot of the metal and I'd ring him later. The fact of the matter was, I was glad to be out of there, away from Pegg. I had thought he was going to shoot me, yet I hadn't been bothered. I hadn't felt nervous or worried, even though I'd been aware of what I thought was going to happen to me. Why hadn't I tried to do something? If I'd thought he was going to shoot me, then surely I could've – should've – done something.

Maybe I just didn't care. Maybe I wasn't bothered.

Thirty-six

Business in the shop was booming. Emma was really keeping on top of things, and when it was really busy Freddie would help out. By now he was an established member of our team. He added a new dimension to the operation and he was good company to be around. Through Ray I had introduced Freddie to Mario, and he was buying heroin from Mario on a regular basis. The heroin was good quality and Mario was reliable; he was sourcing it down the Dirty Dozen, from East London.

Mario was an interesting character; he'd been inside for armed robbery, and had served every day of his long prison sentence the hard way due to his total disregard for the system and the screws. He was a very volatile character, and because of his use of drugs he could easily switch from a really nice guy to an animal.

I was drinking with Mario one night in the wine bar along with Ray, their partners and Emma. We were having a great time and enjoying each other's company. Ray and Mario had slipped off to the toilets a couple of times to 'powder their noses'. Ray was always first to apologise to me whenever I handed him a tissue to deal with that streaming nose he had as a result of the powder he'd stuck up there. After a few glasses of champagne, I told Emma that I was popping to the Gents.

When I got upstairs, I looked behind me and Mario was at my shoulder. I could see the backs of two smartly dressed men in their late twenties, who were stood at the urinals having a wee. Without saying a word, Mario took three steps past me and volleyed the man standing at the closest urinal as hard as he possibly could up the backside. It really was a powerful kick, and completely unprovoked and uncalled for. The young fellow was in shock, but his mate who was stood next to him said to Mario, 'What did you do that for?' Mario spat out his reply: 'Because I fucking can, now do you want to do anything about it?' The two men took one look at Mario and knew immediately that he had aggravation etched all over his face. He was a big, powerful man, and fear was not a word in his vocabulary; he always appeared on the verge of a violent act whenever I saw him.

The two men dusted themselves down and scuttled out of the toilets as quick as they could, without even considering washing their hands. Mario had a huge grin on his face, as if he was proud of what he had just done. I think he saw the disdain on my face, and tried to put things right by asking me if I wanted a 'livener'. I told him to knock himself out, but I was fine. I watched him disappear into the cubicle to have another line of coke whilst I used the facilities.

Back at the table Emma and Chloe were getting on very well, and I admired the way Emma was subtly confiding in Chloe about how happy she was. She told her it was the first time in her life that she'd felt like this was the place that she wanted to stay in forever. Emma explained that we wanted to put down permanent roots in the area. She said that we were looking for houses to buy locally, and that she wanted Ray to help us find one. Chloe was excited at the prospect, and she told Emma how much she and Ray loved our house and how they would really like to move in if we moved out. Chloe was also in the process of setting up her own tanning salon, and with Emma's experience of setting up a business they had lots to talk about.

I spoke with Ray and told him that he better have a word with Mario as he was a little too lively, and I explained what he'd done in the toilets. Ray told me to leave it with him, and after a few more drinks we all left and went to another late-night bar, which was packed to the rafters. We were lucky enough to be given a little corner area by the bar manager and we all continued drinking. Mario was getting louder and louder, and his visits to the toilets more frequent. I had a feeling that it was only a matter of time before he caused a problem or was involved in some aggravation. I told Emma that I thought we should leave after we finished our drinks, and she thought this was a good idea.

I was leaning on the bar chatting to Ray and explaining that we were about to leave, when Mario came over. His nose was running and he had a glass of champagne in his hand. I told him that Emma and I were about to leave and to have a good night. He clearly didn't like what he heard and said, 'You ain't going anywhere until I've bought you a drink.' I thanked him and politely declined, saying we could have a drink another time. He immediately switched, poking me in the chest and putting his face right in close to mine. He lambasted me: 'You think you're something special, don't you, old school? Well, you're nothing to me.'

I could see Ray watching the situation develop. Mario went to grab my jacket by the lapels and I pushed him away. I was in a perilous position; Mario was off his head on drugs, he'd been drinking, and he was physically bigger and stronger than me. I'd seen him attack someone for no apparent reason earlier, and I knew of his violent past. This was only going to end one way.

Ray went to step in and I told him that it was OK. I could see that Mario had put his champagne glass on the bar, and he now had a bottle of Peroni in his right hand. He came in close to me with his hands down by his sides. I looked at him and said if he wanted to take this further, we should sort whatever problem he had with me outside. Emma had seen the row and had come over to me with her coat. She asked Ray what was going on, and Mario just stared into my face from about a foot away, like a boxer at a pre-fight press conference. I wasn't sure whether he was going to headbutt me or hit me with the bottle. I certainly didn't want to turn my back, because whatever he was going to do, I wanted to at least see it coming.

I said, 'Your call, Mario. If you have a problem with me, let's go and sort it out now.' This was a big gamble – some might think it was a stupid suggestion – but it was too late to take my words back. Mario moved his right hand up his body and I waited to see the bottle flash towards my head, but to my amazement I watched as he put the Peroni bottle on the bar. He then wiped his runny nose with his right hand. He straightened up and said, 'You've got some bottle, Joe, but I don't want to fall out with you.' He then held out his hand to shake. I paused for a moment, as all I could think about was the fact he'd just wiped his hand across his runny nose, but I shook it anyway and said, 'I don't want to fall out with you, Mario, but don't ever turn on me like that again.' Maybe I was pushing my luck, but I wanted him to know that I wouldn't stand for him behaving like that.

I turned away and took Emma's arm, and we made our way out of the bar. As the fresh air of the early hours hit me, I realised I'd had a very close shave. Mario was a liability. He was like a bottle of pop – you never knew when he was going to go off.

Ray joined us outside as Emma was ordering a taxi to take us home. He put his arm around me and apologised for Mario's behaviour. I knew that Ray had wanted to help, but I also wanted him to see that I could look after myself. I told

Ray to be careful, because some poor bastard would bear the brunt of Mario tonight and I didn't want it to be him. He laughed at me and said that he'd thought I had a death wish when I suggested taking it outside. I pulled him in close and hugged him as I said, 'Ray, there was nobody more relieved than me when he decided not to.'

Thirty-seven

It was a beautiful May morning and the sun was bouncing off the perfectly still lake; there were a number of tents dotted around the edge. I could see that the fishermen had camped out overnight and were now grateful for the warmth of the morning sun.

I was sat on an uneven picnic table with Freddie, who had just brought me my first cup of tea of the day. I loved this lakeside café – the area was the perfect place for families to enjoy a walk, for twitchers to spot rare birds, and for court-ing couples to walk hand in hand. There were often couples who arrived separately in two cars and subtly looked around the car park before embracing each other, knowing that these were snatched moments before they returned to the reality of their respective spouses. This was a place most people went as a treat for breakfast or lunch, to take in the glorious view and enjoy a summer moment.

I came here because grown men could have adult conversations without fear of being overheard. These were discreet conversations about badness, about deals involving drugs and money and guns and girls. In all the time I had been meeting Ray here, he had never commented on the view or the peacefulness of the lake or the beauty of the migrating birds that fed on the banks. He had been focused on topics that would make him money.

He had called me late the previous evening to say that he wanted a chat. I knew that normally meant there was a problem; it would be something he needed help with. I sat there looking out at the lake enjoying the tranquillity; I stared through my sunglasses and saw one of the fishermen gently removing a fish from his line. I noticed how he stroked the fish, and how he calmly held it in his hand before allowing it to slowly swim away.

Ray didn't like Freddie. He thought he was a recovering heroin addict and a thief; he looked down on him and didn't treat him with any respect. Freddie was aware of this and he used to do his best to keep out of his way.

I could see the smile on Freddie's face drop as Ray screeched into the car park. The serenity of the lakeside was ruined by the exertion of his brakes and the huge cloud of dust that resulted from his arrival. I watched the dust slowly follow the gentle breeze over the lake. The moment of peace had been violated, and Ray was oblivious to this fact.

As he walked up to our table, Freddie grabbed his poly-styrene cup and slowly shuffled off towards the lake. Ray pointed a finger at Freddie and said, 'What's he doing here?' I told him that we had something to do after, and for him not to worry. He looked at me, and said in disgust, 'How can you graft with him – he'd thieve off his own granny, he's worse than a pikey.'

'Go and get yourself a cappuccino and have some choco-late powder as a treat and calm down.'

Ray walked back with a huge grin on his face and started to giggle. His smile was infectious, and he sat down and handed me a cherry flapjack under the table. 'I couldn't help meself. She took me money for the coffee and I had to take two of these.' He was still smiling as he took the first bite out of his flapjack, which was coated in white chocolate. I won-dered for a minute what possessed a baker to cover a flapjack in chocolate, it didn't feel right to me. Ray was still laughing with his mouth full when he said, 'Funny, innit – I always think things taste nicer when they're free.' He spat a piece of oat out of the side of his mouth and it landed in the froth of his cappuccino.

I chuckled to myself. I had read the sell-by date, which had been two months previous. I was sure the two sweet ladies serv-ing in the café might also be having a little chuckle to them-selves. I looked at Ray. 'You're right, Ray. It tastes sweeter when it's chored.' I handed him my cherry one and said, 'You have that for later. I've just eaten.'

He washed the contents of his mouth down with a swig of coffee, but the heat of the coffee clearly caught him by surprise. He tried not to show it, but his eyes began to water slightly.

'What's up, Ray? Why did you want a meet?'

'We have some gear that we need to back, but it's not straightforward.' He paused. 'Someone will have to plug it.' I looked at him in disbelief. There was no way I was going to put anything up my backside for Ray, or anyone else.

I leant across the table and said quietly, 'And why have you come to me?' He said that he thought I might know someone who would plug it for a day's wages and return it to where it had to go.

I shook my head. 'I take it you're winding me up, Ray.' He told me that he'd got this gear from a firm in East London, and they wanted it back as the gear wasn't right, but it wasn't a matter of returning it with anyone. The police were paying particular attention to this firm, so whoever returned it must be able to stand a full Old Bill search. The only way that you could achieve it would be to plug it.

I looked at him and said, 'How much are we talking, Ray?' He said there were four and half ounces. I winced. 'That seems a lot of gear to stick up your arse, Ray.'

I saw his eyes look out towards the lake, where Freddie was stood at the water's edge engrossed in a conversation with someone fishing. It were like a light bulb had lit up in his head; a big smile broke out across his face and I could see the distinctive gaps in his front teeth. I could read him like a book.

He shouted, 'Freddie, come here a minute.' I knew exactly where this was going, and I thought I would have a bit of sport letting Ray ask the question.

Freddie couldn't have walked any slower over to our table. I could see him looking at me, hoping I would give him a clue as to why he had been called over. I was intrigued as to how Ray would approach the inevitable request. Ray put his arm around Freddie, and complimented him on how well he was looking. He pulled the cherry flapjack out of his trouser pocket – I could see that one end of the wrapper had split open and there was a chunk of red cherry in the end – and offered it to Freddie. He had it held out in front of him, flat on the palm of his right hand. Freddie looked at it in bewilderment and declined.

Ray asked him how well he knew East London. Freddie told him he knew it well and had pals that lived Walthamstow way. Freddie was constantly trying to catch my eye to gauge what was going on, but my full attention was now focused on how Ray was going to ask Freddie if he fancied putting four and half ounces of heroin up his arse and driving it to East London.

Ray didn't dance around the houses, he went straight for the jugular: 'How much gear could you get up your arse, Freddie?'

I noticed that a family of four sat on the table next to us had just been served a full traditional English breakfast each. The waitress was asking them if they wanted any sauces. There was a request for both ketchup and brown sauce.

The contrast of the two different worlds on two different tables was not lost on me. Freddie pulled away from Ray and said, 'Are you two on a wind-up? Thanks for the offer, but the days of me plugging things up my Harris have long gone.

Now both of you leave me alone.' I started to laugh and said, 'Don't say you weren't offered.' Freddie walked with purpose back to the lake, looking over his shoulder and shaking his head.

'Fuck it, I knew this would happen. I'll have to do it,' said Ray. We started walking towards the car park, but he was walking as if the four and half ounces were already secreted inside him. He stopped and looked at me. 'I haven't plugged anything up since I took a load of pills over to Ibiza.' You could see the trepidation and angst etched across his face. He bent his knees and squatted down in front of me and said, 'I hoped I'd never have to do this again. Mind you, if people can smuggle a mobile up their arse this will be a doddle.' I could see he was trying to convince himself.

We got to my car and I noticed Freddie looking over, wondering what the hell the two of us were talking about. Ray looked at me. 'I need a plastic bag and a load of Vaseline.' He really was going to go through with this.

I said, 'It may make your eyes water, Ray, but at least you'll save a day's wages.' I told him I had a few plastic bags in the boot, but he said he already had some sandwich bags in his car. I was chuckling to myself; Ray was going to suffer a couple of hours of pain, but I wanted to make sure I got the most out of this situation.

He came back holding a clean sandwich bag between the thumb and forefinger of his right hand. I looked at him and said, 'I haven't got Vaseline but you can use my Molton Brown hand cream. It's expensive but very soft on the hands, I'm sure it'll do the trick on your arse and you'll smell lovely as well.'

I handed Ray the tube that I always kept in my car. I'd never envisaged that it would be required for such a sensitive application. Ray thanked me. Then he walked to his car, removed something from the boot and slowly disappeared into the café. I knew that his destination was the Gents.

I beckoned Freddie, and he bounced over quickly, knowing that Ray wasn't there. 'What the fuck was all that about?' I explained that Ray was currently trying to secrete four and half ounces of brown up his bum. He needed to back it to a firm in East London. I would never have let Freddie do that, but I *was* now going to volunteer Freddie to drive him there so we could find out exactly where the drugs were going. This would also allow Freddie to build up a better relationship with Ray.

Freddie looked at me and told me that he'd been hoping I had a plan, because for a few minutes he'd thought I'd agreed for him to plug the gear. He'd thought I'd lost the plot, but now he understood where I was coming from.

I told him that I'd call him over when Ray came back and tell him to drive him. Freddie nodded and walked back to the lake.

It was a good ten minutes before Ray walked back towards his car. I could see how gingerly he was taking each step, so I saved him a few strides and walked over to him. 'I won't ask you how it is, but I'm going to get Freddie to drive you in case you get into a situation and have to deposit in a hurry. You don't need to pay him, he's on wages with me today, but you owe me one.' I called Freddie over and explained the situation.

Undercover

I opened the passenger door of Ray's car and watched him lower himself, ever so gently, onto the leather seats. He remained still whilst Freddie got in the driver's seat, then slowly put his seat belt on. This would be a long two hours for Ray. I told Freddie to call me if there was any aggravation and I'd see them both at the office later for a drink.

Just as Freddie was about to pull away, I shouted at Ray and the car stopped. Ray put the passenger window down and I said, 'Oi, you cheeky fucker . . . where's my Molton Brown?' He opened the console in between the two front seats and passed me the hand cream. I looked at the remaining contents and then looked at Ray and said, 'That was an expensive operation – half my cream is up your backside.' Ray's window went down without him replying, and the car disappeared out of the car park the same way it had arrived, in a cloud of dust.

Thirty-eight

Ray and I met up again at the posh garden centre. I wasn't sure whether Ray had anything to talk about or he just wanted to come back for a coffee and some cake. Again, we sat as far away from everyone as we possibly could and enjoyed the extensive views across the river. Ray had gambled on a slice of carrot cake and a cappuccino, and I had my usual latte.

Ray did indeed have two reasons for meeting today. As he sipped his coffee, he casually said that Mario could get hold of MAC-10 machine pistols with 9mm magazines. He called them 'rainmacs' and we spoke openly about the prices, with or without ammunition. The MAC-10 was a killing machine: it was an incredibly compact gun designed for close encounters and concealed carrying.

As we were talking about this lethal weapon, we both found ourselves a little too focused on a butcher who was walking towards us. When he was about five feet away from us, I said to Ray that I recognised him. I called out to him and said, 'We've both been looking at you and we know you from somewhere.'

He looked at us and said, 'Do you watch *Come Dine with Me*?' At that moment, both Ray and I remembered him from the TV series – he was a posh butcher who lived in a thatched house. It seemed remarkable that there we were, casually chatting about buying a weapon designed for only one reason: to kill people. Yet at the same time we were talking about a daytime TV programme that normal folk watched in the comfort of their homes.

We finished discussing the rainmacs and I told Ray to let Mario know that if he could definitely get hold of one I'd be interested, but that I didn't want to mess about meeting different people. If Mario had it in his lap, then I would take it off his hands. I told him I wouldn't hold my breath, however, as over the years I'd been promised lots of boxed, unused guns by baddies, but they rarely seemed to materialise.

Ray went on to explain that there was more gear available from Dazza, over in Essex. Dazza was keen to step it up with us, and there was a kilo of coke on offer if we wanted it. I told him that I'd take half a K, but that I wasn't 100 per cent sure about Dazza.

Ray said that he'd make some calls and try to sort a trade out for the Thursday of that week. I was always aware that Ray had an ulterior motive; he was always feathering his nest on the back of one of my trades. I was yet to find out what his angle was on this trade.

We finished our coffees, and Ray said that he was waiting for a call back on the price for a half-kilo. Ray then changed the subject and told me that Chloe really fancied our house when Emma and I found somewhere to buy ourselves. He said that she'd been badgering him to help Emma in her search for a house. He had a mate who was a developer, and this bloke had a number of executive houses that were due for release soon, but he would let us have first choice on them before they were released on general sale. Ray said that he had booked a couple of viewings for Saturday, and he thought he would be able to have a chat with his mate about prices. He gave me some literature on the viewings, and said that he would go with Emma on Saturday and introduce her to his pal. I thanked him and said that Emma would love that.

We parted company, and Ray said that he'd ring me later when he had a price for the half, and he'd have a chat with Mario about the rainmacs.

I went home and had supper with Emma. She cooked her famous sausage pasta, and it was ram-packed with flavour as usual. She had also made a perfect Victoria sponge and gave me a huge slice. What talents Emma lacked in delivering a main course, she certainly made up for with her desserts. She was a dab hand at making delicious cakes and wouldn't have been amiss on *The Great British Bake Off*. If I took the mickey out of her cooking, I reversed this with the amount of compliments I bestowed on her for her baking.

Undercover

Ray rang whilst I had a mouthful of sponge, but I listened enough to agree to meet him for a quick chat down the office. Emma said she didn't mind and offered to drop me off, but I said that I wanted the car as an excuse not to drink. I had a quick brush of my railings, and grabbed my jacket before jumping in the car.

Ray was already sat at our corner table, and he had two of our favourite drinks in front of him. I thanked him as we toasted being millionaires this time next year. He said that Mario was all over the rainmacs, but I just raised my eyebrows in disbelief. He told me that the half-K was on for Thursday. He said Dazza wanted £17,500 for the half and that we would have to go over to their manor to get the gear.

I said I was going to take Freddie with me on this trade because I was a little bit windy about Dazza. Ray replied that he was coming with us, as he needed a chat with Dazza about something else. We agreed that we would take two motors up on Thursday. Freddie could bring the gear away so that Ray and I had nothing in the car.

I told Ray he wouldn't see me tomorrow, as I would have to get the paperwork together. We agreed that I'd ring him when I'd sorted the paperwork and I'd pick him up on Thursday at 1 p.m. I finished my drink, and much to the disgust of Ray told him I was going home. I could sense he fancied a proper drink, but I bailed out before it could get underway.

The following day I met up with Freddie, who had been making great inroads into a number of dealers in the area. I asked him if he'd come to Essex with me and Ray the following day to buy a half-kilo of coke. His little face lit up and he joked that he better come along otherwise I'd only fuck it up, and I'd probably get scared without him. I laughed and told him that's exactly why I'd asked him, so that he could keep an eye on me.

I then explained what I wanted to happen. He'd be travelling in his motor alone, and I'd have the money in my car with Ray. I wanted him to check the gear was OK before I brought the paperwork in and we did the exchange. I stressed he was only to call me in once he was happy with the gear. I told him my reservations about Dazza, explaining that I couldn't put my finger on what it was, but I had a feeling that he was a messer. Freddie was a good pair of hands, and I was glad that we were working together. And I knew that his relationship with Ray had been on a different level since he had chauffeured him to East London to safely return the four and half ounces of brown.

I met up with Dave the following morning and listened to him moaning about the hard work and paperwork that he'd had to complete to get my money. I empathised with him and acknowledged that he had the difficult job of keeping the bosses happy and ensuring all the protocols were being followed. I counted the money out with Dave and joked that it was a thousand pounds short; he didn't see the funny side. He made sure that I signed to the fact that the money was now my responsibility and he wished me good luck. I told him that I hoped to see him later with half a kilo of cocaine.

I knew what was worrying Dave. This was the first time I'd returned to the Essex coast since that long Friday the thirteenth when he didn't think I was coming back.

Undercover

I secreted the money carefully in the car and went to pick Ray up. He was his normal chirpy and bouncy self, and he asked me if Emma had looked at the properties he'd given me the details of. I told him that she really liked a particular one, but of course it just happened to be the most expensive.

I then told him that Emma had seen me in the garden late last night. Ray was aware that I had an 'emergency fund' I kept hidden in the back garden, in case I had to disappear on the hurry-up. I explained that I had been five grand short on the paperwork and that I'd had to make it up from my stash. I said that luckily she hadn't seen me digging, but I'd had to tell her that I thought I'd seen a fox with a puppy in its mouth. He laughed at me, and I said it was the first thing that had come into my head – I knew she didn't like foxes and loved puppies. I said I'd seemed to pull it off and I got the money.

We had arranged for Freddie to meet us nearby so he could follow us. The journey took about an hour and a half, and Ray made and received a number of calls. The plan was to meet Dazza – and a new fella that Ray didn't know – in a pub to have a quick chat. Then the gear would be brought to a gaff they had and we could do the trade there.

At the pub, I told them that I was going nowhere near the gear but I'd brought someone with me to take it away. Dazza seemed more than happy with that and said my fella could leave the money with his people at the gaff when he took the half-kilo away – that way Dazza didn't have to get his hands dirty. The other guy with him was a classic steroid-head; he was juiced up and spent the entire time staring at me with his bulging eyes. Apart from grunting occasionally, he added nothing to the conversation. If he was there to scare me, it certainly hadn't worked.

Freddie waited outside, as I wanted to keep him away from these men. Dazza took a phone call and gave me an address to send my fella to, which was a five-minute drive away. Dazza told Ray to give him a ring when everything was done and we were driving away.

We left Dazza and his ridiculously huge orange friend in the pub. I walked over to Freddie's car and told him what was happening. I gave him the address and told him to ring me if he was happy with the gear, and I'd bring the money in. I said I'd have a look at where the place was and I'd only be a minute away. Freddie was fine with everything and I knew he was more than capable. He did look like he needed a decent meal inside him, but he was happy with the situation.

Ray and I watched him walk up to a door that looked like it was the entrance to a flat above a shop, with a 'To Let' sign outside. I was happy I knew where he was and I saw him disappear inside. I could see that there was a lamp that lit up the first-floor window above the shop, but the grubby net curtains prevented me seeing inside. Ray said he was starving.

I didn't want to look like a couple of detectives on a stake-out, so we drove to a café two minutes from the flat. I grabbed a cup of tea whilst Ray ordered pie and chips. After about fifteen minutes, Freddie texted me to say that the 'thing' was on its way and that he'd ring me in a bit. Ray polished off the last of his chips, then wiped the remaining ketchup off his plate with a triangle of badly buttered white bread and squashed it into his mouth. My phone rang and it was Freddie. All he said was: 'You know where I am, you better come over.'

I could tell from his voice that something wasn't right. I paid for the food and we quickly jumped in the motor and drove round the corner. I told Ray that Freddie wanted me to pop in and see him. He asked if everything was OK, and I said I'd tell him in five minutes. I left the car running and asked Ray to wait for me to get back.

The door was on its latch, and as I pushed it open as far as possible I could see a long corridor that was completely covered in letters, newspapers, and anything else that had been posted through the letterbox. It was clear that this place hadn't been lived in for many years.

The front door only just opened wide enough for me to squeeze through. As I climbed up the carpetless stairs, I could hear voices above me. I pushed open the door upstairs to find two large men and Freddie crowded into a tiny room. I looked around and took in the mess that must have taken years to create. There were piles and piles of newspapers stacked up, and the only light was from a battered standard lamp that flickered in the corner of the room. The smell of damp and cat urine hung in the air. Freddie was sitting on the only surface that was devoid of plastic bags or newspapers, which appeared to be a quarter of a square oak dining table. I could see that he had his Nike drawstring bag on the table in front of him.

I looked at one of the men, who was hovering at the adjoining kitchen door, and I could see that two of the rings on the filthy gas stove were lit to provide heat. I looked at the second man, who was propped up on top of a pile of newspapers in the corner of the room. He held his hand out to shake but I ignored it. 'Nice place, boys,' was all I said.

I tapped Freddie on the shoulder and asked him what was happening. He looked at me and said that the parcel was two ounces light and that we were waiting for the remaining gear to arrive. The one who was sat down called over and said that he didn't know how it had happened but that it was on its way. I looked at him and said, 'Which one of you two is in charge here?' There was a short debate between the two before I interrupted: 'One of you better get on the blower now and tell whoever is bringing the gear that if they ain't here in fifteen minutes, we're gone.' I looked at Freddie and told him either to walk out in fifteen minutes or to ring me when he was happy that the gear was right. I rubbed the top of his head and told him that however much I'd like to stay and chat, I'd be waiting for his call.

I went back to the car and told Ray what had happened. I knew that someone was trying to rip us off. They hadn't banked on Freddie doing his job properly and had hoped that we wouldn't find out that it was light until we got home. Ray got straight on the phone to Dazza and told him that he had better sort the problem out or it would be the last bit of business he ever did with us. It was clear from Dazza's reaction that he knew of the problem and had chanced his luck at trying to have us over with a light parcel. If we hadn't discovered it at the time, he would have denied all knowledge and blamed the two muppets in the flat or Freddie.

I could hear him apologising to Ray, and he said that the gear should be with us any minute. About ten minutes later, Freddie rang me and said that he now had the half-kilo. I couldn't face going back into the flat and told him to walk out with the gear with Dumb and Dumber, and I'd give them the money by Freddie's motor. After a few minutes, Freddie and both of the men came out the door and walked to his car. I got the money from the boot and joined them, and as Freddie got into the driver's seat I threw the bag to the bigger of the two men. I told them that, unlike them, I'd made sure every penny was in the bag. I wasn't going to wait around for them to count it.

I leant into the car and thanked Freddie, and I told him that I'd see him later as I was going to take Ray back. Freddie drove off as the two men disappeared back into the flat, carrying the bag of money. I knew in my mind that Dazza had tried to pull my pants down and have me over, but thanks to Freddie he hadn't.

On the drive back, I told Ray that I didn't like dealing with people like Dazza and I wouldn't do another trade with him. Ray agreed with me and said he actually knew the fella who controlled the gear, the man at the top. He said that they had been in prison together in the past. It was awkward because Dazza knew that Ray knew the man, but Dazza would lose money if Ray dealt directly with this fella.

Ray said that he knew roughly where the guy lived and the exact car that he drove. If he could bump into the guy, all our problems could be solved as he was a top fella. Ray suggested that when we had a spare afternoon, we should go to the area and find the guy, his car or his house, and take it from there.

Dazza rang just as the two of us hatched this plan and he apologised profusely to Ray. He wanted to speak to me, but I told Ray that I had nothing to say to him. Dazza knew that he taken a gamble, but today it hadn't paid off.

Thirty-nine

As my relationship with Ray grew stronger and Emma and I spent more and more time in his and Chloe's company, we became very close. He was still taking more cocaine than he should have and it was at those times that he made the wrong decisions in respect to his unfaithfulness. But he loved Chloe very much, and his devotion to his family and in particular his young son was unquestionable.

I'm sure he considered me a close friend and I really enjoyed his company. The four of us would socialise regularly and it all seemed so natural. One evening when we were out to dinner, I watched his face light up like a schoolboy and he started kicking me under the table. Emma was explaining to Chloe that she had caught me in the middle of the night out in the garden. Emma said she'd thought it strange at first, but it turned out to be sweet as I'd been trying to rescue a puppy from the jaws of a fox.

Emma was doing everything right in the subtle way she fed things into conversations. She had confided in Chloe that she was pleased with the way I was behaving now that I was away from all the bad influences in London. She said that it felt like I was on the straight and narrow and that I wanted to settle down with her. Emma had been with Ray to view houses, and had even taken a tape measure to a second viewing to see if 'our' furniture fitted.

All these things added to the idea that the two of us were staying in the area, and helped put the doubt that Ray had once had about me to the back of his mind. I knew that Ray was completely comfortable with me. I'd bought guns, cocaine, heroin and MDMA with him. I turned down offers of skunk and amphetamines and had refused to meet many other criminals that he'd tried to introduce me to. I'd discussed money laundering, weapons supply, and every possible type of criminality you could imagine. I'd helped him back multiple kilos of base amphetamine. I knew that he trusted me implicitly.

Ray had implied on many occasions that it was only a matter of time before I would meet his mate Frank, the ex-copper, but I had done my best to put him off this idea as it made me uncomfortable. However, Ray thought that the fact I'd not been happy with Dazza opened the door for Frank and me to meet. He explained that Frank could get hold of good-quality gear and that he trusted him, and also he was right on our doorstep and we didn't need to travel. I told Ray I would think about it, and I was only doing that because Ray trusted him.

I had many meetings with Dave and the team about Frank, and what was the best way forwards. There were many things to consider. It could be the case that Frank would try and test me, or even set me up. We knew that he still had contacts in the police, and you could never be 100 per cent sure that there had not been a leak, innocent or otherwise. It was of the utmost importance that we should try our best to assess what threat – if any – he was, and whether he was actually involved in any criminality. At present, all I had was what Ray was telling me.

I came up with a plan that I would tell Ray that I was four and half ounces short on a parcel that I had promised someone else, and I needed to find that amount before I traded with them at the weekend. I thought it was a good starting amount – not over the top – and the story made sense. I knew the timing was right, and I kept my fingers crossed that Ray would suggest Frank. I laid this out for Ray in a very matter of fact way as we were having a coffee at the Spanish café. He jumped all over it, and the first thing that came out of his mouth was Frank's name. He said that he'd go and speak with him face to face and then let me know. I didn't show any enthusiasm, I just asked that he let me know by lunchtime, otherwise I'd sort it out in town myself.

After speaking with him, Ray told me that Frank was willing to trade with me but, like me, was apprehensive about meeting. The first trade was agreed for the four and half ounces of cocaine. The agreement was that Ray would travel with me to a retail park. Frank would park in a separate part of the car park to us, and Ray would take my money to Frank's car and exchange the money for drugs. He would then return to my car. It's fair to say that I was very laid-back about this trade as I thought we should do it on Frank's terms. I thought that if it went well and we all walked away, it would be the first of many transactions and, if necessary, I could be more vociferous in my demands on future trades.

I'd actually seen Frank once before, but only briefly, by chance, when I was with Ray at a garage forecourt. Frank had pulled up to fill his car with petrol as we drove off. We'd nodded at each other, but no more than that.

On the day of the trade, I had the money in the boot of my car. Ray directed me to park at one end of the car park, as he had spotted Frank's car at the opposite end. I casually got out of the car and retrieved the money from the boot, taking my time. I looked over and saw somebody sat in the driver's seat of Frank's car. It was too far away to see exactly who it was, but it was definitely his car. I got back into the driver's seat and handed Ray the money. He told me to wait for him and I watched him walk across the car park and get into the passenger seat of Frank's car. I just relaxed and waited for him to come back. I was supremely confident in my head that if this transaction passed problem-free, Frank and myself would be doing regular criminal business in the future. I made no attempt to get closer and lay eyes on Frank, nor to insist that I take part in the trade. I wanted to make out that four and half ounces of cocaine was only a small trade that I wasn't overly bothered by.

Ray came back with a brown envelope and he said that the gear was inside. I took it off him and put it in the boot. Ray said that Frank was happy that we'd got this first one out of the way, and maybe now we could relax a bit. He also said that Frank would be out on Friday night and that he and I could have a chat and get to know each other a little better. I told Ray that I was willing to give anything a go.

I dropped Ray off and then went to meet Dave and the team. They were all very excited about the purchase. This was a fantastic opportunity to obtain some concrete evidence against Frank. I presumed the team had been busy themselves this afternoon, videoing the transaction or keeping Frank under surveillance. But I could see the mood change when I asked if the team had experienced any problems or issues with Frank that afternoon. Dave's shoulders slumped as he explained that I'd been on my own out there this afternoon. The bosses had been so paranoid about a compromise that they had insisted there was no coverage whatsoever, and they'd relied totally on me.

I was less than impressed. The times I didn't want a surveillance team, they insisted on having one, even if it potentially put my life in danger. When it would have been hugely beneficial to have one – to evidence Frank's movements prior to and during the meeting with Ray, and afterwards to track the movement of the money – they didn't bother. I really couldn't understand their thought process.

I looked at Dave and said, 'Let's keep our fingers crossed that there are future trades with Frank, because the evidence isn't fantastic on that one.' Dave just shrugged his shoulders.

I knew it wasn't his fault, but I needed to vent my frustrations to someone. Dave then confided to me that a decision had been made that it was far too risky to deploy the local surveillance team against Frank again. It would be a matter of trying to beg, borrow or steal a surveillance team from another force if we needed one in the future.

I left the team feeling a little bit deflated, but I wasn't going to dwell on it. I met up with Emma and we went out to our favourite Chinese restaurant. We enjoyed a few drinks together as she filled me in on her day. She said she never really stopped in the shop, and she was fed up with the sound of the bell chiming, which meant that she had another customer. She did impressions of the young white men who came into the shop and did their very best to talk like Yardie gangsters whilst they sold her their ill-gotten gains. She was more than a measure for these thieves, and never allowed them to walk all over her.

I explained the situation with Frank and told her that he would be out on Friday night so she would have to be aware of him. Emma insisted that if we were together she wasn't in any way concerned. As we finished our meal and drinks, I realised that it had been exactly what I needed to deal with the stresses of the day.

On Friday, Emma and I met up with Ray and Chloe at a quiet pub in town before we went on to the main bar where everyone would be. Ray had phoned me the day after the trade and told me that Frank was pleased with the way that things had gone and he would catch up with me for a chat at the bar.

Undercover

The pub was full of locals, and our attendance caused quite a stir, particularly as Ray had parked his car in the tiny car park at the rear. I asked the middle-aged barman for a bottle of champagne and four glasses. I noticed that he had extremely lank and greasy hair and tried to be polite. He took a bottle of Moët off the shelf behind him. It looked like it had been there for a year or two. He looked at me and said, 'Would you like it chilled?'

I was a little bemused by the question and thought I'd throw it back in his court. 'Rather than what?' He certainly wasn't expecting that and he didn't answer, so I continued: 'If you mean rather than drinking it lukewarm, then yes I certainly do want it chilled, very much so.'

In a broad local twang, he said, 'We don't have much call for champagne in these parts.' We felt like all eyes in the pub were on us, and I had now made that situation even worse by ordering champagne. Still, we managed to have a laugh about it and I convinced Ray to move his car, as the locals knew it was his motor and I didn't trust them not to scratch it. After finishing our drinks, we all got into Ray's car. He drove us as close to the second bar as he could and then parked his motor there for the night.

The bar was mobbed, and as we made our way through the crowd I saw that Mario and his gorgeous girlfriend were there. I had already had numerous apologies from Mario for his behaviour last time we'd had a night out, but he still insisted on telling me every time I saw him – and tonight was no different.

We all decided that the easiest way to get drinks tonight was to buy bottles of champagne, and Ray said that he knew the manager so he would negotiate a deal. He came back to me and seemed to have sorted a generous discount on the bubbles if we bought six bottles. I was sure that amongst us all that would not be an issue.. Ray then shyly whispered to me that it was a little embarrassing, but he only had a bullseye on him. He asked if I could sub him £200 until Monday. I gave him the cash discreetly so no one saw. He was very grateful, and promised that he would have it with me first thing Monday morning.

It was really difficult to hear what anyone was saying and we were shoulder to shoulder. As we were spending a lot of money, the bar manager gave us a space at the corner of the bar, much to the disgust of other customers. It wasn't long before Ray brought Frank over; we shook hands and I thanked him for helping me out a couple of days before. I told him that the four and half had filled a gap for me and he'd done me a favour. He said it was no problem and told me that Ray spoke highly of me. Our conversation skirted around any specific details of the previous trade, though it was enough to confirm that he had supplied the cocaine. But the main purpose of the evening was to settle Frank down and make sure that we were both happy to conduct criminal business in the future.

I was happy with our chat and could see that he was comfortable with me. I didn't feel the need to stay in his company any longer than was necessary, so I politely mingled with other people. Ray had a beam that was bigger than ever on his face when he came over. 'I told you that he was OK – I knew you two would get on.'

Emma and I had a few more drinks, but we had achieved what we needed to and I didn't want to prolong our stay. I had a quick word with Ray before Emma and I quietly slipped out of the bar and into a taxi home. It was late by the time my head hit the pillow and I was asleep before I knew it.

I woke very early the next day, and popped out to grab the Saturday paper and some breakfast. I knew that I wouldn't get any notable conversation or enthusiasm from Emma until she had finished her first cup of black coffee, which she had to drink from her bone china cup and saucer, so I left her upstairs to finish that whilst I read the back pages of the paper and enjoyed the weekend peace. I then spoke with Dave on the phone, and filled him in on my encounter with Frank. He was more than happy with the outcome and felt that it was a step in the right direction. The next step was going to be a very important one, and Frank and Ray played an integral role.

I had put Dave in contact with my boss, who had released me to work on this operation, to try and arrange some help with surveillance so that Frank wouldn't recognise the team that was following him. Dave had arranged this, and their services were utilised on a day when Ray was doing some business with Frank.

Ray had phoned me to ask if he could borrow a 'bag of nails' (set of scales) from me, as somebody had not returned his. He told me that he was going to collect a set off Frank, who had hidden them somewhere, and the two of them were due to meet. Later that day, Ray said that he needed to see me; he had met up with Frank, who had spotted a particular car that morning on the way to meeting Ray. Frank had no doubt that it was a surveillance car, and was 'downing tools' as he didn't want to risk trading any more. He was shutting up shop as he thought the heat was on him.

To any criminal this was sensible behaviour – standard practice – but it certainly didn't help my situation and it was a major blow to Dave and the team; they had not had any luck with this side of the investigation. But the fact was, you had to play with the cards you'd been dealt. I would continue my day-to-day activities with Ray, and bide my time until another opportunity came up with Frank. I knew that the overall investigation had been a huge success, and Emma had made huge inroads into local acquisitive crime. She had purchased the majority of stolen property in the area and gained first-class evidence against burglars, robbers and thieves. She couldn't have done any more. Meanwhile, I had identified many multi-kilo, class A drug dealers from the area and had bought considerable amounts of powder from them.

The job was coming to a natural conclusion, and Dave had told me that the bosses were more than pleased with what had been achieved. However, to me, Frank was unfinished business. If I'd known that I only had one opportunity with him, I would have conducted the trade myself.

Undercover

Hindsight is a wonderful thing, but perhaps I should have seized the moment. Because he was ex–Old Bill, I had acted completely differently than if he'd just been another dealer. Perhaps that had been a huge mistake. I would have to wait and see.

Forty

I was making a rare visit back to the small and dingy room at the police headquarters that acted as the official office for the special operations unit. I very rarely attended unless I really had to. It was normally only if I had a specific task to complete or a meeting that needed to take place on police premises. As usual, I snuck up the back stairs and quietly let myself into the key-code security door. I was relieved to find there was no one there, which meant I could get done what I needed to do, and disappear as quickly as possible.

There were four desks in the room, and each of them had a rack of grey plastic trays neatly placed on the corner. There was a whiteboard on the wall, with exactly the same writing on as the last time I'd visited. The most attractive feature of the office was the original set of sash windows, which allowed a draft to naturally cool the room. There was no evidence of me belonging here; you would not find my name anywhere.

I eventually remembered my log-in details for the police computer. I found computers tedious; I could only type with one finger, and my ignorant technical mind had hoped that computers would never catch on. I could think of nothing worse than having a job where you had to look at a computer screen for eight hours. But for the next hour, I had no choice.

As I sat there smashing the keyboard with the middle finger of my right hand, the phone on the desk in front of me rang. Without really thinking, I picked it up. Unfortunately, I never answered the telephone in the corporate way, by identifying who I was and asking how I could help. Instead it was the standard hello.

The voice on the other end paused and said, 'Hello, Joe, we know it's you.' The caller then hung up. The voice was that of a male from the south-east, I would guess aged between thirty and fifty and probably white. There had been no threat in the voice, but someone was making it clear that they knew I was Joe and they knew I worked from the special operations office.

I had always been acutely aware that the greatest threat to my safety and that of my family was from within. I knew from experience that loyalty from colleagues was thin on the ground these days, and I trusted no one. For someone to know that I was in that office, at that particular time, it was either the biggest miracle in the world or something much more sinister.

Whatever the truth was, I knew that I was not going to tell a single person about this. I was going to keep my cards close to my chest. The one thing I did know was that I had to be even more vigilant in what I did and who I told.

I left the office within minutes of receiving the call and slipped quietly down the back stairs, wishing that I'd never made the visit in the first place. Undercover work was often a very lonely existence, but now I knew that I was completely on my own.

Forty-one

I sat in the coffee shop just off the bustle of Victoria Street, sipping my latte with the statutory extra shot. I was wearing a flat cap and sunglasses, and had positioned myself at a corner table with my back to the wall, ensuring that I could see every face that entered to buy their morning hit of caffeine or their pain au chocolate. It was still only 8.15, and at 10.30 I was due to meet Pino for the first time. We had been talking on the phone for a number of weeks now, though – what with one thing and another – we hadn't had a face-to-face meeting yet. But Pino had promised me the world on the phone, in his broken English that was easy to understand even with his strong Colombian accent.

I was there early because I was waiting for Big Tel to come and bring me some money for today's meeting. Tel had asked me to do this piece of work, and was acting as my cover officer whilst I was deployed. A big man, both in stature and in personality, he was one of the good guys. He was a real character, who could tell a story and hold your attention. And he was someone that people naturally warmed to. These were all skills you couldn't teach, qualities you wouldn't get from a textbook – and in the undercover world, these talents were like gold dust.

As I was chuckling to myself about one of the incidents that had happened last time I saw Tel, the door of the café was swung open with such gusto that it hit the chair of a young female commuter. She was sat eating her granola and yogurt, wearing gleaming Nike trainers with her black pencil skirt and crisp white Ralph Lauren blouse. She was startled, and she received an apology from the overenthusiastic customer. I had to do a double take but I recognised him as one of my old team. It was Northern Dave, a really lovely kid who I hadn't seen for about five years. Last I'd heard, he had left the UC world to do some work as a supervisor. It was great to see him, and as usual he had a huge smile on his face.

I eyed him as I held him at arm's length, like a granddad does when he's looking at a relative he hasn't seen for many years. 'Well look at you, Dave, you look great.' And for once I meant it. So often you say those three words when in fact you think the complete opposite – you think they look terrible and life hasn't been kind to them.

Before I could say any more, he pulled out the front of his River Island stretch jeans, and in his broad Manchester accent said, 'I'm Slimming World's biggest loser for the last two months.' He was really proud of his achievement, and in the time we hadn't seen each other I'd probably put on the 'timber' that Dave had lost. This fact wasn't lost on him, and I let him have his five minutes of gloating and baiting. It was really good to see him.

He gave me £2,000, and we nattered and gossiped for well over an hour without realising how quickly time had flown. We hadn't spoken a single word about today's operation. When I looked at my watch, I told him I had better get going. He shook my hand in a formal manner, but I pulled him in for a hug and a squeeze. Dave always liked to have the last word, and before he left he said to me what I had said to him and so many other UCs over the years: 'Whatever you do, don't fuck this up.' We both chuckled like schoolboys, and I watched him disappear amongst the hordes that were scuttling to their offices on Victoria Street.

I paid the bill and started to stroll towards Pimlico, where I was going to meet Pino. It was a lovely day, so I took the back roads near the cathedral and looked at all the mansion apart-ments and beautiful character buildings that made London so unique. I was only minutes from Victoria Station, yet these streets were so peaceful and calming. I wondered to myself what Pino looked like, and pictured in my head a large fifty-year-old man with a monk-type hairstyle, who chain-smoked and would be breathless should he have to ascend a flight of stairs. He would have big hands and deep dark eyes that watched your every move.

My imagination was interrupted by the vibration and shrill sound of my phone ringing. It spoilt the tranquillity of the moment. I glanced at the screen and saw Pino's name. Before I could say hello, he demanded, 'Where are you?'

'I'll be with you in ten minutes. I'll have a latte with an extra shot.' I cut the call off without telling him what he wanted to know. I sensed apprehension in his voice, not the confident manner he had displayed when he'd bragged to me on previous calls, telling me that his cocaine was the best around at the moment, that the supply was regular and that I wouldn't be disappointed.

Over the years, I'd had conversations like this too many times to remember. Men who bigged themselves up in order to lure you into buying their product. It was often the case that they didn't know their product as well as they made out. Sometimes it was a fact that they had bought the gear from someone who had convinced them the quality was high-end, when in fact it was merely 'pub grub'. I'd soon find out whether Pino was full of shit or the real McCoy.

The café was just around the corner from Pimlico tube station and was quite tight for space, although there was a basement with some computer terminals for customers to access the Internet – £1 for ten minutes. At the back of the café, I saw a man sitting with a small espresso cup in front of him; there was another cup and saucer in front of the vacant seat opposite him. I walked over to the clean white Formica table, which had a fresh pink gerbera in a small glass vase sat proudly in the middle. The café was spotless, and there was a tall, skinny, overenthusiastic Eastern European girl busying herself at every opportunity, cleaning the tables with a bright-pink J-cloth. I thought that it was probably her first day or she was determined to keep her job – or maybe she just loved cleaning tables.

I sat opposite the man, held out my hand and said, 'Pino, good to meet you.' We shook hands. Pino was much younger than I had imagined – he was probably thirty years old. His jet-black hair had a natural curl; it was scraped back and hung just above the collar of his denim jacket. He had transition lenses, and they looked dark in the confines of the café.

I waited for him to talk as I broke a corner off a cube of demerara sugar and slowly stirred it into my coffee. I looked up at him as I did this; the clinking of my spoon on the china cup was annoying me, so I knew he would be hoping I stopped. I did, and I sucked the froth off the spoon and placed it on the saucer.

Pino broke the silence by asking me if I had any kids. Not the question I was expecting, but nevertheless I answered him. He said that he had a boy and a girl, and he loved them very much and would do anything for them. We then talked for fifteen minutes or so about his family – about the fact that he had been in London for eight years and they were still back home in Colombia. He spoke warmly about the village he was from and the simple way of life there, so different from his life in London. I purposely waited until he turned the conversation to business. It felt right to let him talk, let him control the tempo of the conversation. I knew he liked to talk, and that certainly suited me.

I studied him for a moment whilst he spoke so freely. He was very dark-skinned and had a slim build – I could see he didn't throw weights around in the gym. He had nicotine-stained fingers, and I could also see three letters tattooed on the inside of his left wrist: 'NFC'. It was a homemade tattoo, the sort Borstal boys or sailors used to have back in the day. He asked me if I smoked as he stood up to go outside. I didn't join him. I hated smoking, and would rather wait and finish my latte whilst he sucked on the Mustang cigarettes he removed from his jacket pocket.

I looked at his shoes as he walked out; I always liked to look at the quality of a man's shoes. He was wearing a traditional black Gucci trainer, with the red band sandwiched by the two green ones. You wouldn't get much change from £350 if you went to New Bond Street to buy them.

I could see him looking at me through the window as he smoked his cigarette and spoke on his mobile phone. Then he threw his cigarette into the street and re-entered the café. He sat back down, and I could smell the smoke from across the table. He looked at me and asked how much I wanted. I had decided before I arrived that I'd ask for two kilos, but I wasn't going to do it today.

I looked at him and waited for the skinny girl to wipe our table and get out of earshot before I replied: 'I tell you what, Pino. I want two units a week – regular, no nonsense, a reliable grown-up relationship – but before I do that, I want to be sure the car drives as well as I hope it does. I want a sample today. Can you get me an ounce, so that I can road test it over the weekend and this time next week we can do the two units.'

He asked why I hadn't said on the phone to bring it with him. I explained that until we'd sat down and chatted and got to know each other I wouldn't do that, but now I was asking him if he could get me an ounce as a sample. He got up and said, 'Give me ten minutes.' He told me it'd be £1,800. Pino then left the café, and I watched him cross the road and get into a green BMW that had another dark male sat in the driver's seat. I noted the registration number and allowed myself a little smirk, knowing that we had a 'job' on now.

About fifteen minutes later, Pino rang me and asked me to come outside the café. I could see him in the BMW's passenger seat, the same driver alongside him. I got into the back of the car behind the driver. The car smelt of a showroom, it had rubber see-through covers on the seats, and the wood veneer gleamed from a recent polish. Pino opened the glovebox and I could see a number of folded Costa coffee napkins and a tube of wet wipes. He took out a knotted, white plastic bag and handed it to me. I was confident that the weight was about right, and the smell of cocaine was pungent so I passed him £1,800 in £20 notes. Pino counted them and put them into his trouser pocket.

I leant forward between the two front seats, apologised to Pino for the inconvenience and thanked him. I said that if I was happy with the 'thing' then we could make arrangements for two units next Thursday. I held out my hand and he shook it firmly. I told him not to phone me Saturday as I was at a family christening but I would ring him Sunday evening. I put the bag in my inside jacket pocket and got out of the car.

I crossed the road, waved down the first 'flounder' I could see and told the cabbie: 'St Thomas' Hospital, please.' I had no intention of going there, but I wanted to ensure Pino and his sidekick weren't following me. Once I had satisfied myself that the two South Americans were nowhere near me, I told the cabbie to pull over. I paid the fare and alighted on a quiet side street just round the corner from Shepherd's restaurant. Then I phoned Roger and told him to come and meet me at The Barley Mow on Horseferry Road. He said to give him ten minutes.

I took a slow stroll, knowing that I'd get there before Roger. I ordered a pint for myself and a lime and soda water for Roger, as he'd said earlier he wasn't drinking. I sat in a quiet corner and read the *Standard* until Roger joined me. I explained what had happened, went through all the intelligence, and passed the knotted bag under the table. He asked me if I thought Pino was for real. I told him that I thought he was capable of two kilos a week, and that the sample was definitely 'off the block'. Roger said he'd have to let me know the quality of the cocaine tomorrow, as he had his weigh-in tonight and didn't want to miss it.

We said our goodbyes and Roger disappeared. I was quietly pleased with my day's work. It made me smile that I was so matter of fact that a Colombian gang had agreed to sell me two kilos of their finest cocaine every week. But I knew that I should really get back to the job I was officially on. Roger and the team were unaware that I was moonlighting in London but – as I was often told – what they didn't know couldn't hurt them. I finished my pint and ordered another, wondering what the remainder of the day would hold for me.

Forty-two

Following a series of meetings amongst senior officers, a decision had been made that the operation Emma and I were on should be brought to a conclusion. It was probably the correct decision for the police force we were working for, but I felt that as an undercover operation we were on the cusp of compromising a number of significant national targets.

This is where the difficulty lay. We were employed by the police force to combat a particular problem. This force had to justify their spending to a police authority (a separate organisation responsible for overseeing the activities of the police force), and also to evidence their reduction in crime figures and the increase in clear-ups of recorded crimes. With that in mind, this operation had more than achieved its targets. So for a parochial senior officer, responsible for only that force, why should he or she be concerned with a drug dealer who is operating on a national basis? That dealer does not directly affect any of the figures that the senior command team's performance is assessed against. Sad as it seems, drug dealers are not on the radar for most senior officers, as they don't impact on their performance indicators.

This was very frustrating because all I'd ever wanted to do was put bad guys behind bars – the badder the better, to my mind. Dave was equally frustrated, but we had both been around the block long enough to know that we were far too low on the food chain to have an influence on the decision.

Emma was gutted that the job was coming to an end. She had put her heart and soul into the operation and had sacrificed many things at home to ensure the job was a success. She also had a huge amount of work to do to make sure that everything was brought to a close professionally. She was meticulous in dealing with the important matters that needed to be tied up before the end of the job.

The senior management team had decided the specific date that the arrests would take place. This involved a planning team, and the assistance of staff from a number of other police forces. The logistical support needed in order to conclude the arrest phase was enormous.

Now that the arrest date was confirmed, Dave asked me to try and work out a way that the main subjects could all be together in the same place the night before. He wanted to be in a position where he could arrest Ray, Mario and Pegg all at the same time, and he asked if I could make that happen. I assured him I would come up with a cunning and devious plan, and to leave it with me. This was one problem that I could take off his hands.

We had about six weeks until the date when the operation was going to close. Ray and I continued our daily activities together, and Emma worked hard in the shop. We had become truly settled in the area. After a year; it felt comfortable and it was a really nice place to live. It was going to be hard for both Emma and me to return to the reality of our own lives. This had been the norm now for such a long time. I had already received phone calls about the possibility of me starting another long-term job once this one had concluded. But I wanted to concentrate on bringing this operation to a successful and professional ending before I let my mind drift on to the next.

Emma and I proposed that we would try and get the three main players and their respective girlfriends to a formal meal. We would make it a special occasion and let them know that we were picking up the tab. We decided to choose somewhere out of town that was quite exclusive – somewhere we knew they would be excited about having dinner at. Emma picked the perfect place: a secluded, red brick manor-house hotel, covered in ivy and steeped in history. The grounds were stunning, and there was a beautiful walled garden, overlooking a lake, where drinks could be served. It was a picture, and if the weather remained as expected it would be a glorious evening. The hotel's dining room was traditional and stylish: wood-panelled walls that dated back centuries; elegant, white linen tablecloths topped by immaculate glassware and gleaming cutlery. It was the perfect place for a special meal.

Emma told Dave what she'd decided and that she planned to ask people to come to ours first for drinks. She thought that Ray and Mario would probably go straight to the hotel, as it was closer to their houses, but Pegg and his girlfriend would probably enjoy a drink at ours and a lift in our car. Emma had suggested that I should leave her speak to the girlfriends and invite the men through them, and she would make out that it was a bit of a surprise for me.

Dave insisted that he would have to visit the restaurant to satisfy himself that it was a suitable place to make a number of arrests safely. Emma and I both knew that meant that Dave would be eating dinner in the restaurant one day this week. Dave also needed to be sure of exactly who was attending. Emma was happy with this, as it was natural to need numbers when one was booking a decent restaurant.

After Dave had eaten at the restaurant and the head of the tactical arrest team had checked it out, Emma was given the green light to make the arrangements. I knew that as soon as Ray was told about the meal, he wouldn't be able to keep it a secret and he would tell me immediately. Sure enough, that's exactly what happened. He also confided to me that Chloe was pregnant and that everything was OK after the first scan. I knew that Chloe had told Emma, but I made out that I hadn't a clue. I congratulated him, but inside I really felt bad. I knew what was coming for Ray – in three weeks he would be going to prison for a very long time.

Undercover

Ray said that he fancied a drink, and asked if we could pop down to the office. I could see the happiness in his face and I wanted to share in that, but I knew that I was being completely two-faced. I really liked Ray – he was a funny, happy, full-of-life character. He had a family and a mortgage and bills to pay, just like everyone else. Only Ray had made the decision to support his family by committing crimes. I didn't have a problem with that – it was his choice, he knew the potential consequences of his actions and he would have to live with them.

However, I understood the reality of those consequences. The fact was, Ray's son or daughter would be born whilst he was in prison. Chloe would have to fend for herself and her life would become unrecognisable overnight. She would struggle to bring up a new baby whilst trying to pay the bills. She was a tough woman, but the challenge that she was soon to meet would break most people. She had done nothing to deserve the pain that was coming her way, and the child that was soon to enter this world would now have a completely different start to their life.

All these things hurt me – they tugged at my heartstrings and they played on my mind. Ray was my pal, and him being in this position was entirely my fault. I was ruining a number of lives just by doing my job well. At that exact moment, I wished I hadn't done a good job, and I wondered if I could somehow tell him, warn him what was coming. But I knew I couldn't and I wouldn't do such a thing. I just had to get on with it, and deal with the emotional fallout, which was considerably less than what Chloe and the kids were going to have to cope with.

I came up with a lame excuse not to go to the pub, and told Ray that I'd meet him the next day and we'd have a proper catch-up then.

My job would have been so much easier if I had no emotions, no heart, no feelings – if I could just say, 'It doesn't bother me, and he got exactly what he deserves.' But the reality of life is very different, and if anyone thinks that they will never be affected by the fallout from relationships that they develop on these types of operations, they're very wrong.

Finding a mechanism to cope with the way I would inevitably feel was essential, but I was yet to find the perfect technique. Perhaps my way was to submerge myself into the next job.

I met Ray for a drink the following day, and as usual he had another dealer that he wanted to introduce me to. He said that he had been put in contact with this fella by chance. He had known him from years back but they had lost contact, and that he trusted him. He said that the fella had 'trainers' that came as a pair, and also some good-quality powder. I laughed at him and said, 'Ray, has anyone ever told you this is really shit gear – everyone just tells you it's good quality.'

The trainers were kilos of amphetamine and were sold in pairs, so you had to buy two kilos at a time. I was aware that the team had enough work to be getting on with, so I told Ray I'd have a think about it. I used the Frank situation to my advantage, saying that I was keeping my head down until the heat blew over. In the back of my mind, I thought it would be a good idea to try and tie up this proposed trade on the evening of our meal.

Emma was up to her eyes in organising our move and shutting the shop. There was also a phenomenal amount of paperwork involved that would be needed in court. Everyone was working flat out to ensure that we were ready for the arrest date. And it was very important to keep up the story that we were settling permanently in the area. We didn't want any alarm bells to ring or for people to think that we were suddenly upping sticks.

There was a lot of pressure on everyone involved at this time. It was the hard, gritty part of the investigation, ensuring that all the 'T's were crossed and the 'I's dotted. But, ultimately, it was Dave's job to ensure that everyone was doing his or her job properly, and that the paperwork was up to the required standard.

The days were passing us by, and Emma and I spent a lot of time sat with the team, trawling through paperwork. If truth be told, neither Emma nor I wanted this job to finish. We understood that it had been a tremendous success, but we both felt that we were in a good position to take it to the next stage and the next tier of criminality. We got on very well and gelled as a team, and we had certainly settled into a routine. There were very few people that I liked deploying with, but it seemed to have worked really well with Emma. This was unusual as I preferred to work on my own. That way I didn't have to rely on anyone's ability except mine. And I didn't have to worry what a colleague was saying in another part of the room or to a separate baddy. I was confident in my own skills, in my personality and my ability to talk to people naturally. I always had a nagging worry in my mind when I was working with someone else.

I had decided that my best mate Don should come to the meal as well. He had met Ray before, and his presence would show some depth to my background. He was one of the few people that I could go anywhere with; he could speak to anyone and I'd never worry about what he was saying. We had known one another so long that everything was completely natural.

I had also managed to arrange a trade with Ray for nine ounces of cocaine on the evening of the meal. I had told him that one of my people was travelling down from Manchester and that he would be at a particular hotel close to the Dirty Dozen at 8 p.m. I said I'd give Ray the fella's number that evening, and he could forward it to his man. The two of them could conduct the transaction whilst we were enjoying a sumptuous feast at the manor house. It was clear that Ray was on an earner again for the introduction on this transaction as he was overly keen to make sure it happened. If he'd had his way, Ray, his fella and me would have done the trade ourselves, then gone on to the meal.

Don and I had a bit of fun with Peter, the UC who was going to buy the nine ounces. Peter was working with Don at the time, and I asked him if he fancied coming and helping on the operation. I ran through the entire job with him and he was really enthusiastic about getting involved. I explained to him that it was the final day of a long operation and that he would be meeting a dealer that Ray had referenced to buy nine ounces of cocaine. I said the only issue was, I'd told Ray to tell the dealer that my fella spoke with a broad Manchester accent and always wore a beanie hat.

The silence on the phone was deafening. Peter came from somewhere hundreds of miles from Manchester, and his accent was anything but Mancunian. I broke the silence by saying that he had a week to perfect the accent and to make sure he went and bought a beanie. I put the phone down before he could ask any further questions. Don later said that whenever he and Peter spoke in the build-up to his deployment, Peter spoke in a Manc accent.

Emma and I sat down with Dave and ran through the plan for the evening. We knew that Pegg and his girlfriend were coming to have drinks at our house and then we would drive them to the hotel. In their minds, they were going to share a cab with us coming home. We were then going to meet Ray and Mario and their girlfriends at the manor house, where Don would join us. Emma had arranged for us to have a few glasses of champagne on the lawn outside, and we were going to sit at the best table in the restaurant. Dave assured us that the team had practised their approach and they would be completely invisible to us until they actually entered the restaurant to make the arrests. Dave anticipated this would take place whilst we were eating our main courses. As Peter would be about fifteen miles away at another hotel conducting the cocaine trade, Dave also had to consider the impact of the arrests and the risk to Peter.

Before we knew it, the day was upon us. It was a beautiful summer morning and the weather was balmy. I was in the kitchen before 7 a.m. and had the espresso pot on the stove. The birds were in full voice in the back garden, and I opened the patio doors and sat on the decking. The sun was warm on my face as I closed my eyes, and at that moment it dawned on me that I had spent my last night in this house. If I'm honest, I felt a little sad – this had been the place I called home and it was going to be hard to leave.

I could smell the aroma of the coffee and I poured a cup for me and one for Emma. I called up to her, and a few minutes later she came down and joined me. She was wrapped in a pretty patchwork quilt and she looked like she was still sleepy. She sat next to me outside on the decking, our backs against the wall. Neither of us said a word to each other for a while as we enjoyed the warmth of the sun. Then Emma looked at me and said, 'You have no idea how much I'm going to miss this place, mister.' She had made this house a home, and she had worked so hard to make this operation a success, and now it was over.

I went to get up, but she stopped me: 'Please, just sit here for a bit longer.' We both sat, comfortable in each other's company, without saying another word.

There were many things to be getting on with during the day. I met with Don and Peter at their hotel. Peter now sounded like one of the Gallagher brothers, and on this warm summer day he sported a beanie hat. Don took me to one side and asked me when I was going to tell Peter that the Mancunian accent was a wind-up. I said that I had no intention whatsoever of telling him, and I thought that he'd practised it for so long that he may as well go through with it.

Undercover

The three of us went over the plan again. Peter knew that he should wait in the bar of the hotel, and Ray would tell me when the fella was on his way. I would give Peter his number and the two could make arrangements to complete the trade. I arranged to meet Don at 7.30 p.m. in the bar of the hotel. I wished Peter good luck and said I'd ring him later, to which he replied in his broadest put-on Manc accent, 'No mither, our kid.' I chuckled to myself as I left the two of them.

I got myself ready for the evening in minutes, and left Emma upstairs to finish. She asked me to put a bottle of fizz in the champagne bucket and fill it with ice, in anticipation of Pegg and his girlfriend Alicia arriving. We'd both made an effort to dress up for the evening. I wore a plain blue suit, with a cream Smedley and Gucci loafers. Emma was wearing a pretty summer dress and a pair of Karen Millen shoes, and she had a shawl over her shoulders. She came into the kitchen and said, 'We don't make a bad couple, do we?' I said that she looked great and I poured her a glass of champagne. I clinked her glass and toasted her success.

It wasn't long before Pegg and Alicia walked up the drive to the back of the house. Alicia had really dressed up for the night, and it looked like she had bought Pegg a brand new shirt to go with the smart pair of jeans and nice shoes he was wearing. He was holding a carrier bag in his hand, and said to me after shaking my hand, 'Give me one of them and put the other five in the fridge, I don't want to have any of your poncy drinks.' He grabbed one of the six tins of Stella he'd brought and then handed me the bag.

I poured Alicia a glass of champagne and we all chatted for about thirty minutes, in which time Pegg polished off another two cans. I locked the doors for the last time and we all climbed into my car. Emma and I had both packed overnight bags, which sat in the boot of the car unbeknown to our two passengers, as we wouldn't be returning to this house ever again.

I looked at Emma as we pulled out of the driveway for the last time, and I could see that her eyes were welling up. Pegg interrupted the awkwardness instantly when he started talking about eating a 'nice bit of grub'. Alicia said that he fancied himself as a bit of a chef and loved it in the kitchen. He was still drinking from his third tin of Stella. Pegg drank almost as much as he smoked skunk and snorted coke. He liked to live life to the full. There was very little to him physically, but he had a reputation as a nutter. I think most of this was down to his harsh upbringing in London and the fact that he was scared of absolutely no one.

We drove for about twenty minutes before we pulled off the main road onto a tree-lined lane. This led the mile or so to the beautiful, old wooden gates that lay open for us. The red brick building was a picture as we left the smoothness of the lane for the noisy gravel of the horseshoe pull-in. I could see that Ray's car was already there and I knew that he was bringing Mario and his girlfriend Sara. Pegg wasted no time in describing it as a 'proper fucking gaff' and said he bet that it had some treasure inside. Alicia linked arms with him and told him to be on his best behaviour and not to embarrass her.

Undercover

We walked through reception and past the restaurant to the bar at the back of the manor. Emma had made the arrangements, and she went and spoke to the maître d'. Ray and Mario were chatting to Don; I kissed Chloe and Sara and gave them each a glass of champagne. I asked them to bring their drinks out through the open doors into the walled garden, where I could see Emma escorting the waiter outside. He had a beautiful champagne bucket with two bottles and a number of flutes in it, which he placed on one of the parasol-covered tables. Ray was so happy his smile was huge. He came over to me, a glass of champagne in his hand, and said, 'We must be doing something right – this is the life.' As always, he wanted to talk business and he said that the fella with the thing had just left and should be with my man in an hour and half. Ray gave me the fella's number and I rang up Peter, who answered in his Manc accent. I gave him the number and asked him to ring me when it was done.

Everyone had dressed up properly. Ray, Mario and Don all wore suits, and the girls had really made an effort and wore dresses. Chloe said she'd been worried about fitting into hers as she was already showing. Everyone was so relaxed, and the surroundings made you feel like you had stopped in time. Pegg had disappeared, and Ray said straight away that he bet he was thieving. Ray said he couldn't help himself, it was in his blood.

We had all had a couple of glasses of champagne when the maître d' came over and told us that our table was ready. As we walked inside, Ray pointed to Pegg coming down the stairs, he winked at me and said, 'I told you.' I called to Pegg and told him we were going through to the restaurant.

The large round table was laid out beautifully; it had clearly taken someone considerable time to set it so elegantly. I sat down with Mario on my right and Ray to my left, then Don and Emma either side of them. Chloe, Alicia, Sara and Pegg, who was next to Don, completed the seating plan. The staff treated us with the utmost respect, even though we were far noisier than any other table of diners and probably very different to the normal clientele. Seated at the closest table to us was an elderly couple who were impeccably dressed. I saw the girls looking over at them with a smile after Emma explained that it was their fiftieth wedding anniversary.

The waiter came over and took our orders for starters and the main course. In my mind I knew we probably wouldn't be eating our main, so I ordered what I considered the biggest starter. This happened to be the braised pig's cheek. I could see Emma making faces at me as if she was going to be sick. There was no way she would even consider eating anything like that.

Mario had ordered a rib-eye steak for his main, and the waiter brought him a huge, wooden-handled steak knife. As soon as the waiter removed one of his knives and placed it to the right of his place mat, I began to worry. Mario picked the knife up and held it by the wooden handle, with the gleaming sharpness of the blade facing up to the ornate ceiling. He only let the knife go to drink from his wine glass, but picked it up as soon as the glass returned to the table.

Undercover

I could feel the pressure building inside me, but I was showing no outward sign of nerves. It was like the feeling when you know you're going to crash on the dodgems or before you're punched in the face in the boxing ring, or when you pull the trigger on a gun knowing that it's going to go bang. Soon, all the hard work and dedication we had put in would be over. This would be the last time we ever sat round a table together, laughing and joking without a care in the world. Tonight would be a defining moment for many people, and a number of lives would change forever. I needed to play my part; there was no backing out now, what was done was done.

Everyone had now eaten their starters, and people were discussing the pros and cons of their respective selections. In a whisper, Ray asked me if I'd heard anything from my man. I said I hadn't, but I knew it wouldn't be long. At that very moment, out of the corner of my eye I saw a large police van stop on the gravel outside one of the windows. I was transfixed as I watched at least ten officers jump out of the van. I could see they were wearing black riot overalls and helmets. I tried to avert my eyes as quickly as I could, but Mario had seen my face and he saw them too. He looked from them to me, as if he was trying to work out why they were there. I wondered whether he could see the guilt in my face, whether my reaction had given something away. He had the steak knife in his hand, and for a split second I thought he was going to sink it deep into my neck.

Then the tranquillity and ambience of this historic room was shattered in an instant. As the police officers stormed in, the noise and intensity was deafening. I watched as Mario began to stand up, but for some unknown reason, he immediately sat back down and released his grip on the knife. I could see the shock on Emma's face – it had caught her by surprise.

Pegg was the only one on our table to resist. Each of us had two officers allocated, and Pegg knocked over the elderly couple's table as his two officers struggled to restrain him. Alicia was shouting for him to calm down, but her words were making him worse. He was calling them 'mug cunts', and for a very slight man he still had the better of two very large police officers. Eventually, four or five officers managed to get him onto the ground. Each of us was handcuffed and we sat at the table looking at each other. Chloe was desperate for the toilet, and being pregnant her need was even greater. They wouldn't allow it, and for some reason this was really bugging me. I shouted at one of them to take her to the toilet, but they were having none of it.

Pegg was literally carried out – kicking and screaming and swearing – by his hands and feet. Then the rest of us had our names called out, and we were formally arrested and escorted out of the restaurant. As I was led out, I saw the elderly couple staring at me; they looked a little bit frightened and I wondered what they were thinking about me. I saw the man hold his wife's hand gently in both of his. I thought to myself that, even in the chaos and mayhem and violence they had just witnessed, there was nothing that could stop their love for each other. It was a surreal moment.

The culmination of over a year's work stopped at that very moment. This was the end of the operation.

Forty-three

I was standing at the front of a lecture hall that was full of detectives, investigators and support staff. I had been asked by a friend to deliver a presentation on UC work to an audience who had been described to me as 'the future of undercover work' in the region in which he worked.

The audience had just finished a free lunch, which was normally enough to ensure that the majority remained for at least the first presentation of the afternoon. The head of the undercover unit introduced me, but I wasn't really listening to what he was saying. Instead, I looked at the faces of the people who filled the seats in front of me. Some stared back and smiled, while others averted their eyes nervously as if they had done something wrong. Sat in the back row on the left was a group of about six people I knew as undercover officers from the local unit.

My first question to the audience was: 'How many of you have previously been involved in undercover operations?' One smartly dressed gentleman in the second row put his arm bolt upright like a keen schoolboy answering his teacher. He had a neatly trimmed beard and wore a tweed jacket and a smart cream shirt. I asked him if he minded sharing his experience with the audience. He was a stocky man, and I couldn't help noticing the thatch of hair that was protruding above his shirt. He explained very eloquently how he had supervised the delivery of a package containing cannabis to a local criminal on his patch. It was not the most exciting story, and I found myself thinking that I hoped there was a better example. A second man put his hand up. He was in his late twenties and was very confident when he told the audience that he had once trained as a test purchase officer. He went on to say that he had previously deployed on the streets to buy heroin, but that he hadn't enjoyed the apprehension he felt in the build-up to meeting the dealers, so he'd stopped working in the role. I was impressed by his honesty, but hoped there would be some more experience in the room. 'Anyone else?' I threw the question out for the last time, more in hope than anticipation. The audience fell silent.

I never prepared for these presentations; I knew what I wanted to get over, and always used audience participation to make the presentation interactive. About an hour in, I paused and surveyed the faces in the audience, and the majority of them were open-mouthed. I could tell they had only really ever imagined that the police conducted these types of operations and would never be involved in such work in the future.

I continued for another half an hour, giving them examples of previous operations and discussing the dangers as well as the outstanding results that can be achieved in undercover investigations. I had always promised myself that whenever I delivered these presentations, I would only ever give examples of cases or operations I had personally been involved in. I would never tell someone else's story and pretend that it was mine. This always guaranteed authenticity, and you could never be caught out telling a lie about an operation.

I had finished what I wanted to say, and I asked the audience if they had any questions. A few senior officers asked some relevant legislative and policy questions, which I answered. Then, from the middle of the audience, a very ordinary-looking man with silver-rimmed spectacles put his hand in the air. He had a brown cord jacket on, and an oversized manbag that hung diagonally across his chest. His hair was receding and he was about forty years old. He stood up and I noticed he was taller than I had expected. He waited for me to acknowledge I had seen him before he asked his question. I recognised the local accent as he said, 'How do you sleep at night?'

I stared at him for a number of seconds. I wasn't sure whether he objected to the type of work I was involved in, or the lies and deceit that I had employed to stay alive. Or was he actually trying to indicate that it was a brave role and he was acknowledging the dangers involved? I really couldn't work it out, so I answered slowly: 'Like a baby.'

I now knew, for sure, that if this was the future of the work that I had dedicated twenty years of my life to, it was time to move on.

Forty-four

I manoeuvred my Porsche Cayenne Turbo off the M62 as I glimpsed the sign for Stalybridge. I was jaded from another late night, and my Gucci sunglasses protected my bloodshot eyes from the autumn sun. I was wearing my Hugo Boss black suit, a white cutaway collar shirt with a thin black Boss tie, and a pair of black Loake country brogues. Hanging up behind me was my favourite Crombie coat – a coat that has its own story to tell at some stage, but now isn't the time.

I shouldn't really have been driving; one or more too many Courvoisiers during another day and night deployed in the country pub had taken their toll. But nothing would've stopped me from making this journey. I had thought a lot about this over recent weeks – the fact that he had died so suddenly, the fact he hadn't told anyone he had cancer. I could close my eyes and see his face as it had looked the last time I'd seen him. He'd been sitting next to me at Doncaster races, drinking a pint of John Smith's with a wee glass of whisky next to it.

Today was the funeral of a dear friend: a colleague, a hard man, a man who didn't show emotion, a man who cared, a quiet man, a man that you and I owe a great deal to. This man had saved many a young child from the dirty, mucky claws of sick men – men whose only desire was to harm children, harm them in ways that are difficult to comprehend.

Jim hadn't taken the sexy, five-star undercover lifestyle. Jim had worked from the late 1980s in the testing world of paedophilia, a world that was new to undercover work, a thankless world, where sometimes only you as the operative recognised that you had saved the life or protected the innocence of a child. This wasn't a world that was spoken about. I knew about the exceptional work Jim had done, and I'm sure that as he lay in his coffin, the nightmares that he had would no longer have.

I felt really emotional, which wasn't a word that I would ever use to describe myself. I didn't cry – to me it was a sign of weakness – instead I bottled everything inside and always had.

I turned the volume on the CD player up and the lyrics rang through my head. It was Slow Moving Millie singing, and each word hit home. I played it over and over as I fought back the tears. Had it happened to me? Had I let a good man turn bad? These were thoughts I didn't want in my head.

Undercover

The track was on repeat and was interrupted only by a knock on my window. I hadn't remembered any of the journey, I hadn't remembered parking the car, I was lost in my own world. I could see a man recognised, and his words brought me back to reality as he banged on my window: 'I knew it would be you as soon as I saw the motor pull into the car park, you flash cockney. I take it you're still working, Joe?' It was an old DI who had run the Manchester undercover unit for many years but had been retired a while. He and I had always got on well. I was pleased to hear his voice because it brought me back – back from thoughts I didn't want to have, emotions I wanted to hide away – he rescued me from the very place that I didn't want to go.

'Come on, Joe, take them daft sunglasses off and let's have a brew.'

I climbed out of my car, and Graham put his arm round me and gave me a squeeze as we walked into the café at Morrisons. He looked well; I didn't think he had changed. He had ruled the undercover unit from the day he'd started the job. He did things 'Graham's way', and his team became accustomed to what that was. It was the right way, a tried-and-tested way, and it worked.

I had done many jobs for Graham and we had a mutual respect for each other that had grown. He trusted me and I trusted him. I'd always known that whenever I worked for him he had my back, and in over twenty years working undercover, I could count on one hand how many people I could say that about.

We drank coffee and shared memories about Jim; we laughed and it felt good remembering. We had been together the last time we had seen him. The three of us doing the things we enjoyed: betting on the horses, drinking and telling stories. Graham expressed how glad he was that we'd made the effort to meet at the races and said we must promise each other, the two of us, that we'd do it again soon. He held his hand out and gripped mine. 'I mean it, Joe. Let's not let life pass us by.'

I agreed, but knew the reality of our friendship. Before I'd met Graham at Doncaster, I hadn't seen him for eight years. I knew it could be another eight years before I saw him the next time.

I decided to stroll up to St Paul's, a big lump of a church off the Huddersfield Road. There were people gathering in the car park and outside the doors of the church. These were people that probably hadn't seen each other since the last 'job' funeral they'd attended. But I didn't want this to be just any funeral – this was Jim's, this ought to be different. It deserved to be, we owed him that.

The hearse arrived and I took a deep gulp and pictured Jim lying inside, and I wondered what he'd be thinking. I bet there were one or two people who'd turned up that he would've had a few choice words for. I knew he'd be glad I was here, and I knew what I wanted to say to his wife. A lady I'd never met, a lady that had answered his mobile for him and helped him send text messages to me. A lady I often had a three-way conversation with when I rang his mobile to ask if he had any tips. Betting was a pastime they'd both enjoyed, and it's fair to say his wife Mary enjoyed considerably more success than Jim did, though he seldom admitted that.

I stood in a rear corner of the church, lost in the moment. There were hymns being sung, but they weren't registering in my mind. I glanced up just as an ordinary-looking lad climbed the stairs to the pulpit. He looked like he'd been raised above us. He announced himself in a broad Lancastrian accent as Jim's nephew. He said they'd called him Captain Jim, from his days in the merchant navy. When they were boys, Jim had told them of his many adventures at sea. The lad said that Jim had taught them how to fight, how to smoke and how to gamble. He'd also lent them money when they lost at gambling, but insisted on charging them interest. This made me smile, it made me happy – this was the real Jim, the Jim I knew. He ended by saying that he missed Captain Jim, missed him so very much. He began to cry as he descended the stairs of the pulpit. I wanted to cry too. I wish I had, I should have, but of course I didn't. I wanted to get out of the church, get away from this place.

I was the first to leave. I didn't say any goodbyes – I just left. I had rehearsed what I'd say to Mary over and over in my head, but in the end I said nothing at all. I left before I'd told her what a great man her husband was and how he'd always told me that he loved her. That she was his rock and that without her he felt weak. But I didn't; I turned away without saying a word.

As I walked slowly back to my car, I stopped momentarily. It was in this very second that I felt a strange clarity. I think I realised that, for me, nothing had changed. All my effort and emotion was devoted to my job as an undercover officer, as it had always been. I had lost any semblance of a work–life balance a long time ago. I'd allowed all the issues in my 'real' life to fester. I hadn't been a man, hadn't been the head of my family, had broken promises, ignored responsibility, hidden within this shell I'd invented. I hadn't tried to sort my life out or mend my broken relationships or heal the wounds I had inflicted.

I had let it all drift. I'd let it drift because, in my head, the job I was doing was so important, because without me, 'the job' would crumble. I had believed that I was more important than anything else, that I was above the world, that behind my mask I was untouchable.

In a way, I realise now that it was my pre-programmed coping mechanism – I have always buried my head in the sand. I wasn't as strong a man in my real life as I was as 'Joe'. As Joe, I felt that I was invincible. I would take on any operation, any baddy – the more impregnable the better. I thrived on such challenges, on the imminence of danger, on an acute proximity to violence and death.

But in real life, I had let down the people I loved the most. I'd failed that challenge; in fact I hadn't even fought the battle. In many ways I was a coward. I had run away from my issues, using my work to hide from the problems of normality. I know all these things now, and I understand it may be too late to put things right, and I suppose I have to live with that.

I reached my car and climbed in. I knew exactly what I'd do – what I did best. I'd drive the two hours back to the pub where I was deployed on my new job. I'd lose myself in the company of the people I called my 'friends'. People I didn't really care for, people I'd walk away from in a breath. I would sit and tell lies and drink until it was time to go to bed.

And that's what I did.